T0397568

Stop & Frisk and the Politics of Crime in Chicago

Stop & Frisk and the Politics of Crime in Chicago

WESLEY G. SKOGAN

OXFORD
UNIVERSITY PRESS

OXFORD
UNIVERSITY PRESS

Oxford University Press is a department of the University of Oxford. It furthers the University's objective of excellence in research, scholarship, and education by publishing worldwide. Oxford is a registered trade mark of Oxford University Press in the UK and certain other countries.

Published in the United States of America by Oxford University Press
198 Madison Avenue, New York, NY 10016, United States of America.

Library of Congress Cataloging-in-Publication Data
Names: Skogan, Wesley G., author.
Title: Stop & frisk and the politics of crime in Chicago /
Wesley G. Skogan.
Other titles: Stop and frisk and the politics of crime in Chicago
Description: New York, NY : Oxford University Press, [2023] |
Includes bibliographical references and index.
Identifiers: LCCN 2022029915 (print) | LCCN 2022029916 (ebook) |
ISBN 9780197675052 (hardback) | ISBN 9780197675069 (paperback) |
ISBN 9780197675083 (epub)
Subjects: LCSH: Crime—Political aspects—Illinois—Chicago. | Police—Illinois—
Chicago. | Stop and frisk (Law enforcement)—Illinois—Chicago.
Classification: LCC HV6795.C4 S45 2023 (print) | LCC HV6795.C4 (ebook) |
DDC 364.109773/11—dc23/eng/20220902
LC record available at https://lccn.loc.gov/2022029915
LC ebook record available at https://lccn.loc.gov/2022029916

DOI: 10.1093/oso/9780197675052.001.0001

For Barbara, as always

Contents

Acknowledgments

Financial support for some of the work described in this book was provided by two Chicago-based foundations, the John D. and Catherine T. MacArthur Foundation and the Joyce Foundation. Both have been important in supporting both research and reform. The findings and conclusions expressed in this book are my own, and do not necessarily reflect the positions of the MacArthur or Joyce Foundations.

My thanks extend to a long list of research partners and co-authors, reporters and data-driven journalists, insiders who tolerated my being there, informants who helped me understand what was going on, journalists with good questions, willing purveyors of underground data, readers of draft chapters, statistical explainers, and role models whom I admire. The list includes a few supporters of earlier projects in Chicago that laid the foundation for this study and influenced my thinking the entire way. A final thanks is to Meredith Keefer at Oxford University Press, who kept this project moving in the right direction.

Ellen Alberding	Mick Dumke	Jamie Kalven
Jack Benigno	Joe Ferguson	Candice Kane
Curtis Black	Al Ferreira	Dan Kivel
Richard Block	Beth Ford	David Klinger
Glen Brooks Jr.	Richard Fowles	Timothy Lavery
Marc Buslik	Warren Friedman	Jonathan Lewin
Tom Byrne	Craig Futterman	Dan Lewis
(the elder)	Jeremy Gorner	Jim Lewis
Amy Campanelli	Adam Gross	Lori Lightfoot
Paul Cassell	Rich Hagen	Bruce Lipman
Ralph Chiczewski	Cari Hennessy	Howard Lodding
Tony Chiesa	James Hickey	Freddie Martinez
Maurice Classen	Terry Hillard	Terry Mazany
Fay Lomax Cook	Craig Howard	Garry McCarthy
Richard M. Daley	Mark Iris	Tracey Meares
Victor Dixon	Nola Joyce	Chip Mitchell

Angel Novalez
Ted O'Keefe
Andrew Papachristos
Jennifer Parsons
Susan Popkin
Elliott Ramos
Charles Ramsey
Charlie Ransford
Matt Rodriguez
Dennis Rosenblum

Ilana Rosenzweig
James Roussell
Sarah L. Ryley
Mark Sedevic
Karen Sheley
Tracy Sitka
Gary Slutkin
Julia Stasch
James K. Stewart
Randolph Stone

Justice Tankebe
Flint Taylor
Matteo Tiratelli
Bob Tracey
Jeremy Travis
Tom Tyler
Maarten Van
   Craen
Nina Vinik
Chuck Wexler

1

The Era of Stop & Frisk

In 2014, Chicago police stopped, questioned, and often frisked more than 718,000 people. That was a big number for a city of 2.7 million. It was more than three times the stop *rate* in the place best known for its aggressive stop & frisk policy, New York City. Chicago's chief of police was under fire and 2013 had been a bad year, seeing by its end a 20 percent jump in murders. The powerful head of the teachers' union pronounced Mayor Rahm Emanuel "the murder mayor," and it was rumored that late in the year the mayor threatened to oust Police Superintendent Garry McCarthy. The media were coming down hard on police headquarters and city hall. In a press conference the mayor took responsibility for bringing down the rate of shootings and killings in the city. At headquarters, the chief of police ratcheted up the pressure on his commanders to produce more "numbers." Already at a record high, the stop & frisk count jumped again during 2014. Murders promptly dropped by 20 percent, so everyone knew what the future held. Until it did not. Within a dozen months stop & frisk had collapsed, the mayor was clinging to his seat, the chief of police was out and plotting revenge, and Chicago stepped over the precipice into an historic spike in gun violence.

This is just a sampling of events in the era of stop & frisk in Chicago. It began a decade earlier and stops waxed and waned during the firing of a previous chief and the early resignation of a third in the face of scandal. More news was to come later in the era, in a period featuring lawsuits, federal and local investigations, new legislation aimed at constraining the exercise of police discretion on the street, and the election of a reform-minded mayor determined to do something about her police department.

So, while this is a book about stop & frisk, its main message is that policing strategies raise intensely political and social concerns. A description of its legal and operational features does not address most the core issues they raise. Actual evidence of its effectiveness is thin. The biggest crime problem facing Chicago police was a collapse in their ability to solve crimes, largely due to factors outside their control. That, plus the rise of a distinctive culture of gun violence. Together these seriously undercut the standard model

Stop & Frisk and the Politics of Crime in Chicago. Wesley G. Skogan, Oxford University Press.
© Oxford University Press 2023. DOI: 10.1093/oso/9780197675052.003.0001

of policing that evolved during the twentieth century and stop & frisk looked like the way forward. But during its peak year of 2014, 90 percent of those stopped were African Americans and Hispanics. From 2013 to 2015 more police enforcement actions were taken in Chicago's predominately African American neighborhoods than there were people living there, every year. Putting cops in hot spots to conduct stops and other enforcement activities had consequences. Stops also undermined trust in the police among the 30 percent of Chicagoans who were being stopped in a year. Surveys of the city showed many Chicagoans did not trust the police, and a survey of officers documented that most did not trust Chicagoans. Still, about 20 percent of city residents were hard-core supporters who stood behind expanding police stop & frisk powers. When a tsunami of gun violence swept over the city, the claim was the collapse of stop & frisk was "what dunnit."

Why Stop & Frisk?

While this is a case study, stop & frisk is not just another Chicago saga. It has become a subject of political contention throughout the United States. During the past 25 years, American policing moved from a focus on responding to crimes in progress or (more often) already committed toward proactive strategies for preventing or deterring future crimes from occurring in the first place. The earlier standard model of policing involved responding rapidly to emergency calls, interviewing witnesses, gathering evidence at the scene, and identifying individuals for further investigation or arrest. The causes of crime were beyond them. Jerry Wilson, once the chief of police for Washington, DC, told me I would never meet a better sociologist than a district commander whose crime rate was going *up*. They would be surprisingly fluent regarding crime's social and economic roots. Then, their every-day performance was evaluated by how fast their officers could drive to the scene after being dispatched via radio.

Now, rather than cleaning up in the aftermath of crime, police have taken responsibility for its occurrence. This was a political choice. Police leaders were emboldened to take ownership of crime during the post-1991 period during which it was in steady decline. The argument that this decline was their doing gained them new public support and justified their budgets during economic and crime downturns. During the 1990s and into the early 2000s, police tried a variety of new policing strategies, most notably community and problem-solving policing, and claimed success for all of them. But in the 2000s, violent crime stopped declining and changed in character. A larger proportion of it involved guns, and a great deal of violence was linked to gangs and drugs. The ability of police to solve violent crime declined to sometimes alarming levels. Crime remained low in parts of many cities, but in other areas it was growing and it was more violent. The neighborhoods still impacted by violence were even poorer and more disorganized than in the past, and it proved difficult for police to make much progress there using innovative strategies. But police now had responsibility for crime, and this led almost inevitably to more heavily targeted and aggressive police tactics.

Attesting to stop & frisk's importance, William Bratton, twice Commissioner of the New York City Police Department, argued:

> Stop-and-frisk is such a basic tool of policing. It's one of the most fundamental practices in American policing. If cops are not doing stop-and-frisk, they are not doing their jobs. It is a basic, fundamental tool of police work in the whole country. If you do away with stop-and-frisk, this city [New York] will go down the chute as fast as anything you can imagine. (Toobin, 2013)

In broader scope, stop & frisk is a popular component of a larger class of "proactive policing" strategies that pit officers on the street directly against members of the general public who happen by. Another example from Chicago is "seat belt missions" during which officers block street traffic to inspect cars and question drivers as they wind their way through a maze of traffic cones and burning flares. These missions focus on crime hotspots, and the form officers fill out documenting their accomplishments includes counts of their felony and misdemeanor arrests, as well as traffic citations. Chicago officers are also empowered to issue dispersal orders to gangs (defined as a group of three or more persons) suspected of loitering or being drug dealers gathered in public places. Those who fail to obey or are seen to engage in further loitering are subject to arrest (there is more on this in Chapter 7). Traffic stops play a very large role in policing the public, in Chicago and elsewhere. They may have a somewhat more limited role to play in deterring violent crime, but they provide more and highly flexible legal opportunities for police to stop and question passers-by. Two fine books have been written about traffic stops, by Charles Epp and colleagues (Epp, Maynard-Moody and Haider-Markel, 2014) and Frank Baumgartner and others (Baumgartner, Epp and Shoub, 2018). During 2018 Chicago police initiated almost 700,000 traffic stops. Chapters 6 and 7 address their local relationship to stop & frisks and to crime.

One feature these efforts have in common is that they involve large numbers of stops that prove unwarranted. As we shall see, most Chicagoans walk away from stop & frisks with no legal consequences. Following traffic stops, many drivers move on after a verbal reprimand, without a ticket being issued. Large scale "catch and release" practices seem to be a requirement for promoting general deterrence through stopping people. Another feature of these stops is they still can be fraught with risk for the parties involved. Officers are trained to fear for their lives while conducting them, while some of their subjects respond to the aggression and disrespect they too frequently experience with a mixture of fear, anger, and defiance. Chapter 4 documents how stop & frisks undermine public confidence in the police.

Stops deserve attention because they can have terrible consequences for those involved, as well as for the standing of the police in the community. Stop & frisk ranks high among the policing tactics that have riven the country. They take place at the intersection between crime, race, and potential violence. Many high-profile instances of police-initiated violence began as routine proactive encounters. Eric Garner died in 2014 in a chokehold during a routine New York City street stop investigating whether he was selling loose cigarettes from packs without a state tax stamp. Daunte Wright was killed in 2021 by a police officer in a brief struggle protesting a traffic stop in suburban Minneapolis, when, in the heat of the moment, the officer drew her firearm rather than a taser. Other situations certainly provide opportunities for encounters between police and the public to go sour. In 2020 George Floyd was killed in Minneapolis following the police response to a routine 911 call. In 2017 an off-duty Chicago officer driving his pickup truck spotted a developmentally disabled young man who had been reported as a missing person. From his truck the officer opened fire and wounded the unarmed man, whom he claimed was walking toward his vehicle. The head of the city agency which reviews such cases was "mortified" when she saw the video, but it was not released to the public for another 15 months (Kalven, 2018). "No-knock" police crash-ins in the middle of the night exude danger for everyone involved. What is distinctive about stop & frisk is that there are no complaining victims, no named suspects, no advance confirmation that any offense has even occurred, and precious few reasons to make "pretextual" stops based on some observed infraction like a misfunctioning turn signal. Rather, officers who have been sent out to make stops must somehow spot enough "reasonably suspicious" people who happen to be passing by to keep their lieutenant happy.

Further, Chicago's experience during its era of stop & frisk addresses other questions of continuing relevance around the country:

Can proactive encounters be better targeted and handled? Do so many people have to be stopped for proactive policing to be effective? Will officers be more intentional in how they treat subjects of their stops?

Are there inevitably trade-offs between over policing and under policing? African American neighborhoods in Chicago experienced both, at the same time.

What happens in the face of "de-policing," or when "the police footprint" is reduced meaningfully in size? Chicago's stop & frisks dropped by 80 percent in one month and stayed down. There were many views regarding the consequences.

Do cops necessarily "go fetal" or otherwise surrender in the face of withering criticism by the media and some communities? What does "not doing stops & frisk" mean? Does the agency just switch tactics, and not necessarily in a better direction?

Can better policing build public support and enhance their legitimacy. In the 2020s American police faced a catastrophic legitimacy crisis. What do we know about rebuilding it?

What is the political base of support for stop & frisk? About 20 percent of Chicagoans wanted more of it, and tougher too. Is there political space for a law-and-order backlash even in progressive cities?

What are the *alternatives* to stop & frisk, not general and future-focused plans but concrete steps promising to effectively respond to the specific crime problems facing neighborhoods next weekend?

Stop & Frisk as an Organizational Strategy

Stop & frisk is certainly not confined to the United States. In the UK, searches are regulated and reported nationally. In 2008–2009, the last year that encounters not leading to a search were recorded in the UK, police recorded more than 2.2 million stops and almost 1.1 million searches in a 12-month period (Shiner and Delsol, 2015). What Americans call stop & frisk is astonishingly prevalent in poor immigrant neighborhoods in France. The most common police activity there is demanding "*vos papiers*" (your papers). These identity checks usually involve no offense or even any real suspicion, and the officers often know their subjects well through repeated stops. The real role of identity checks is to reinforce their authority (Jobard, 2020). This is a tactical choice. In a cross-national study the German police made fewer stops than the French and did not come down extra hard on immigrant youths (de Maillard, et al., 2018). Summarizing the results of a national survey of young people in France, Jobard, et al., (2012) report that 28 percent of respondents recalled being stopped at least once in the previous year. In Britain, the comparable survey-based figure for 2010 was 10 percent of everyone age 16 and over (Jackson, et al., 2012). The only equivalent national data for the United States comes from a nationwide survey conducted occasionally by the U.S. Bureau of Justice Statistics. In their 2015 survey, one percent of the national population age 16 and older reported being involved in a street stop ("being stopped while in a public place or a parked vehicle") during the past year (Davis, Whyde and Langton, 2018). On the other hand, Chapter 4 reports the one-year survey-based overall stop rate for Chicagoans ages 16 and older was *30 percent*; 22 percent were stop & frisks While some U.S. cities (such as New York City) release reports of their stop & frisk practices based on administrative data, many are not so transparent. Chicago's transparency was imposed on the city by the Illinois State Legislature and the American Civil Liberties Union, in events that are described in Chapter 6.

To be sure, there is nothing new about cops making stops. Officers routinely take note of people's actions, as well as the setting in which it is situated. They may choose to intervene directly based on their own informed suspicions. They might conduct a pat-down search for weapons to ensure their own safety. Moreover, they can search more thoroughly if they have cause for suspecting criminal misconduct. Tactics such as these for responding to events and people are exercised often. Descriptions of the "craft" of policing feature vignettes illustrating the knowledge, skill, and judgment that officers acquire through daily experience and how they apply it to decision-making on the street (for samples of police wisdom from Chicago see Preib, 2010; Fletcher, 1990). Whom to stop is among the most frequent of these decisions.

However, my interest here is not in individual stops and how they are handled. This book views stop & frisk as an *organizational strategy*. As a strategy rather than a tactic, stop & frisk takes on additional features. Stops are not just reactions to events or people. Officers set out on patrol with instructions to conduct them. It is part of their mission because their managers expect them to conduct stops and "lay hands on people" (a Chicago phrase for conducting a search). Officers need to record them and "make their numbers" to keep their bosses happy. Their managers monitor the numbers, and they frequently call for yet more during roll call meetings and supervisory encounters. District commanders and watch supervisors insist on stops being made because they, in turn, are being held accountable by headquarters. The numbers generated by various units will be used to identify those that do not hit their quotas, and there can be consequences for any shortfalls. In the many agencies using versions of a CompStat-style performance management process (there is much more on this in Chapter 3), the consequences can include on-the-spot professional humiliation, and unit commanders can lose their position. From headquarters, top executives will describe what they are doing as "vital to crime prevention" when they report to their political leaders and address the media and the public. They will interpret the numbers as evidence they are doing their utmost to combat crime. This resonates with the many segments of society that have bought into the idea that routine policing must be proactive, not just reactive. If there is any downward movement in crime police leaders will claim success; but, in the era of stop & frisk, just demonstrating high-volume *activity* has become a performance measure as well.

Stop & Frisk and Deterrence

Stop & frisk as a prevention strategy embodies the principles of deterrence. The idea is a relentless focus on "hot people"—persons known or suspected of criminal involvement, and perhaps even included on a hot list—increases the risks they face when they choose to carry drugs or weapons. On their side, potential offenders will balance the increased risk-to-reward ratio associated with carrying contraband, and they may decide not to do so. This will deter crimes that stem from hot people carrying guns and drugs, including shootings and drug dealing. Being stopped and identified also threatens individuals with a backlog of unpaid tickets on file or warrants out for their arrest. Their numbers can be considerable. During the 1990s, Chicago began to replace arrests for many minor nuisance offenses with a ticket requiring paying a fine or contesting it at a hearing. Currently there are 75 offenses on the list. Few who receive them show up at their hearing, and about two-thirds of the required fines go unpaid. Their names are "in the system" and stops can identify them. The theoretical link between stops and offending is that they increase the *certainty of being apprehended* for these infractions. Compared to other aspects of deterrence, including the severity of punishment or the speed with which it is rendered, certainty is seen as the strongest tool in the crime deterrence kitbag (Nagin, 2013; Apel and Nagin, 2011). Actual arrests will matter, of course, but under most stop & frisk regimes they occur in only a fraction of stops. Police leaders in New York City have claimed that not finding anything during a stop & frisk is evidence that stops are working. Stop & frisk also promises to be *disruptive*. It may force drug dealers to make elaborate arrangements to stash their drugs in out-of-the way places, or for groups to move hidden "gang guns" from hand-to-hand as needed rather than carrying them conveniently in their pants. Possessing stolen credit cards gets riskier. Of course, motivated offenders may adapt their tactics to accommodate shifts in police strategy; this is known as "offense switching" in criminology. However, this also raises the complexity and thus the costs of offending, and it may expose them to new risks. The deterrence rationale for stop & frisk essentially celebrates intimidation by police that is achieved by fear of being questioned, searched, and sanctioned.

The hot people rationale for stop & frisk, and why they are seen pivotal to public safety, was explained to a reporter by the head of Chicago's major police union:

> You have a corner loaded with guys you know are up to no good and have historically been up to no good, because you've been working the same beat for . . . years. They're in the same spot every day. If they're out there throwing narcotics or involved in gang activity or intimidation or street robberies, we know these individuals. You [need to] ask if they're there for a lawful purpose, if they're wanted on warrants or in possession of narcotics or weapons . . . [Y]ou don't give up the corner. If you lose the corner, you lose the block. (Spielman, 2017)

Other features of a stop & frisk policy should weigh in on behalf of deterrence as well. Surely fewer crimes will be visibly committed while police are patrolling nearby. The real test is whether the shadow of a *possible* police presence is dark enough to ward off criminal activity when they just *might* be there. Deterrence requires communication of this risk. If the strategy is to be effective in the aggregate, risks created by stop & frisk need to be widely understood; hot people must perceive they are real and widespread. Stopping potentially hot individuals is one form of communication, but an increased frequency of police patrols and the visible presence of officers on the street confronting people of all temperatures may spread the message more widely. On warm summer nights stops draw onlookers, and the story gets around. The *general* deterrent message is that the neighbors should not even consider carrying contraband in the first place. There also may be some room for educational campaigns aimed at instilling fear of the police. Decker (2003) described extensive advertising campaigns mounted as part of the federal Project Safe Neighborhoods program. These campaigns were aimed at increasing public knowledge of the consequences of involvement in gun crime—the message was "hard federal time for gun crime." However, in most places the message that police are omnipresent is communicated largely by stopping enough people, enough to spread the required level of fear around the community. Of course, the number of stops that is sufficient is a key detail, and the upper ranges of that number were tested in Chicago in the mid-2010s.

A goal of this book (there are several) is to address the deterrent effectiveness of stop & frisk, distinguishing it as much as possible from the many other moving parts that make up a big-city police department. In a landmark study, Franklin Zimring (2011) attributed New York City's drop in serious crime—which for a long period was roughly twice the average decline nationally—to the city's proactive policing policies. The New York story will be addressed briefly in this book, but Zimring confessed he could not determine which of the city's grab-bag of policing tactics were working, and which may have been window-dressing. Chapter 7 sorts them out for Chicago.

There is also, of course, some slippage between deterrence theory and practice. Can officers focus on truly hot people in an efficient manner? There are not so many truly hot people. In a review of research, Martinez, et al. (2017) concluded about five percent of the population accounts for about half of all crime, and within the five percent the most prolific offenders account for most offenses. However, there is usually no handy offender hot list. Instead, it is standard practice to focus on hot neighborhoods, stop large numbers of likely-looking suspects, and hope to scoop up a useful number of guns, make crime-deterring arrests, and intimidate everyone else. This book documents that Chicago police were quite good at neighborhood focusing, following the principles of hotspot policing. But, as the program scaled up, this led to an immense number of unwarranted stops of "cold" people. To be a general deterrent, stop & frisk relies on volume, with most who are stopped just going about their own business. One of the negative features of stop & frisk is that doing nothing wrong does not protect citizens from being swept up by the police, when that is the organization's mission. Stop & frisk in practice raises serious equity issues. This includes who bears the brunt of *unwarranted* stops. Throughout this book the victims of unwarranted stops are a principal concern.

Research indicates tightly focused and carefully managed proactive policing tactics including stop & frisk can be effective. However, when stop & frisk becomes an agency's principal crime prevention strategy, tight focus and careful management often go out the window. The balance of the number of people stopped who turn out to be hot against those who are not is known as the "hit rate." Based on Philadelphia police data, stop & frisks during 2014–2015 uncovered contraband of any kind (including weapons and drugs) in just three percent of stops (Hannon, 2020). In New York City during the early 2000s the hit rate was also low, but the data collected was more detailed. During 540,000 stops in 2008, 0.15 percent yielded a firearm, and 1.2 percent a weapon of any kind. Other kinds of contraband, mostly drugs, turned up in 1.7 percent of stops. About six percent of all stops resulted in a ticket arrest, and another six percent an arrest. Subtracting out stops resulting in arrests, citations, and seized material, fully 88 percent of New York City stop & frisks during 2008 were what the local chapter of the American Civil Liberties Union dubbed "innocent stops" (Jones-Brown, Gill and Trone, 2010). Chapter 8 evaluates Chicago's hit rate (which was higher) as an "efficiency" issue, but it will have larger implications when we turn to the impact of stop & frisk on its targets' lives.

While the Supreme Court has expressed the hope that stop & frisks will be "momentary," being stopped in Chicago was not just an inconvenience. As we will see in Chapter 4, perhaps surprising numbers of innocent residents reported being handcuffed, pushed around, and even threatened during stop & frisks before they walked away. It was common also for Chicagoans to be stopped *repeatedly*. These experiences can, in turn, lead to what Manski and Nagin (2017) dubbed "legitimacy costs." Here we examine their corrosive impact on trust in the police. For many, unwarranted stops undermined their confidence that police would respect their rights, make decisions that are right for their neighborhood, and be trustworthy. This influenced their willingness to assist the police and obey their requests, both important features of a law-abiding society. Legitimacy questions reappear in several of the upcoming chapters.

Stop & Frisk in Law

In law, officers can stop a person (that is, temporarily restrain them from moving away) if they have "reasonable suspicion" the suspect has been involved in a crime or is about to commit one. Illinois law is clear that during these stops people can be asked to account for themselves and their presence at the scene. They can get in trouble if they do not cooperate. Furthermore, officers may "pat down" (or frisk) the outer clothing of a suspect during the encounter if they have reasonable suspicion to believe the subject is armed and poses a threat to the officer or to the public. Such searches are to be directed only at the discovery of weapons, not other forms of contraband or evidence of criminality. The stop is to prevent or interrupt suspected criminal activity, and the frisk is to promote officer and bystander safety. If actions by officers in such cases are challenged in court, they must be able to explain to the judge the reasonable basis of their suspicion. As in every aspect of policing, a large body of case law describes what is and is not a protective pat down and how far officers can push their search-like powers.

At the time these rules took formal shape (in a 1968 decision by the Supreme Court) they were viewed as a grand compromise. They balanced the personal freedoms of Americans (protected by the Fourth Amendment to the Constitution) against the risks presented by an increasingly armed society which was experiencing an epidemic of violent crime. The Court itself acknowledged that investigatory stops and frisks "must surely be an annoying, frightening, and perhaps humiliating experience" for the individuals singled out for attention (*Terry v. Ohio*, 392 U.S. 1, 1968, pp. 24–25). However, the case brought to them described stop & frisk of a particular form. It involved an experienced detective who was working his regular beat in the center of Cleveland when he noted three unfamiliar faces peering into the windows of jewelry stores. He followed them discretely for some time, taking note of their actions. As the three gathered in front of one shop, the detective approached them and got what he described as a "mumbled response" when he asked what they were doing. He then conducted what would become known as a "Terry stop," named after one of the suspects. The detective made what was described as a cursory search of each of them, finding two of the three were carrying firearms. One suspect quickly confessed they were intent on robbing the store. John Terry wanted the Court to exclude the evidence that was seized as the "fruits" of his search. It was argued the arresting officer did not have cause to do the pat down (which was described as a search, as it was at the time) and, therefore, the evidence was unlawfully obtained. When the Court considered the admissibility of the evidence, they thought its discovery stemmed from good police work, and that the officer had acted reasonably to protect his and others' lives. The Court endorsed the tactic as described to them.

What *Terry* gave us was a legal justification—reasonable suspicion—for officers to conduct a new kind of search that was not a search, but a pat down. To be "reasonable" their suspicion must be backstopped by what the Justices described as "specific and articulable facts" that led them to this view. This rule means officers need to be able to describe the basis of their reasoning during criminal court hearings, relying on their official pocket notebook if need be. The term "reasonable" has generated a great deal of case law all by itself. The Court gave some guidance in their pronouncement that a reasonable stop-and-frisk is one "in which a reasonably prudent officer is warranted in the circumstances of a given case in believing that his safety or that of others is endangered, he may make a reasonable search for weapons of the person believed by him to be armed and dangerous." Having found this reason, officers are not supposed to dig very deeply into a suspect's clothing during a pat down, unless they sense something additional that might present a danger to them or others on the scene. The Supreme Court also thought Terry stops would mostly be momentary, another justification for allowing this intrusion into Americans' personal space by the state.

A further legal standard is involved in justifying conducting what is now considered to be an actual search for contraband or evidence. The standard is that the officer has "probable cause" to believe a crime has been or will be committed by the involved individual. A bad actual search taints any ensuing arrest. There can be no lawful arrest without probable cause, which again the officer needs to be able to describe in court if called upon. This requirement is also rooted in the Fourth Amendment, in a very short and murky section that uses the term but gives no clue as to it means. The Court itself has referred to probable cause as fluid and contextual, which means (to me) that you know it when you see it.

Stop & Frisk in Practice

But this book is not about law; it is about practice, with an empirical focus on the origins and implementation of stop & frisk in one great American city. There is a great deal of discretion involved when officers consider the legal rules in the field. Practice is about identifying suspicious looking people plus hanging a bit of factual decoration on that insight. Out on the street the precise details of the rules are not very important. Few officers know much about the law in any event. Instead, they follow various rules of thumb picked up from others or developed through their own experience. In Chicago, a U.S. Department of Justice investigation of the department's training in constitutional policing concluded it was terrible. The report noted that "the Academy program relies on outdated materials that fail to account for updates in legal standards, widely accepted law enforcement standards, and departmental policies" (United States Department of Justice, 2017, p. 95). They noted the department's training video on use of force was 35 years old and was made ". . . prior to key Supreme Court decisions altering the standards used to evaluate the reasonableness of use of force. The tactics depicted in the video were clearly out of date with commonly accepted police standards of today" (p. 95). They found not much training time was spent on searches. White and Fradella (2016, p. 6) organize much of their book-length study of stop & frisk in New York city around this disjuncture, pointing early to the "disconnect between stop & frisk in principle and in practice." They note that stops are ". . . constitutionally permissible and are grounded in historical and legal tradition dating back hundreds of years." Two long chapters of their book provide a detailed overview of both this tradition and the specifics of Constitutional law as it is applied to stop & frisks. But later they note that events on the ground "tell a very different story. It is a tale of gross overuse and misuse of the strategy" (p. 7). Their analysis, like this one, then turns to police misuse of their discretion and its impact on their lawfulness and legitimacy in the eyes of the public. In the end they hang responsibility for this on the failure of police departments to "properly guide and control" their use of discretion. The conclusion in this book is a bit different. It is that Chicago police and political leaders got pretty much what they wanted from stop & frisk, until it collapsed.

Chapter 2 sets the scene for stop & frisk, describing trends in crime in Chicago. After peaking in 1991, crime in the city declined steadily for more than 20 years. Then this welcome trend came to a halt. At the time, the spike in shootings and gun murders in Chicago during 2014–2015 was almost unique among large American cities. Residents could no longer be reassured their fear of crime was unfounded. Gun violence began to change in character. More shots were being fired, and they involved higher-caliber and more deadly firearms. Most of the gun-related crimes that were spiking remained unsolved; Chicago's "clearance rate" was collapsing as police were increasingly unable to solve gun crimes. This in turn threatened the city's standard business model for policing: to respond quickly when called, conduct investigations, identify suspects, and make arrests. When this model stopped working, there was concern the deterrent value of the criminal justice system itself was at risk, and this did not bode well for the city's safety. Political pressure to "do something" mounted, and one strategy that promised to fill the breech was more stop & frisk. By the mid-2010s the city's police and political leaders found it an attractive option.

Chapter 3 charts the rise of stop & frisk as a key organizational strategy of the Chicago Police Department (CPD) for dealing with violent crime. The review begins with leadership, as the city's recent Superintendents of Police have varied in their enthusiasm for stops. Because Chicago's police leaders serve at the pleasure of the mayor, they also need their mayors to trust what they are doing. Trust can be fragile in city politics. Political and leadership factors driving stop & frisk have varied by administration. Important for both the chiefs and the mayors have been the twin pressures of media attention to crime and their standing in the political environment. Chicago's hotly competitive media can make life miserable for public officials, and crime is one of their favorite clubs to beat them with. Any resulting dips in their polling numbers become fodder for even more discussion of how they failed to quell crime. The chapter describes how the dynamic worked in Chicago during the reign of two mayors and four chiefs of police. It examines how police executives translated the strategic and operational priorities they set into actual practice in the field. In Chicago, their primary mechanism for doing so has been CompStat, a management style that has swept the policing world. There is a description of how CompStat in Chicago strayed from its original purpose, which was to enhance the effectiveness of a traditional model of policing through its intelligent, data-driven application. As the breakdown of that model became apparent, CompStat morphed into a forum for imposing a massive number of stop & frisks as the principal solution to the city's violence problem. There is an analysis of how effective management was in focusing stop & frisk in the highest crime areas and some of the consequences of this focus for the city's African American residents. They were the hardest hit by stop & frisk, but also by a longer list of sometimes confrontational but always punitive police interventions into community life. Home by the mid-2010s to 780,000 people, the city's predominately African American neighborhoods were the target of more than *two million* police-initiated encounters during 2013–2015 alone. Proactive policing was a daily feature of their lives.

Chapter 4 turns from police data on whom they stopped toward the experiences of the targets of stop & frisk. It examines the findings of a community survey designed to measure the frequency of stops, what happened to city residents who were swept up in them, how well stop & frisks matched principles that officers had been trained in, and the impact of their experiences on trust in the Chicago police. The survey found that during 2014–2015 *22 percent of all adults* reported being stopped but then released in the course of a year. These are frequently referred to as "innocent" as well as "unwarranted" stops. African Americans and Hispanics withstood the worst of these often aggressive yet unwarranted stops, leading to serious equity issues. They described more frequent stops, and they were more often searched, handcuffed, and subjected to the use of force when they were stopped—and then released. The chapter then turns to an assessment of the quality of stop & frisks, using as a standard the procedural justice approaches to managing them that Chicago officers had been trained in. From the point of view of those caught up in them, there was a great deal of variation in how well officers hewed to those principles. African Americans and Hispanics were more likely to think they were treated disrespectfully and unfairly by the police, that officers paid little attention to their side of the story when they tried to express it, and that their situation was not addressed in a factual and neutral manner. In turn, the experiences of Chicagoans at the hands of the police affected their trust in the police as an institution and as a local resource for addressing neighborhood problems. Good practice helped grow trust, bad practice undermined it, and bad practice was particularly concentrated in African American neighborhoods. The chapter concludes with a discussion of the roots of support for a "law and order backlash" that animated perhaps 20 percent of the city's adult population. Stop & frisk had a lot of supporters.

Chapter 5 turns to the other side of the police–community relationship, what officers think about the public. From their point of view, the public was one of their problems. They thought their relationship with the citizenry was bad, people did not understand them or their job, and—mostly— people could not be trusted. They were disdainful of two key community institutions providing public and democratic oversight of the police: the news media and political leaders. The chapter documents importance of *where they worked* in shaping officers' views of the community and their job. One was the racial composition of their beat. White, Hispanic, and African American officers alike saw their views of right and wrong aligned with residents of largely White neighborhoods. They were all "blue" in their response to neighborhood conditions. Community context also affected whether officers felt acting in accordance with the principles of procedural justice could work. Again, this seemed a standard more relevant in predominately White neighborhoods. A second contextual factor was where cops were making stops. Officers working in high intensity stop & frisk beats felt overworked and more at risk, two of the banes of police work. They also perceived themselves as most estranged from the community and the least likely to have anything in common with residents. The wedge between police and the community in Chicago was largest in the places where potentially abrasive encounters between them were concentrated.

Chapter 6 details a dramatic period in the city's history, the collapse of its stop & frisk regime during the waning months of 2015. The number of stop & frisks dropped by 85 percent in two months and stayed down for several years. The collapse came on the heels of scandal. A previously concealed video came to light that graphically documented a horrific episode of police violence. The scandal was compounded by a more than year-long cover-up campaign intended to protect the reelection chances of a mayor. The unraveling of the cover-up set loose a cascade of political events. The chief of police was driven from office, followed quickly by the head of the city's civilian police review agency. Her political party abandoned the local prosecutor, who was defeated for re-nomination by a reformer just two months later. Investigations of the Chicago police were launched in short order by an independent local commission and by the U.S. Justice Department. The tsunami of press coverage all this generated put intense pressure on local leaders regarding police reform. The crisis was reflected in local opinion polls documenting new and widespread skepticism of the mayor and the police among White voters, as well as a continued erosion of support among African American and Hispanic Chicagoans. At the same moment, earlier agreements between the city and the local chapter of the American Civil Liberties Union, plus new rules regulating stop & frisk from the Illinois State Legislature, came into effect. These imposed further restrictions on local policing practices. In the face of all this, stop & frisk collapsed.

Chapter 7 captures the continuing agony of the city. The third-largest violent crime surge in Chicago's modern history quickly followed the collapse of stop & frisk, leading many to tie the two together. This chapter documents which crimes spiked, yielding some clues as to their causes. It then reports the conclusions of a detailed statistical analysis of the impact of stop & frisk on shootings and killings over its entire span, beginning in 2004. This involved developing measures of many factors that could have been competing to drive violence both up and down. Large and complex cities like Chicago have many moving parts and stop & frisk is just one of them. The chapter comes to the uncomfortable-for-some conclusion that stops had deterrent value, but (uncomfortable for others) only a moderate impact. The effects of stop & frisk lay well within the range of other proactive policing interventions that have been carefully and positively evaluated. This is a range of impact in which possible tradeoffs among proven policing strategies can be debated, and where other important social and political values could be accommodated.

Chapter 8 begins with the question "is this anything new?" Noting that cops have always made stops, it places stop & frisk in the context of other policing crackdowns in Chicago's modern history and concludes that it was indeed something new. The chapter summarizes what we learned regarding the efficiency, effectiveness, and equity of stop & frisk as an organizational strategy. It concludes that stop & frisk was quite inefficient, of unimpressive effectiveness, and raised serious equity issues. A toxic mix of both under-policing and over-policing was going on at the same time. There is a discussion of options for improving stops, including statistical optimization, pushing procedural justice harder within the organization, and relying on body worn cameras to change police and public behavior. The chapter concludes with what should be a continuing conversation about the comparative merits of *alternative* strategies for preventing crime that compete with stop & frisk on these evaluative dimensions while still addressing the realities of crime on the ground.

Stop & Frisk in the Three Chicagos

Virtually every issue examined in this book involved digging into how racial differences played themselves out. This reflects the fact there are three Chicagos, not one (Skogan, 2006b). The city's large White, African American, and Hispanic neighborhoods differ dramatically in character, including in their distinctive crime problems and their relationships with the police. In important ways residents live in different worlds. Largely White Chicago neighborhoods are generally quite safe. Problems residents have with the police would not call for a book-length discussion. In our survey, White residents were mostly pleased with the crime-fighting performance of the police, and they saw themselves on the same team when it came to supporting community norms. When they were stopped—which was not often—most White Chicagoans reported they were treated fairly.

The violent gun crimes featured throughout the book were heavily concentrated in predominately African American areas. When gun violence surged in 2016, that is where it spiked. By every measure, resident's problems with the police were concentrated in the same areas, and they were where the police were most suspicious of the motives of the people they serve. Stop & frisk became the phenomenon it was because of the volume and abrasiveness of stops in predominately African American neighborhoods. Residents there reported being fearful of crime but also deeply distrustful of the police, putting them in a tight spot. Unlike other areas, the African American community in Chicago has been shrinking and getting poorer, and it is increasingly isolated from more prosperous neighborhoods. We see in Chapter 7 these factors were robustly linked to crime trends.

The city's diverse Hispanic population is divided by language and culture, factors shaped by the origin and timing of immigrant flows into the city and nation. Hispanic numbers expanded tremendously during the 1980s and 1990s, and more than 30 percent of the Latinos interviewed for this study had to be questioned in Spanish. However, by the end of the period we are examining this immigrant stream had slowed to a trickle. The city's total population remains almost constant because African Americans are being replaced by young, better-educated Whites, while the size of the Hispanic population has become virtually steady-state. Compared to the African American community, recorded crime is generally much lower in concentrated Hispanic neighborhoods. Trends there often more closely parallel those characterizing largely White neighborhoods. By many measures the risks Hispanics face during encounters with the police more closely resemble those of White residents than of African Americans. At the same time, Latinos report generally positive feelings about the police. They broadly support them and by a large margin were not as heavily targeted by stop & frisk. They were, in fact, the group most likely to favor *expanding* the stop & frisk powers of the police. This was driven in part by high levels of fear of crime. However, when they were stopped encounters involving Hispanics were frequently abrasive, which undermined trust in the police, and this was particularly true for recent immigrants and Spanish speakers. While it is common to talk about "the black and brown community" in Chicago, when it comes to crime and the police, they are sometimes in two different places entirely, and sometimes not.

Disclosures

Finally, I have been watching, riding with, surveying, talking with, and formally interviewing Chicago police officers for (at this writing) 30 years. Over the period I have evaluated a number of their initiatives, and written dozens of books, articles, and research reports on what they have been up to. I have sat in on numerous training sessions for rookies, sergeants, senior executives, and serving officers needing refreshing on topics such as community policing and procedural justice. I have given training lectures (always *pro bono*) to sergeants and lieutenants on these and other topics. I explained their community policing program to many visiting delegations of police and public officials from the United States and abroad. I attend every union meeting I can, and I have interviewed multiple union presidents. I sat in many dozens of CompStat meetings, starting when they began locally in the early 2000s. I have served on department committees, including the Superintendent's Advisory Committee (during the term of Police Superintendent Garry McCarthy), a Diversity and Policing Forum (under Terry Hillard), an on-going Training Advisory Committee which vets lesson plans and PowerPoint© decks, and the Superintendent's Community Policing Advisory Panel (for four chiefs, so far). I was actively involved in the reform work of Chicago's

Police Accountability Task Force; their efforts are described in Chapter 6. Along the way I have met many remarkable people. Readers will have to judge for themselves the extent of the sympathy, cynicism, and impatience these experiences have left me with, and how they may have influenced my assessments of stop & frisk.

2

Twenty-first Century Crime

This chapter sets the stage for events to follow. It focuses on the trends and conditions propelling Chicago toward a crime strategy emphasizing stop & frisk. In brief, a precipitous decline in crime over a 15-year span had come to a screeching halt. There followed a decade during which the violent crime rate remained stable, at a level so low the city had not seen the same since the late 1950s. However, even during this period the character of crime was changing in ways close observers saw as disturbing.

First, not everyone was included in the generally good times. During the "crime is flat" decade homicide began to grow again in the city's African American neighborhoods. This could be seen clearly in the violence *rate*. But between 1991 and 2015 the African American population dropped by 25 percent, or more than 240,000 people. As a result, the numbers in predominately African American neighborhoods did not look as terrible as the risks actually faced by those living there. During the 2010s, the gap between crime rates in African American and White Chicago grew.

Second, violent gun crime became the issue of the era. From 2010 to 2015, gun homicide crept up, but other categories of crime, and even violent crimes, subsided. As a result, the crime totals cited by the police department (they always pick the most favorable) continued to drift down, and alarms did not begin to ring for a few years. The stopping power of weapons in the hands of criminals also went up as they shifted to larger-caliber and rapid-fire guns. As this chapter details, *gun* violence was the most pressing crime problem facing the city. During this period Chicago's non-gun homicide rate was comparable to the pretty good numbers reported by New York City and Los Angeles, but its gun-related homicide rate was three times New York's and twice that of Los Angeles. Widely recognized, this became part of debates in the city over crime control.

Next, violence was extremely concentrated. Many neighborhoods were not impacted by these changes. Most homicides occurred in only a few places, where they remained seemingly impervious to the prosperity generally returning to the city in the twenty-first century. When police began

Stop & Frisk and the Politics of Crime in Chicago. Wesley G. Skogan, Oxford University Press.
© Oxford University Press 2023. DOI: 10.1093/oso/9780197675052.003.0002

to cast about for policies responding to renewed pressure to "do something," these pockets of crime presented tempting targets for tough enforcement strategies. The same places were *already* facing seemingly intractable social and economic problems, and this new attention became another burden residents had to bear.

Fourth, it became apparent police had stopped solving crimes. The percentage of violent crimes police could attribute to someone had been sliding down for some time, and into the 2010s it fell into single digits in many categories. By 2015, Chicago police were claiming to have solved only one-quarter of murders and 13 percent of shootings. For all cities that year the solution rate for homicide was 60 percent, and for big cities it was 66 percent (Federal Bureau of Investigation, 2016). The city's "clearance rate" crisis later became a national story, but its real importance is that it presented a fundamental challenge to a modern model of policing. Driving to the scene quickly in response to reports of crimes, then gathering evidence and information from those on the spot, and quickly catching someone stopped working. The question facing police headquarters and city hall was, what policing strategy could replace it?

Finally, the end of the crime drop led to the re-emergence of deadly gun violence, its enormous concentration in places already presenting seemingly intractable problems. The realization Chicagoans could seemingly shoot someone without consequence eventually became a political problem for the city. The media and the public began to take notice. At this point in the stop & frisk era, pressure to *do something* was being felt by all the players in the local criminal justice policy game.

Crime Was Down for Decades, But . . .

The history of crime in twentieth-century Chicago is lurid. It includes the Al Capone era and the fatal fallout from the city's Beer Wars during Capone's tenure. During the last three years before Prohibition the city averaged 137 murders per year; during Prohibition's last three years (1931–1933) the average was 342 killings per year. During the Great Depression and World War II years that followed, the homicide count fluctuated around 200 to 300 killings per year, showing no particular trend. Then came 1959, when Chicago's murder count jumped by 33 percent in one year. Killings continued to rise on an almost yearly basis. The count peaked at 970 in 1974, and it remained above 800 for each of the next seven years. After a brief pause at a high plateau (in the 700s) during the 1980s, murders were back up to 940 in 1992.

But while the early 1990s looked ominous at the time, their arrival signaled the beginning of a historic drop in American crime, including in Chicago. The decline in crime that occurred in American cities beginning in 1991–1992 was unexpected news. Researchers and practitioners have puzzled over this pattern and argued about where credit should be given (Weisburd and Majmundar, 2018; Rosenfeld and Weisburd, 2016). Some pointed to demography and the economy, others to the waning popularity of crack cocaine at the end of the 1980s and its associated homicide spike. There are supporters of the effectiveness of mass incarceration, and many present examples of smarter or more aggressive policing (which are not the same thing). For the evidence, analysts point to crime trends in cities pursuing this strategy or that strategy, but there is almost always a notable counterfactual; for example, another city evidencing the supposed cause of crime decline where it did not go down by much or dropped at a different and causally inopportune time. Many explanations point to factors that peaked too soon, or too late, relative to changes in crime. Other researchers have identified causal factors for which there are typically no appropriate over-time data, but they need to be taken seriously because the proposed explanations are in accord with as much as a century of criminological research. An example would be the social cohesion and organizational capacity of city neighborhoods (Sharkey, Torrats-Spinosa and Takyar, 2017). The absence of supportive evidence of crime rising and falling in concert with shifts in community capacity over time does not mean such claims are untrue. Rather, the problem is there often is no local, over-time data reflecting some of the most important ideas in criminology. Instead, a careful review of many potential sources of crime decline in Chicago came to the discouraging conclusion that ". . . it remains a puzzle" (Chicago Crime Lab, 2017, p. 3). There simply are too many holes in the data through which causal influences on crime could flow, and many of those flows remain unmeasured.

Despite being unexplainable, Chicago participated in this trend—for a while. The detailed data on Chicago crime examined here begins in 1991, at or near the peak year for many categories of offenses. Figure 2-1 presents trends in Chicago crime for a few illustrative categories. Because the city's population fluctuated over this 25-year period, the trend lines represent

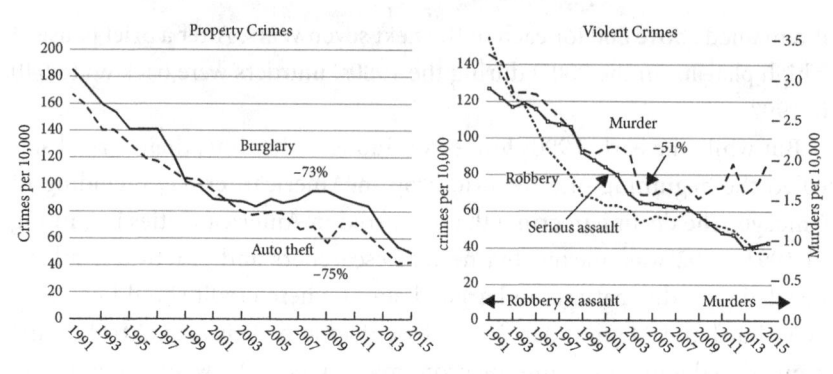

Figure 2-1   Trends in Crime 1991–2015

crimes per 10,000 residents, based on Census Bureau estimates of the size of the local population each year.

The right-hand panel of Figure 2-1 presents trends in murder and two other categories of violent crime.[1] Murders are much less common than assaults or robberies, so they are presented on a separate right-hand scale. Over this entire period murders were primarily gun crimes, and by the mid-2010s as many as 95 percent of homicides fell in this category. As is apparent, the drop in the city's murder count was sharpest during the 1990s, and then leveled off during the mid-2000s. The turning point, which was around 2004, is marked in Figure 2-1 by notes reporting the extent of crime decline in each category. Between 1991 and 2004 the murder rate dropped by half. Then the drop stopped, and the number of murders grew again. The 2015 homicide surge illustrated in Figure 2-1 is noticeable, and, as we will see, became a subject of public debate. Figure 2-1 illustrates another important feature of crime in Chicago. During the same time shootings, gun crimes, and murders plateaued, many other categories of crime continued to drop. All robberies and serious ("aggravated") assaults declined even further following 2004. The same was true of most categories of property crime (which is not shown here). In Chicago, it was specifically *gun*-related crime that was reemerging.

The left-hand panel of Figure 2-1 documents a long period of declining property crime in the city. Burglary and auto theft—two "crimes of acquisition"—dropped fairly steadily from 1991 to 2015. Each dropped by almost three-quarters, a headline if anyone had noticed. We often hear that property crimes are much more frequent than their violent counterparts. In this case, while 2015's national burglary rate was almost *five times* the national robbery rate, in Chicago there was almost as much robbery as burglary. Both clocked in at just above 40 per 10,000. Nationally, serious assaults were more than twice as frequent as robbery, but in Chicago they were just 10 percent higher (Federal Bureau of Investigation, 2016, table 1). Crime in Chicago was exceptionally violent.

However, Chicago *had* become a safer place because of these general trends. To illustrate the magnitude of the decline in crime, conditions in 2015 can be compared to a "what if..." world in which crime did *not* decline. For example, between 1991 and 2015 the yearly serious assault count declined from 35,190 to 13,900, with victims piling up during each of the years in between. Imagine if the aggravated assault count had not declined but had instead remained at its 1991 level throughout the period. If this had been the case, 287,000 *more* people would have been attacked than actually were. The (hypothetical) drop in the number of people who would have been killed were it not for the 1991–2015 drop in crime totaled 8,396 saved lives. The numbers were just as stark in other high-volume offense categories. If the crime drop had not occurred, there might have been 564,200 more robbery victims, 540,120 more burglaries, and 517,290 more cars stolen. Those are large numbers, and they help illustrate the social and economic significance of what took place in Chicago, and around the nation, toward the end of the twentieth century.

On the other hand, a detailed analysis of when and where crimes were occurring during the 2010s pointed to a disturbing situation. Not everyone was equally safe, and these benign trends were not being felt everywhere in the city.

Another way to analyze crime data is to link it to the communities in which it occurs, by geocoding incident address. This produces crime trends distinguished the predominate race of the residents of each of the city's census tracts (the crime incident data do not include any characteristics of victims or offenders). Adding together tracts home to generally the same groups formed geographical clusters for tracking crime rates over time. It was not required that these clusters be geographically contiguous, but most were. In 2010, 268 of the city's 788 inhabited tracts were principally home to African Americans, and the people living in those areas constituted 27 percent of the city's total population. Another 22 percent of the population lived in the 202 tracts that were classified as predominately White in composition. Hispanics were heavily clustered in 155 densely populated tracts, home to 23 percent of the city's population. Finally, many tracts—167 in total—were sufficiently diverse that they could not be thrown into a more descriptive pot. The diversity of these tracts came primarily from their mix of Whites, Hispanics, and the city's growing Asian population. A key point about Chicago is that the city is sharply segregated. Few African Americans live in predominately White or Hispanic census tracts, and few (but somewhat more) live in diverse areas. Together, residents of diverse areas totaled 24 percent of the population. Comparable population counts were used to calculate crime rates (per 10,000 residents) for each cluster. The computer algorithm for classifying tracts by race drew on interpolations of decennial census data until the early 2010s, when the Census Bureau began distributing yearly census data by tract. Each year it recalibrated the racial classification of each tract, adjusting for shifts in the city's population over the decades.

Figure 2-2 presents trends since 1991 for crimes in two categories that became politically salient during debates about stop & frisk: murders and shootings. "Shooting" was not a statistical category in crime in Chicago until the arrival in 2011 of a new police chief from New York City. Shootings were a big focus of New York's media, and he insisted on adding it to press releases from the Chicago department. It quickly became a local favorite. This category (which we will see a lot of) combines any crime during which someone is shot, including the many victims who lived through the experience as well as those (fewer) who died.[2] During 2015, for example, the survived-versus-died ratio in the shooting category was about 6-to-1.

Early in this period the trend in both murders and shootings had been down in White, African American, Hispanic, and diverse areas of the city. As Figure 2-2 illustrates, these crimes declined most dramatically in African American communities through the mid-2000s. Shootings and homicides declined the least in predominately White areas, where they were not very

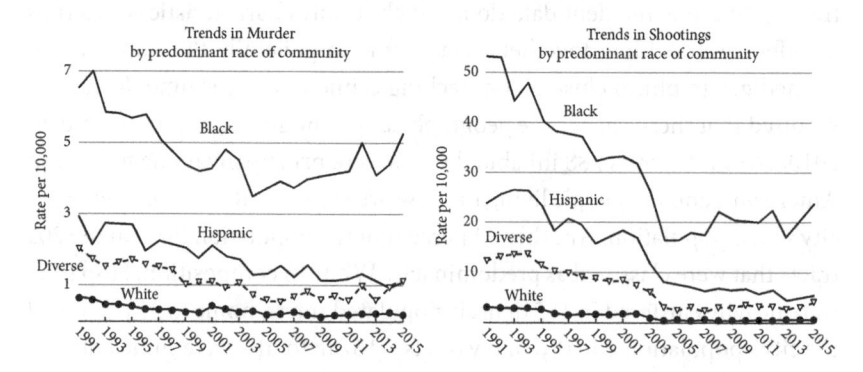

Figure 2-2 Violent Crime Trends by Race 1991–2015

high at the outset. However, in percentage terms, even White areas (although it is hard to see) enjoyed substantial declines in violent crime during the 1990s.

Then violent crime stopped dropping. In predominately White areas, shootings and killings continued at about the same rate for another decade and more, while in Hispanic areas they drifted down a bit further. However, shootings in African American areas staggered back up, ending in 2015 at more than 30 percent above their 2004 low. Murders surged upward after 2008, and by 2015 murders made up about two-thirds of the ground it had lost over the previous twenty years. Around this time, the overall death rate per 100,000 for African American males in Chicago was 109; for Latino males it was 26; and among White males it was 1.9. Firearm-related death rates for African American males aged 10–24 years were *50 times* higher than for young White Chicagoans (Kemal, et al., 2018). There was a lot of change in Chicago's African American community, much of it for the worse.

What About the New York Miracle?

Chicago's crime shifts attracted local, and even national, attention. At that moment, crime was *not* rising in most big cities—a point not lost on the city's critics. Many cities continued to enjoy historic declines during this period, while in other cities crime just leveled off. Looking at city-level changes in crime from 2014 to 2015, just two cities—Chicago and Baltimore—accounted for one-quarter of the *national* increase in big-city murder in 2015 (Rosenfeld, et al., 2017). By June 2015, the Chicago media had begun focusing on their newest crime wave. The summer shooting season started early, and the *Chicago Tribune* headlined (on June 8), "Chicago's gun violence up from a year ago, topping 1,000" (Ford and Gorner, 2015). Adding up the numbers, they noted that, since 2012, "this is the earliest in the year 1,000 people have been shot." Chicagoans prefer high benchmarks, but too often they still exceed them. The *Tribune* also noted the comparable total for Los Angeles shootings over the same period was only 438, and in New York City it was just 510.

Chicago is not New York City, but New York is the media capital of the country, so trends there were well known locally. Figure 2-3 presents comparable murder rates for New York and Chicago, with the national trend over this period illustrated as well. Perhaps the most remarkable feature of

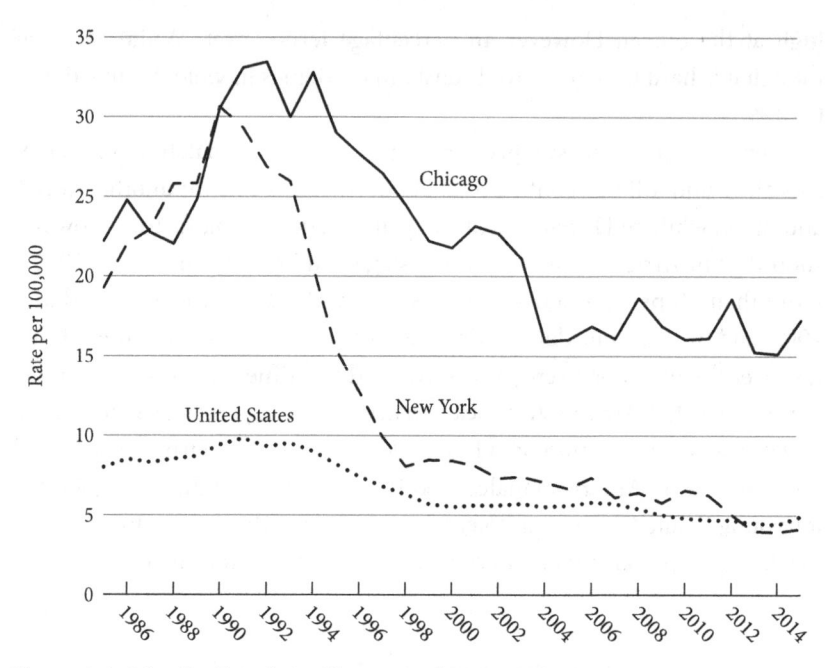

Figure 2-3 Murder Trends in Chicago and New York City

the chart is the convergence of New York with the homicide rate for the nation as a whole (Rosenfeld, Terry and Chauhan, 2013). City size is generally one of the strongest correlates of violent crime, but by the end of the 1990s this city of more than eight million residents resembled the rest of the country. Chicagoans, on the other hand, took away another message from these comparisons. During the 1980s, Chicago and New York experienced about the same rate of homicides, and they traced about the same trend. In fact, their trends had tracked one another since the middle of the 1940s. However, after 1990 the two cities began to diverge. The "New York miracle" began earlier than any serious decline in Chicago's murder rate. In rapid order, New York was tagged "the city that became safe," to quote the title of Franklin Zimring's (2011) book on this remarkable period. Chicago, on the other hand, did not look so safe, except in contrast to more-violent earlier decades. From their side, the *New York Times* asked itself, "So what's going on in Chicago?" The paper replied—in a self-congratulatory essay—"It's complicated, but a comparison with New York is good place to start" (Fessenden and Park, 2016). Nationally, during the 2016 Presidential election campaign it was reported that candidate Donald Trump (of New York) likened Chicago to a "war-torn country," and opined "I think Chicago needs stop and frisk." Later (on January 24, 2017), he threatened to "send in the feds" if ". . . Chicago doesn't fix the horrible carnage going on . . . ."

As we will see in Chapter 3, such comparisons—highlighted by the 2011 arrival in Chicago of a new police chief imported from New York City—added to continuing political pressure to do something about gun violence. This was a moment when Chicago contributed a case for textbooks on police organization. As predicted by "institutional" theories of organizational adaptation and change, the city reached out for a culturally and politically validated response they could point to as a solution to the gun violence crisis. There are plenty of examples of Chicago and other cities acting this way on other occasions. These include the adoption of units serving special populations, community policing programs promising to restore neighborhoods, local anti-terrorism units of (often) no particular utility, data-driven CompStat management formats, and large investments in body-worn cameras (for more on this see Jurek, Matusiak and King, 2022). In this instance, "validated" meant that "it worked in New York." Whether it would work in Chicago was unknown, but "the New York Miracle" of declining crime during that city's stop & frisk era cast everywhere an almost mythical aura of legitimacy over the adoption of aggressive proactive policing on a very large scale. There was plenty of support in various communities for other paths toward crime prevention, but they were not media and political favorites. Stop & frisk looked more like "real policing."

It Was All About Guns

The crime crisis that emerged in Chicago by mid-2015 was specifically a crisis regarding *gun* violence. The murders dominating the headlines were virtually all attributable to firearms, plus there was an increase in the use of guns in robbery and serious assaults. Gun murders have long dominated homicide statistics. In 1999, Zimring and Hawkins (1999) noted that 70 percent of Chicago's homicides involved guns. This was high for the times, but not later. As they pointed out, killing someone—especially an alert young man—with a knife or a tire iron is close-in work and risky for both parties. And it easily leaves DNA traces and blood stains, which are convincing physical clues. Zimring and Hawkins argued it was the ready availability of guns and a willingness to use them, not any unique preference for violence itself, that

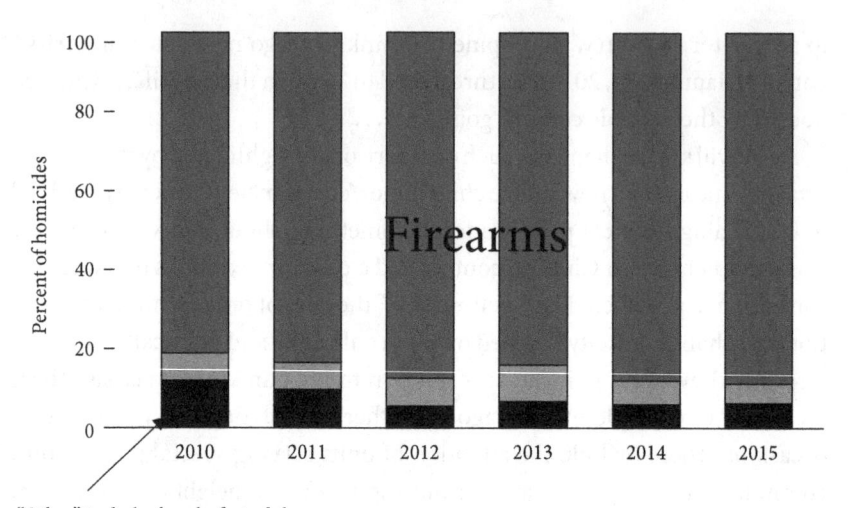

"Other" includes hands, feet, clubs,
vehicles, burning, poison, strangling and all unknown

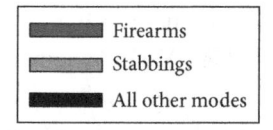

	Firearms
	Stabbings
	All other modes

Source: Chicago police department reports

Figure 2-4 Weapon Types in Murder

determined America's standout ranking on national homicide lists. Looking across countries, they concluded, "our rate of assault is not exceptional; our death rate from assault is exceptional" (pp. 122–123).

The continuing role played by guns in Chicago homicide is illustrated in Figure 2-4. It contrasts gun murders with others. The "clubs" category includes baseball bats and hammers; strangulation may be by hand, rope, or phone cord; "burning" frequently involves gasoline. Except for the knives and screwdrivers used in stabbings, other types of weapons are used too infrequently point to trends. For many years (but not recently) Chicago police published a detailed list of the weapons involved in homicides. An intriguing one was "refrigerator." By 2015 homicides were almost all about guns.

Figure 2-5 presents a broader view of the rise of Chicago gun crime just during the 2010s. It illustrates the mix of gun and non-gun murders, noting the number of gun killings registered each year. It is apparent that the upward spike in fatal violence in Chicago during this period was a spike in gun

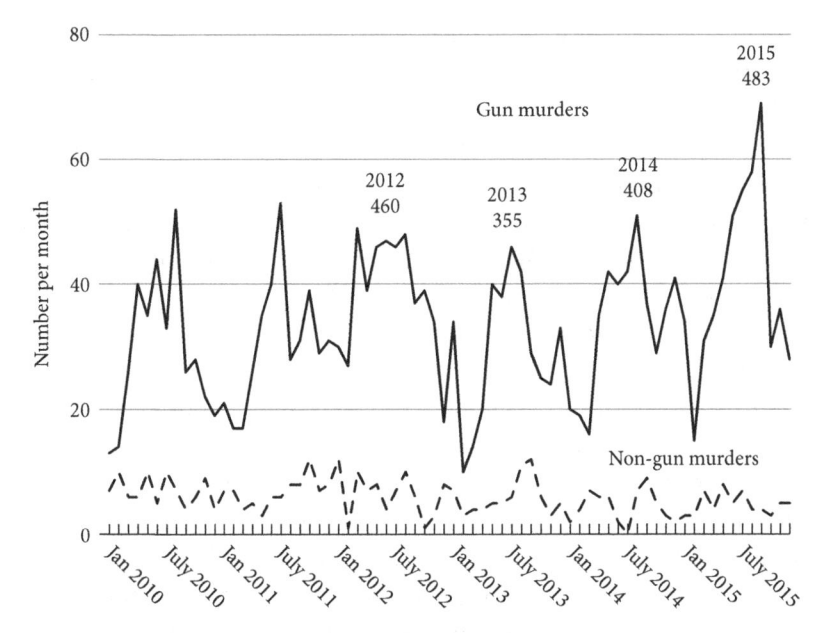

Figure 2-5 Trends in Gun Use in Murder 2010–2015

violence. While the number of non-gun killings plodded along at constant pace, between 2013 and 2015 the number of gun murders went up by 36 percent (from 355 to 483). As a study of this period noted, while Chicago's non-gun homicide rate was comparable to rates in New York and Los Angles, the city's gun-related homicide figure was three times larger than New York's and twice that of Los Angeles (Chicago Crime Lab, 2014).

Another feature of Chicago's gun problem was the increasing proportion of *heavy* weapons working in the gun mix. Continuing research on firearms has documented the emergence, and greater lethality, of heavy street weapons. Braga and Cook (2018) found shootings with larger caliber bullets are more likely to result in death, even controlling for where, and the number of times, victims are shot. They noted that if offenders grow more likely to use large-caliber, high velocity guns, murder rates could increase rapidly. Lauritsen and Lentz (2019) concluded that in recent years the national increase in homicide has not been driven principally by more violent crime incidents or increased gun use, but by the increasing *lethality* of the guns being toted.

In Chicago, a local newspaper documented changing patterns of weapon use. Reporters reviewed medical examiners' reports on everyone shot to death during the month of August in 1992, and again 14 years later. They found the average homicide victim was shot almost twice as many times in 2006. In addition, more were shot by hollow-point bullets designed to fragment into multiple pieces, scattering through victims' bodies. These "R.I.P." bullets—short for "radically invasive projectiles"—create multiple wounds from a single shell. Both trends reflect the more frequent use of semiautomatic firearms fed by high-capacity magazines that can spray bullets around with ease. Worse, rifles like the AR-15 employ shells that rattle around in the victim's body and leave large and jagged wounds. With an AR-15 one can—with skill—hit a target 650 yards away. In 1991—simpler times—six-shot, hand-held revolvers were the most common murder guns (Main, 2018). However, as a rule, young men on the street today prefer large-caliber, large-magazine semiautomatics, when they can lay their hands on them. In Boston, this means being willing to pay about twice the legitimate-market price (Hureau and Braga, 2018). The only factor involved in homicide that seems to have improved over this period is the emergency medical treatment delivered by the city's hospital trauma centers. This good news is leavened by the fact that *access* to its trauma centers remains stratified by race and class (Wandling, et al., 2016).

My own data include details on weapons only for the years since 2012, but even during that period the potential lethality of the guns used in homicide rose. Ratings of the range and "energy transfer" (e.g., stopping power) of various weapon calibers classified them into low, moderate (comparatively), and high lethality. The latter ranged upwards from .40-caliber bullets, including popular 9mm, 10mm and .45-caliber handguns, plus all shotguns. The percentage of known murder guns in the highest lethality category grew from 30 percent in 2012 and 2013 to 40 percent by 2015. Much of the movement was from the slightly-less-lethal category, which included guns in the popular .357-caliber and .38-caliber range. Scattered earlier police reports described the frequent deployment of smaller, cheaper guns through the 1990s, but by 2015 the .32-caliber and under range constituted only four percent of the guns involved in homicides. It is important to note firearm characteristics can only be determined when investigators recover a bullet or shell casing; they cannot reliably be classified based just on the bodily damage they inflicted. However, this physical evidence frequently is not successfully gathered and inventoried.

Where did all these guns come from? Originally, they mostly come from the legitimate gun market. People who commit crimes with guns can get their hands on the weapons in several ways. In 32 states, gun owners can sell weapons in unregulated private sales not requiring background checks. One major study found almost 60 percent of the crime guns recovered in Chicago between 2009 and 2013 were first purchased in nearby Indiana and Wisconsin, as well as in Mississippi, states which did not require background checks for sales at guns shows or on the Internet (Chicago Crime Lab, 2014). An important source of crime guns is via "straw purchasers," or individuals who buy guns from licensed dealers on behalf of others who cannot because of their age or criminal record. Studies in Chicago have found about 15 percent of crime guns are acquired through straw purchasers.

Another source of guns is theft. The criminal supply chain is fed by thefts of household guns during burglaries, for example, and from larger-scale thefts from gun shops. In 2012, Chicago police apprehended two members of a gang that had recently stolen 450 guns from eight gun shops. In the same year, Chicago police recovered 57 firearms stolen from one gun shop in the immediate suburbs, while in 2013 a Chicago resident led an armed takeover of a gun shop in nearby Indiana, netting 40 guns (Main, 2017). In addition to retail thefts, Chicago is a major railroad connection point and, during the period we are examining, several significant thefts of guns took place in its rail yards. Based on news reports, thieves stole 319 guns from boxcars parked in Chicago in December 2009. In May 2014, 130 guns were stolen from freight trains. In the same year another group (apparently) stole 111 guns from a boxcar train traveling through Chicago from a Ruger factory in New Hampshire. Only 19 of the 111 were recovered directly; the remainder disappeared, doubtless into the illicit market for firearms. It is almost certain that thefts like these were based on insider information, from informants who identified which of the thousands of rail cars passing through the city each week presented these opportunities. Thefts on this scale could be responsible for notable spikes in violence, as they surge into the underground economy in large numbers. Earlier, resales of guns stolen from the CPD evidence room were also part of the mix. In 2007, a secret internal report was released on evidence theft during the 1990s. Guns vanished and were later recovered from criminals. Only in 2001, after an officer stole 44 pounds of cocaine from the evidence room, did the department begin to seriously manage its holdings (Main, 2007).

Violence Was Very Concentrated, Calling for Concentrated Responses

An important feature of violent crime in Chicago is that it was heavily concentrated in just a few parts of the city. The concentration of violence was most notable in Chicago's most disadvantaged African American communities on the west and south sides of town. There, the general decline in crime following 1991 was less steep, and it stopped dropping there first. Papachristos, Brazil and Cheng (2018) document how the gap between Chicago's safest and most dangerous areas grew dramatically beginning in the late 2000s. The gap was particularly driven by rapid improvements in safer neighborhoods, increasing the gap between have-crime and have-not-crime areas.

As a result of this concentration, in any given year only a few areas in Chicago experienced most of the city's shootings and killings, some incidents were scattered about, and more than one-half of the city's neighborhoods had virtually no violent gun crime at all. Chicago is traditionally divided into 77 well-defined community areas. The names of many of them are widely referred to by residents, and most maps and statistical descriptions of the city divide the data by community area. Differences in trends between those 77 places reflect the concentration of crime. During the entire period of 2004 to 2015, one community area (Edison Park, on the city's northwest side) did not experience a single shooting. On the other hand, residents of three community areas—Austin, North Lawndale, and Englewood—witnessed at least one shooting *every month* during the same 144-month span. Homicide is less frequent and even more concentrated than shootings. However, during the same 144-month period the Austin community area experienced only 14 murder-free months, while Edison Park again scored 144 monthly zeros.

Why is crime so concentrated? It is because gun violence clusters people, places, and behavior. Part of the story is that *offenders* are concentrated. They are not spread thinly everywhere (Lurie, Acevedo and Ott, 2018). They concentrate crime because most do not travel very far, very often, in search of victims. Also, they are often networked with their peers in the area, concentrating their focus on nearby locations. Andrew Papachristos and colleagues find homicides and shootings in Chicago are strongly concentrated within small social networks. Analyzing CPD arrest data, they uncovered a social network consisting of only six percent of the city's population accounted for 70 percent of nonfatal shootings (Papachristos, Wildeman and Roberto, 2015). Importantly, offending is even concentrated *among* offenders.

Research indicates most crimes are committed by chronic offenders, who stand out even among other lawbreakers. Few people are responsible for a very substantial proportion of all crime. Martinez and colleagues (2017) report that the most prolific 10 percent of offenders (note: not people, but offenders) account for more than one-half of all crime.

Another reason crime is concentrated is that it is concentrated among *victims*. There is inevitably a trail of repeated victimization—and even re-victimization by the same offenders—characterizing just a few of them but accounting for a disproportionate percentage of all crime. The numbers can be significant because repeat victims are themselves concentrated at places. A study in Britain, for example, found the principal difference between high and low crime areas was the pileup of repeat victimizations (Hope and Trickett, 2008). Those most likely to carry out shootings are also extremely vulnerable to becoming gunshot victims themselves. In the small networks driving shootings, the line between perpetrator and victim is often blurry. Gunshot survivors are at a heightened risk of committing firearm-related crimes, as well as returning to the hospital with another violent injury. It is the social—and thus importantly geographical—proximity of young men within networks of gun offenders and other victims that increase their risk of become a shooting victim (Papachristos, Hureau and Braga, 2013; Papachristos, Wildeman and Roberto, 2015). These groups—in Chicago, primarily young men of color—are thus trapped in a cycle of violence.

Finally, features of *places* concentrate crime. The kinds of offenses we are considering here require victims and offenders to intersect somewhere. For example, Wrigley Field (home of the Chicago Cubs) regularly brings together 40,000 potential victims (they usually sell out) and crews of pickpockets. Neither victims nor offenders usually live or (otherwise) work there, but this crowded, boisterous environment facilitates victimization. Another example is neighborhoods that are home to fearful, discouraged residents who have given up cooperating with the police and have been unable to generate any sustained community efforts against crime. Weisburd, Groff and Yang (2012) report that the exercise of informal social control is less common in higher-crime places, creating more opportunities for crime.

So, as elsewhere, an important feature of crime in Chicago is that it is not spread evenly over the city's 256 square miles of real estate. Rather, crime maps reveal both mountains and valleys of crime, cut by rivers of expressways and streams of streets. This varying typography reflects "Weisburd's Law" (2015), which posits that a small proportion of places in any jurisdiction will account for a disproportionate fraction of all crime. A great deal of research has focused on these concentrations and their implications for crime control. For example, Braga, Davis and White (2012) found five percent of city blocks and street intersections in Boston generated 74 percent of shootings between 1980 and 2009. In a review of numerous studies, Lee, et al. (2017) concluded about 43 percent of all crime is found in the top 10 percent of places within cities. On a crime map, hot spots flash red, warning where mountains of trouble have accumulated.

The concentration of crime in hot spots obviously has important implications for social and economic policies, as well as for effective law enforcement. It is not to be forgotten that crime reports count *victims*. They flag the locations of the homes, workplaces, and activity spaces where victims live out their lives. Concentrated crime signals concentrated human misery. Some recent research on hot spots concludes that crime co-concentrates there along with emotional and physiological stress, high blood pressure, and a variety of related measures of physical and emotional ill-health (cf., Weisburd and White, 2019). Emergency medical teams are dispatched to crime hot spots with disproportionate frequency. Knowing where crime is concentrated, especially in stable, chronic fashion, should signal where agencies of all kinds should focus their efforts.

When it comes to policing, well-organized departments make aggressive use of crime patterns to deploy their officers. Relying on the metaphor of old-style crime maps, which marked the location of offenses with colored pins so patterns might appear, this means "putting cops on the dots" (Maple, 2000). In fact, a review of police research released in 2017 (Weisburd and Majmundar, 2018) concluded that focusing resources on crime hot spots in this way was potentially the most effective use of police resources in terms of reducing crime. Police can address a substantial proportion of all crime in a city by focusing on a small number of high crime places. To guide themselves, police should be asking questions like, what is it about specific places that leads to the concentration of crime? For example, research indicates hot spots form at the convergence of motivated offenders and likely targets in places where social factors and the physical layout facilitate victimization (Groff, 2017). Officers with proper problem-solving skills should be able to identify those factors. This leads to the next question: What are the best policing and alternative strategies for addressing these crime generators, and dealing with the problems created by crime there? Answering those questions takes problem-solving skills as well.

However, in Chicago during the 2010s, it was more likely that concentrations of crime would be treated as targets for aggressive stop & frisk than as the locus of chronic problems needing solving. For police, and for a public worried about the incursion of crime into *their* neighborhoods, the question was whether the crime spike was due to the increased intensity of victimization in the usually suspect locations, or whether it was spreading into hitherto less threatened areas.

Aggregating crime and census data for each of the city's 2010 census block groups identified the extent of violence concentration in Chicago. Census block groups are very small areas—there are 2,170 of them in the city, and in 2010 they had an average population of 1,230.[3] To examine trends systematically, area boundaries were fixed so that they remained the same over the entire quarter-century of data. For each year, the highest concentration places were those falling in the top five percent of block groups. Using this cutoff value flagged the 108 most dangerous small places in the city each year. The percentage of shootings and killings falling in the top 10 percent of block groups (216 block groups) yielded a parallel measure. By either measure, the stability of crime concentration in Chicago was remarkable. Despite fluctuations in the level of crime over this period, the top five percent of block groups consistently accounted for about one-third of all shootings taking place in the city. In 1991, the top three percent of concentrated violence pockets accounted for 2,294 shootings, or 33 percent of the city's yearly total. During the period when crime was dropping, shootings and killings declined by roughly the same proportion almost everywhere, and my estimate of Weisburd's Constant for Chicago did not change much at all. In 2017—26 years later—33 percent of shootings again took place in the top five percent of places. All of this is in accord with a corollary to Weisburd's Law: "crime concentration stays within a narrow bandwidth across time, despite strong volatility in crime incidents" (Weisburd, 2015, p. 133).

Figure 2-6 details the concentration of crime for a half-decade. Seen in detail on the right-hand side, stability in the concentration of shootings is apparent. Over this period, just the top five percent of block groups were home to 30–33 percent of shootings. Stepping back to the top 10 percent of groups, they accounted for 50–54 percent of shootings over the long haul. Murders are fewer in number each year (in 2010 shootings were 16 times as frequent), and in 2010, 85 percent of Chicago's block groups did not have a single murder. Because of the smaller numbers involved, the year-to-year proportion of homicides in the top five percent of block groups will fluctuate

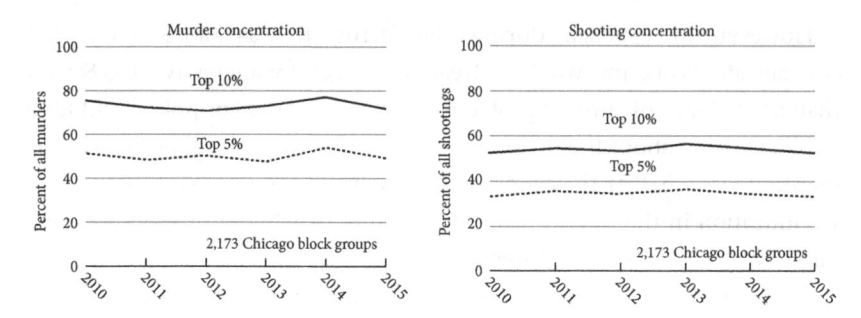

Figure 2-6 Trends in Violence Concentration 2010–2015

a bit more than the comparable series for shootings. In 2015, the most concentrated pockets of violence in the city accounted for about 50 percent of all murders, and the top 10 percent (still just 208 small areas) accounted for just over 70 percent of murders. The key point is that there were not many "dots" to focus the cops on if they did their homework. Concentrating heavily on a few pockets of violence promised to be an informed start toward crafting an effective gun-focused strategy.

As an aside, this stability did not mean violence had to be concentrated in the *same* small places each year. Empirically, the highest-crime communities sit close to one another, and many showed up repeatedly on the hot list, but police must display some agility in moving around in response to shifting crime patterns. When it came to shootings, the most consistently dangerous block group in the city was in the West Humboldt Park community on the west side of Chicago. Shootings in this area—home to about 1,200 people in the 2010 census—were both frequent and persistent. Block group 2315/6 remained among the top five percent for shootings in the city for *25 straight years*, from 1991 to 2015. Over that period almost 330 people were shot there. During 2015, 2315/6 tied for *first place* citywide in the number of shootings, recording 11 of them. Notably, over the entire period of 1991–2015, 2315/6 also recorded the largest homicide total in the city—a total of 72 people died there.

Group 2315/6 did not stand out in other readily apparent ways. It and many other persistent pockets of violence are not particularly different from the much larger number of poor areas to be found throughout the city. In the Census Bureau's 2015 community survey, 96 percent of 2315/6's residents were African Americans. Almost one-half of the households in 2315/6 were receiving food stamps, and more than one-third of households consisted of single mothers and their children. Only 29 percent of adults in the area were in the labor force, a very low number. One-half of adults had not graduated from high school. Comprising 25 standard-sized Chicago blocks in a roughly five-by-five grid, 2315/6 is almost completely residential. No large housing developments are sited there. Most residents live in modest two- and three-story buildings. A cluster of about a dozen new scatter-site, assisted-rental single-family homes are grouped in one corner of the area. Each is on its own lot, with a fence. The area is home to one elementary school, not unusual because there were then 660 of them in Chicago. I counted three storefront churches in the area, but only one grocery store—and it was boarded up. There are many vacant lots where abandoned buildings have been knocked down and clawed out, in line with the city's fight against blight. The 2016 Census survey found 25 percent of the still-existing residences in the area were vacant. But there are also trees, and many front yards look well-tended. Like 2315/6, Chicago's highest-crime hot spots generally are not statistically distinguishable from other poor neighborhoods by their composition or poverty, nor by measures of the many other afflictions co-locating with race and poverty. To identify 2315/6 required crime analysis.

As we will see in later chapters, awareness of the importance of crime concentration influenced Chicago's policing strategies in significant ways. During the 2010s they put cops on the dots in a massive way. The Chicago Police Department certainly noticed block group 2315/6. Between 2004 and 2015 they made an astonishing 11,600 stops in this neighborhood and its surrounding arterial streets, including almost 5,000 stop & frisks during the 2013–2015 period when stops were ramping up in the city. But during this entire period, shootings in 2315/6 still closely tracked those for African American Chicago as a whole.

Getting Away with Murder

The final—and perhaps most significant—feature of crime in Chicago was a collapse in the ability of police and the rest of the criminal justice system to successfully solve crimes and bring offenders to account. In earlier days, police were capable of resolving most murders but by the mid-2010s most were going unsolved. In 2015, they solved only 14 percent of shootings. For robberies ("Your money or your life!") the solution rate was 18 percent, and for all gun crimes it was one-in-five. Property crimes were worse; the solution rate for burglaries was nine percent.

Chicago was not alone in this. According to the FBI's national figures for 2015, 46 percent of violent crimes and only 19 percent of property crimes were solved. For murder, the national solution rate was 62 percent, and it was 54 percent for serious assaults. Robbery, which was solved only 29 percent of the time, brought down the violent crime total. Nationally, only 13 percent of burglaries were solved. Earlier these percentages had been higher, but during the 1990s and 2000s they remained stable at the national level (Pew Research Center, 2017). That said, this apparent national-level stability masks a great deal of variability in the ability to solve crimes. The solvability of crime varies widely across cities, and it shifts from year to year within cities, all for ill-understood reasons (Scott, et al., 2018). Cross-city studies of crime do not clearly link solvability differences to police budgets, equipment, or organization. Studies of individual cities, on the other hand, have found effective management, the hours of effort invested in cases, extensive follow-up visits, forensic testing of physical evidence, paying serious attention to nonfatal shootings, and an organizational commitment to crime solving can make a difference in solution rates over time (Braga, Turchan and Barao, 2019; Pizarro, Terrill and LoFaso, 2018).

Why is this important? First, the erosion of crime fighting created a crisis regarding the effectiveness of the model underlying the organization and operation of policing. That model is to react quickly to citizens' calls, gather physical evidence and interview witnesses, and make arrests. But by the middle of the 2010s Chicago police were not catching very many people, even when it came to crimes that were the focus of public and media attention. This could not help their standing in the eyes of the voters and taxpayers. In 2013, a local magazine featured a story claiming homicide clearances were the lowest "in memory." The headline was "Chicago criminals are getting away with murder" (Jackson, 2013, p. 1). More fundamentally, the inability of police to catch many offenders undercut the effectiveness of two causal mechanisms which can be activated by reactive policing: individual and general individual deterrence. The fact that actual shooters and killers were not being brought to account meant they—and their guns—were not being taken off the street, and they were not paying a price for their actions. This was not likely to encourage them to hang up their holsters. The inability to solve crimes also sent a message of sorts to the neighborhoods afflicted by gun violence: the police could not protect them, even from criminals in their midst. They were, in this sense, seriously under-policed despite being the focus of intensive policing. Declining solvability could also undermine the general deterrent effectiveness of reactive policing when it comes to discouraging people from carrying weapons around and even thinking about using them in the first place. In the absence of a meaningful risk of being caught if they used their gun, the possible benefits of carrying them—which included self-protection and control of their street corner, as well as the power to have their way with people—could look more attractive.

And this was not the end of it. The crime clearance crisis could have even wider implications, including for the legitimacy of policing. The inability of the police to bring offenders to account was seen by many as a signal their communities were not worth the effort it would take to protect them. Police were accused of being indifferent to minority victims, their families, and their communities. Many city residents just assumed police were doing better in better-off neighborhoods, as usual. This raises the issue of "distributive justice," which arises when groups of people think they are collectively getting the short end of the stick (Tankebe, 2013). Perceptions of distributive justice are intimately related to people's beliefs about the legitimacy of the institutions serving—and controlling—them. In my 2015 community survey, more than 75 percent of African Americans agreed the Chicago police did not provide the same quality of service in all neighborhoods. When asked, "How likely is it that police are providing a better service to the rich than to the average citizen?" 54 percent of African Americans replied they "definitely" did. The cynical view of Chicago police was, "they don't really care about people like me."

Further, when people see bad deeds going unpunished, their faith in the rule of law is at risk. When people do not trust the police, they may stop cooperating with them. One of the foundational hypotheses regarding procedural justice theory is that trust in the police encourages more crime reporting, more cooperation with police investigations, a greater willingness to exchange information with the authorities, and greater involvement in crime prevention activities. But if the system is seen as both unfair and ineffective, neighborhood residents could be pressed to take matters into their own hands. They may begin to carry weapons for self-defense, acting on their own when loved ones are threatened, and exacting retribution when they see bad deeds are going unpunished. Smith and Uchida (1988) called this the "collective security hypothesis." They pointed out that the tradition of communities "taking the law into their own hands" when formal institutions have failed to protect them is as old as American history. The San Francisco Committee of Vigilance was formed in 1851 to chase down criminals and exact private justice because the political establishment could not. The Committee added a word to our vocabulary.

From the point of view of the police in Chicago, the practical questions were: How could they prevent shootings when the deterrence model was broken? How could they stop crimes if they couldn't solve them? How could they continue to deter people from committing them in the first place? Their business model was not working.

Unsolvable Crime

Figure 2-7 charts the percentage of shootings and gun murders solved by the police, beginning in 1991. Recall that gun murders are a subset of shootings, which are mostly nonfatal. Over this period, the solution rate for gun murders dropped from 72 to only 26 percent, a precipitous collapse. Detectives were able to put more time into murders than almost any other crime, but by

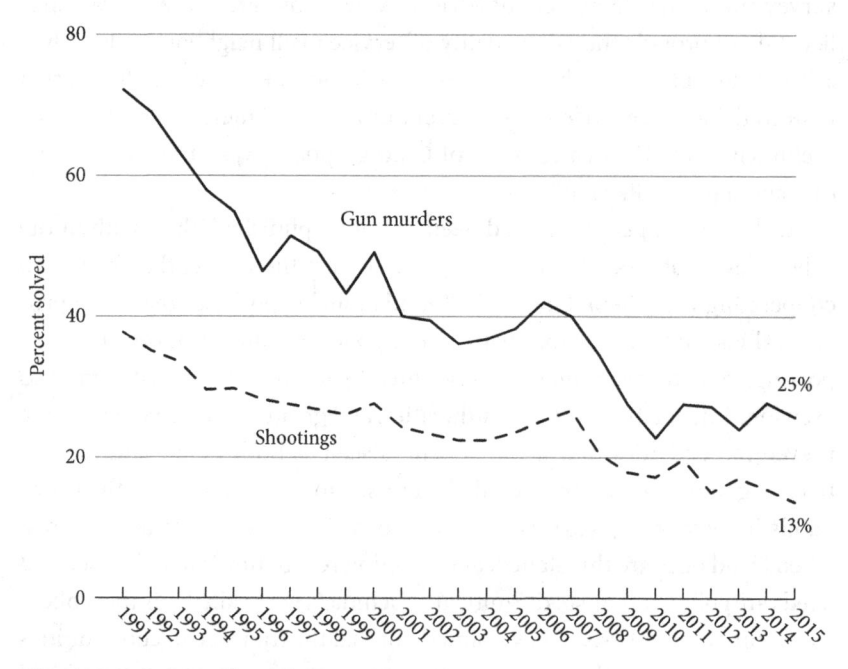

Figure 2-7 Solving Gun Violence 1991–2015

2015 they were solving them only about one-quarter of the time. A review of media reports and statistical summaries issued by the police indicate that well into the 1960s the Chicago department was claiming to solve more than 90 percent of murders. (I should add there was some suspicion even at the time about the veracity of these claims.) Between 2010 and 2015, a period in which the homicide solution rate apparently lingered at its lowest level in history, about 1,800 gun murders went unsolved.

As Figure 2-7 documents, the numbers for shootings were worse. Unlike homicide, it has always been the norm that most shootings in Chicago go unsolved. But during a 2015 uptick in shootings their solvability declined even further. There were more than 2,370 shootings during 2015, and about 86 percent were never successfully resolved. During 2010–2015, a total of more than 10,000 shootings went unsolved. In addition, just during this period the solution rate for serious assaults and robberies dropped by about 10 percentage points.

What contributes to solving crimes, and why has crime clearance dropped so discouragingly? In Chicago, the easy-to-solve ones are known as "smoking gun" cases. When they arrive at the scene in response to calls from neighbors or bystanders, officers may find the protagonists still assembled there. Domestic violence cases and within-family homicides often fall in this category. In others, the alleged perpetrators are "known, but flown." Think fights in bars, where there were many witnesses. In these cases, the alleged perpetrators may have taken off, but bystanders can have a great deal to share with the police regarding what happened. In her book on Chicago, *What Cops Know*, Connie Fletcher (1992, p. 18) noted, "that's when you know who did it, you got an eyeball, an actual witness, or an earball—somebody who knows who did it." Known but flown cases are mostly cleared up. The hard-to-solve cases, on the other hand, frequently remain in the category of "mystery." In Chicago, it is the growing number of mysteries that is the source of the clearance rate crisis.

Homicide clearances used to be higher because a large percentage were crimes of passion or fueled by alcohol. They involved offenders who were known by, or even related to, their victims, or they arose out of public disputes. They were usually easy to solve. However, much of the nationwide decline in homicide since the 1990s has in these categories. Between 1991 and 2011 (after which Chicago police stopped releasing crime reports), the percentage of murders in Chicago classed as "domestic situations" declined by 98 percent, down to 0.2 percent of the total. This is in line with a rapid decline in domestic homicide nationally (Dugan, Nagin and Rosenfeld, 1999). During the same period, the proportion of Chicago's murders stemming from gang and drug-related violence doubled. A problem, of course, is classifying homicide types in this way is dependent on knowing "whodunit" and why. When it is possible to figure out the motive, about one-half of Chicago's murders now involve gangs and/or the drug business. However, in a parallel shift, a much larger percentage of homicides are now classified as "motive unknown" and "relationship unknown" cases. This is in line with the decline in clearing violent crimes, flagging they have become more difficult to solve. In 1972, Chicago police claimed to solve 87 percent of homicides. Their detailed homicide report indicated they could not uncover much about offenders—for example, even their relationship with the victim remained unknown—in eight percent of homicides. By 2000 the "relationship unknown" fraction was at 42 percent, and police were solving 47 percent of homicides. In general, these shifts have also increased the similarity of victims and offenders. The character of contemporary homicide is signaled by the fact that in 2011 (this was the last such report), 77 percent of Chicago's murder victims had previously been arrested; for their killers the arrest figure was only a bit higher, 87 percent (Chicago Police Department, 2012).

One cost of this low solution rate was that it became widely believed that detectives practice "victim devaluation." On radio talk shows and activist blogs there were constant claims that police simply did not try as hard when victims were African American. In this view, the age, class, race, and sex of victims determine how thoroughly cases are investigated (Pizarro, Terrill and LoFaso, 2018). This is not hard to credit. To quote a 2015 blog comment by an officer whose views were widely shared by other vocal participants:

> The majority of those killed: they are almost exclusively gang banging pieces of shit, involved with narcotics in some aspect and/or career criminals. They contribute nothing meaningful to society . . . . Society is better off without them.

There is a fair amount of research on crime solving. Clearing crime is in part dependent on situational factors. Late-night crimes are harder to solve because there are fewer witnesses. In the Chicago data, the clearance rate for murder drops by 10 percentage points when the sun goes down, between the hours of 9pm and 5am. Murders occurring in public places are also hard to solve. During 2015, police cleared more than 50 percent of homicides taking place in residential locations because these more often involve a relationship among the parties. The few remaining domestic violence cases and disputes between neighbors can also be easy to solve. Murders in shops, at the workplace, and in other commercial locations were also solved more frequently; 44 percent of them were cleared. Murders in the streets and alleys, in parking lots, and at parks and along the lakeshore largely remained mysteries.

Research also has identified community-level factors linked to crime clearance. In general, crimes prove easier to solve in stable neighborhoods characterized by solidarity and high levels of trust among neighbors, frequent participation in community affairs, and high levels of collective efficacy (Mancik, Parker and Williams, 2018). The neighborhood correlates of crime clearance rates in Chicago are certainly in accord with these findings. In 2015, clearance rates for murders and shootings were positively related to measures of affluence and residential stability. Clearances were more frequent where residents turned out to vote in large numbers, signaling some commitment to the political system. On the other hand, clearance rates were lower in census tracts where income inequality *within* the area was high, perhaps flagging low levels of neighborhood cohesion and more limited familiarity among residents. Clearance percentages were much lower where there was a lot of violent crime, reinforcing the view offenders in the toughest areas enjoy greater immunity from the law. The ability of police to solve crimes was also lower where African Americans lived in larger numbers, but unlike some other studies it was not related to the concentration of Latinos (see Mancik, Parker and Williams, 2018). Finally, clearance rates were lower where police were making many stop & frisks. Chapter 4 examines in detail the relationship between stops and the views of residents who are caught up in them; suffice it to note here many stop & frisks generated cynicism regarding the justice system and undermined confidence in the police.

Importantly, the *cooperation* of victims, witnesses, and family members is likely to be the key to solving violent crimes (Wellford and Cronin, 1999). They must be willing to talk to police and tell officers what they know. This can be a problem. As one officer described it in a blog post:

> In many cases it is a matter of survival. Dude gets shot or killed. He is not anything to you. Are you going to stick your neck out? Do you want your garage torched, bullets thru your windows or family threatened? Does anyone with any sense think that the police can protect them? Can you promise

victims/witnesses protection in all honesty? Remember the "snitches get stitches" shirts?

Some observers write off victim and bystander non-cooperation to a "code of the street." This code largely develops in poor and embattled communities. The code, they claim, calls for people to watch their own back and mind their own business. It is said that "no snitching" is the rule. However, after years as a Chicago journalist, Alex Kotlowitz (2016, p. 2) concluded instead "most victims and witnesses stay quiet because they're afraid of retaliation by friends of the shooter, not because of some unwritten code of the streets." Fearing retaliation means people doubt the ability, or willingness, of police to keep them safe. Recall that most of the large number of shootings reported in Chicago each year has a *survivor*. Officers report to me that victims often know much more than they are willing to tell, even though they were the ones who were shot.

The Implications of Crime for Chicago Policing

The levels and trends in crime depicted here, their concentration in a few neighborhoods, the emergence of gun crime as the poster-child crime of the stop & frisk era, and the inability of police to solve very many of them, all had implications for the crime strategies employed by Chicago during the first half of the 2010s.

First, the changing character of crime during the mid-2010s created pressure to do something more effective in response. After the public and the media had been reassured for more than 20 years that it was on a continuing slide down, violence was no longer in recession. During the 2014–2015 period it rose. It was not then a national crisis. Media and scholarly reports of crime trends for the period urged cautious optimism. In a report for the federal government on changes in crime between 2014 and 2015, Richard Rosenfeld (2016, p. 8) concluded only 10 among the 56 largest cities accounted for two-thirds of the total increase in all of those big cities. He noted, "had homicides not risen in these cities, it is likely the homicide increase in 2015 would have generated far less attention and controversy." Unfortunately, Chicago was second on Rosenfeld's list of 10. We have seen the largest increases in crime also were largely confined to the scariest ones: seemingly random, apparently unstoppable shootings and gun murders. Chicago also stood out regarding this important detail.

Second, it was apparent that gun violence was concentrated in just a few areas of the city, and it was increasing primarily in poor, African American areas. They had been the biggest winner during the great crime decline beginning in 1991 (recall Figure 2-2), but now they were falling behind. In 2015, just 216 of the city's 2,160 Census block groups recorded 70 percent of all murders and 50 percent of all shootings. The Chicago police were long accustomed to being asked why they did not allocate their resources very smartly, by focusing officers on the highest crime areas. Earlier federal investigations found officers were overly concentrated in primarily White police districts, while the number of violent crimes per officer was much higher in African American neighborhoods (Illinois Advisory Committee to the United States Commission on Civil Rights, 1993). This persisted because powerful White politicians wanted it that way. They were not about to face constituents angry because "their" officers were being moved somewhere else. For more than a decade I watched the police department's research and development group struggle to redraw beat and district boundaries to reflect the changing distribution of both residents and crime. Their proposals were always rejected by City Hall, for fear of upsetting the political applecart. After a new administration and a new chief arrived in 2011, the police department began to move large numbers of officers to roving units that specialized in making stops, which helped in focusing cops on the dots. Aldermen complained bitterly.

As we shall see in ensuing chapters, adopting this strategy meant coming down harder on African Americans. The logic of focusing policing resources on crime hot spots seems impeccable: why go where crime isn't? Research certainly confirms hot spots concentrate hot people carrying hot guns. But the co-concentration of crime with poverty and race played a powerful role in creating tremendous inequalities in the distribution of unwarranted street stops, and this alone became a centerpiece of debates over the wisdom of the policy.

Third, as suggested at the outset, crime solvability has important implications for the criminal justice system, and for society. Over time, the collapse in crime solvability increasingly threatened the standard business model of policing. The mid-step in this process involves interviewing victims, their families, bystanders, and other potential witnesses because the standard business model is to be reactive to events. As the clearance rate for shootings dropped toward single digits (it got there in 2017), it was clear this model had stopped working. In Chicago, crime solution rates declined in both heavily Hispanic and African American neighborhoods. Beginning in 1991, homicide solvability there declined from the upper 70s to the lower 20s, and the solution rate for shootings dropped from around 40 percent to about 15 percent.

Another implication of declining solvability is deterrence threatens to disappear. Deterrence is another bedrock feature of criminal justice policy. *Individual* deterrence occurs when police catch someone who committed a crime. The ensuing price they will pay should encourage them to walk the straight and narrow in the future. *General* deterrence is exerted on a larger pool of potential offenders, who should abstain from offending in the first place because they face an unacceptable level of risk of punishment if they do so. But, if hardly anyone is getting caught—as was the case in Chicago in 2015 and beyond—deterrence may no longer play an effective role in ensuring community safety. The risks and rewards associated with other choices could begin to loom larger in the eyes of potential offenders. These could include young men on the street arming themselves for self-defense. Further, a collapse of deterrence could encourage them to resort to *preemptive* violence to protect themselves. Waiting patiently to shoot back is generally a losing strategy. If you want to live, shoot first. Finally, the crisis emerging from the collapse of crime solvability could stimulate *retaliatory vengeance*. Victims have friends and families and may belong to street organizations capable of exacting an eye for an eye. Considering all of this, an economist friend remarked that the threat of retaliatory vengeance may be the most important remnant of deterrence that is still operative in this new world. That's vigilantism, and he asked why it should be discouraged. It's all we have.

These ideas will return in Chapter 7, which examines the Great Chicago Crime Spike of 2016. As bad as things looked in 2015, they were going to get worse.

3

Stop & Frisk as an Organizational Strategy

Cops make stops. Officers routinely take note of people's actions. They may intervene, they might conduct a pat-down search for weapons, and they could conduct a thorough search if they have cause to suspect criminal misconduct. But we are interested here in a particular aspect of stop & frisk—its role as an *organizational strategy* for addressing crime. As a strategy, stops are not just reactions to furtive activities; officers set out on patrol intending to conduct them. Making stops is their mission because their supervisors demand they do so. Their organization wants numbers, and they need to come back at the end of their shift with some completed paperwork. One mechanism for encouraging doing this is to impose quotas, or specific numeric goals for officers to meet. This can be legally shaky, however, and in some jurisdictions (including Chicago) formal law enforcement quotas are forbidden. The public also does not like them, especially if they involve traffic enforcement. This chapter describes some other ways by which officers are incentivized to make their numeric goals anyway.

Stop & frisk reports become working numbers when they are entered into the agency's data system and the people who run the organization begin monitoring and using them to manage it. The emergence of systematic performance measurement and assessment has been one of the most significant changes in contemporary policing. Earlier, the attention of the top brass was focused on crimes and arrests, but then stop & frisk counts began appearing in their daily briefings. Managers at the district level insist on numbers because they, in turn, are being held to account by executives at police headquarters. In Chicago, as in many other large police departments, the performance numbers generated by various units are utilized centrally. Commanders are challenged to remedy their units' shortcomings, which are usually flagged by declining numbers. By 2000, Chicago had adopted a format for numbers-driven management already common elsewhere—CompStat. We shall see in this chapter how CompStat was used to manage stop & frisk.

At the top, executives will describe what they are doing as "vital to crime prevention." At a 2013 news conference, Chicago Police Superintendent

Stop & Frisk and the Politics of Crime in Chicago. Wesley G. Skogan, Oxford University Press.
© Oxford University Press 2023. DOI: 10.1093/oso/9780197675052.003.0003

Garry McCarthy noted, "The most important thing that we need to focus on is reducing violence in the city, and one of the ways that we do that is by seizing guns" (Mitchell, 2016). They will interpret their numbers as evidence they are doing a great deal to combat crime. Of course, stop & frisk reports measure effort and not accomplishment. That is true of much of the data flowing through police organizations, but many outsiders have lost sight of the point. In any event, police leaders will warn that any move to question their priorities will put the public at great risk. Stop & frisk is how they keep the lid on. This was especially seen to be true in Chicago, which (as we saw in Chapter 2) was experiencing declining arrests and a growing inability to solve gun-related crimes. The traditional model of reactive policing was not working, and stop & frisk was promoted by headquarters as taking up the slack.

In short, this chapter examines stop & frisk as a *strategy*, one deliberately drawn up, vetted politically, and systematically executed and monitored. This is important because stop & frisk has become the crime-prevention strategy of choice in American policing. For generations, policing largely operated as a reaction to crime. The police came when they were called, mostly, and their job was to clean up the mess that had already occurred. One prominent performance measure during this era was response time; getting to crime scenes fast was a measure of good policing. During the early 1990s, thinking about policing began to shift. In this new era, police are increasingly expected to prevent crime from occurring in the first place. Before, they deterred crime by responding quickly, investigating what happened, and apprehending offenders. Now, they deter crime by posing a risk to potential offenders through their intrusive presence in the neighborhoods. This book examines how this shift happened in one great American city.

This chapter first traces the development of stop & frisk as a strategic initiative in Chicago. It begins with leadership, and the city's recent Superintendents of Police have varied in their enthusiasm for stops. Because Chicago's chiefs of police serve at the pleasure of the mayor, they also need their mayors to trust in what they are doing. This has also varied by administration. Important for both the chiefs and the mayors have been the twin pressures of media attention to crime and their standing in the political environment. Chicago's hotly competitive media can make life miserable for public officials, and crime is one of their favorite clubs to batter city leaders with. Any resulting dips in politician's polling numbers become fodder for even more discussion about how the public is unhappy because they have failed in quell crime. Here I describe how this dynamic worked in Chicago during its period of peak stop & frisk. The chapter also examines how police executives translate the strategic and operational priorities they have set into actual practice in the field. Their primacy mechanism for doing so during the period of peak stop & frisk in Chicago was CompStat. There is also an analysis of how effective this was in focusing stop & frisk in the highest crime areas, and some of the consequences of this focus for the lives of the city's African American residents.

Stop & Frisk in Chicago

Figure 3-1 traces the growth of stop & frisk, beginning in 2004. The program ramped up quickly and totaled almost 215,000 stops during the first year. In 2007, the peak year for stop & frisk during the 2000s, police recorded about 471,000 stops. Then there was a downward slide in their monthly numbers. The slump hit bottom in 2011, a year when stops totaled only 380,000; in December 2010, only 19,400 stops were recorded. Then stop & frisk took

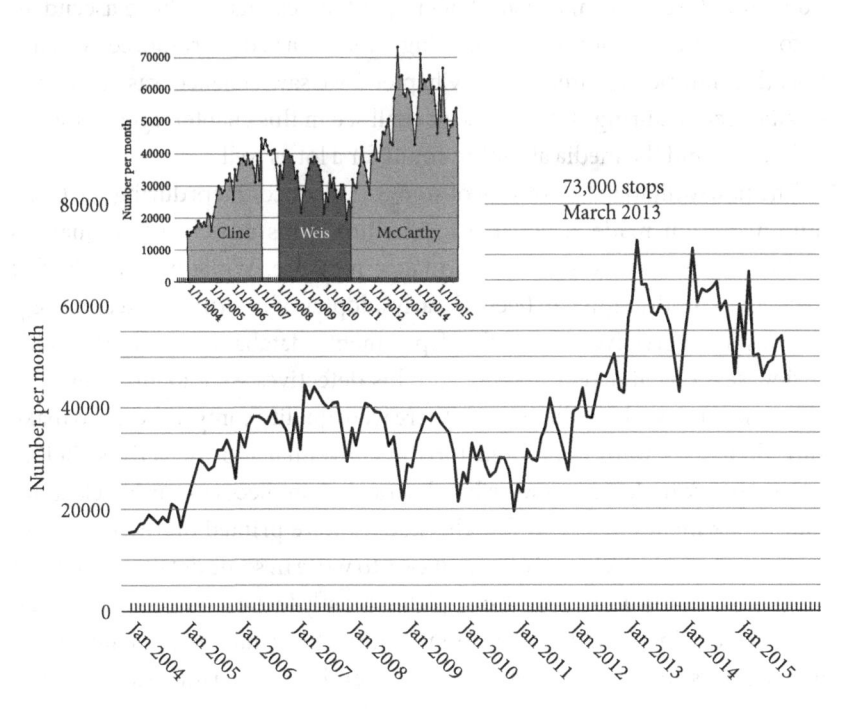

Figure 3-1 Trends in Stops 2004–2015

off. Two years later, annual stops totaled more than 700,000, and March 2013 witnessed peak stop & frisk, with 73,000 stops. Chicago officers reported 718,000 stops during 2014. This was more stops than were recorded in New York City during its peak year, even though New York is more than three times as populous.

How did this happen? What explains the roller coaster of stops described in Figure 3-1? Why did it grow exponentially after 2011? Was any of this simply in response to trends in crime? First, let us look at leadership.

Figure 3-1 also summarizes stops during the administrations of the three chiefs of police who served during this period. They each had a distinct taste for stop & frisk as a core policing strategy for Chicago, and this is reflected in the volume of stops on their watch. The first Superintendent, Philip Cline, served from late 2003 until April 2007. A detective, the son of a Chicago firefighter, and the father of a police detective, Cline was appointed Superintendent in October. He was chosen, rather than a more community-oriented candidate, because of a media-inspired crime scare. The apparent crisis was created by a leading local newspaper (the *Chicago Tribune*), and it led the mayor and Cline to refocus the department on guns, gangs, and homicides (see Skogan, 2006b). Policing initiatives that had been ascendant before, including community policing, were starved of resources to support this new policy direction. In Chapter 2 we saw violence was actually in steady decline during 2003, but as we shall see in this chapter, agendas set by politicians and the media attention count for a lot as well.

The newly digitized recording of stop & frisk encounters during the Cline administration made it possible to monitor stops at police headquarters and used them as a district performance measure. While he was Chief of Detectives his division had been an early adopter of information technology. He was an aggressive user of the department's databases during homicide review sessions aimed at making sure his detectives were identifying solvable cases and working them hard. There were quality control checks to make sure that cases were not closed for the convenience of detectives. Before Cline, stop & frisk reports were hand-scrawled on pieces of cardstock about four by six inches in size. A few checkboxes were printed on these "contact cards" and space was boxed off for officers to write in some details about what happened. Contact cards were completed mostly by beat officers. The actual cards were held in the district stations, where they could be consulted when investigators wanted to know who was around when a crime occurred. The cards were to be destroyed after six months, to allay concern about police "keeping files on people." The department had gotten in trouble for this before, including for keeping investigative files on political activists and progressive union leaders.

The paper form continued to be used, but beginning in late 2003, the information was digitized to track officer activity. In time, more of the data being gathered was directly entered into squad car computers. The newly computerized records included subjects' age, sex, race, plus their name and address. Officers noted if they had any visible scars or tattoos. The reason for the stop was entered as text in the form, and later someone classified the reasons into five uninformative categories. Officers were to record a contact whenever they made what was dubbed an "investigatory street stop." If they arrested, ticketed, or gave a summons to someone they stopped, they did *not* complete a contact form. Instead, officers filled out the other paperwork required to process such cases. The first newly digitized stop & frisk in my database occurred late in 2003, just after midnight in the city's Humboldt Park neighborhood. He (a male; no names were included in the public file) was stopped for being a "suspicious person" and the officer tagged him as a 32-year-old Caucasian Hispanic affiliated with the Maniac Latin Disciples street gang. This was an investigatory stop, so he was doubtless questioned, but the contact form did not include a field documenting whether he had been frisked. He was in the stop & frisk database because he had not committed any actionable offense, and so there was no other paperwork to complete instead.

The number of digitized monthly stops built up slowly and at different rates in various police districts, so in the analyses presented here we will track them only from January 2004, when stop & frisk became a fully operational strategy. But the key point is stop & frisks recorded in Chicago were all "innocent stops." They did not include persons arrested for what they were doing or carrying, nor because there was a warrant outstanding for their arrest. Individuals who were issued a ticket for something were likewise excluded. Those in the database were all in the same moral category—no action was warranted in their case.

Figure 3-1 depicted the ramp-up of stop & frisk during Cline's administration. Stops on his watch peaked in March 2007, when they exceeded 44,500. He resigned the first day of April. He had been musing about retiring, but his term, like that of many Chicago Police Superintendents, was cut short by scandal (Fan, 2015). He left on the heels of two lurid police misconduct cases concerning officers involved in bar brawls. In both cases, police units called to the scene somehow failed to accurately report what had happened, neglected to note that police officers were the aggressors, and did not manage to list the names of the police participants. But both incidents were recorded on security cameras, and the video returned to haunt the department. Worse, these cover-ups by police coincided with a scandal involving crews of officers robbing drug dealers and conducting home invasions aimed at stealing money, drugs, and guns.

There followed a messy and unsuccessful search for an internal candidate to replace Cline. The next in line within the department was clearly unsuited for the job, and further down the bench there were no starting players. In my view, decades of political meddling in promotions by the mayor had decimated the leadership of the organization. The city's Police Board conducted the required official search and (by law) presented the mayor with a list of three candidates to choose from. The mayor would not appoint any of the candidates they put forward; nobody he would support was on it. The resulting 10-month hiatus in leadership is depicted in Figure 3-1. Eventually, Mayor Richard M. Daley took the unpopular step of "going outside" for his next chief of police. He found Jody Weis in the Philadelphia office of the FBI, where he was the Special Agent in Charge. He was the first outsider appointed police Superintendent in more than 50 years. Weis was not impressed by what he saw when he arrived in Chicago. He quickly fired a large contingent of top officials, including 21 of his 25 district commanders. They had risen to the top through a long-established system of political patronage and family-and-friends favoritism. Displacing them made Weis enemies among powerful people. Through his entire tenure, media coverage of Weis rarely failed to mention this bloodletting. He lost further support among traditionalists by daring to wear a Chicago police uniform that (it was charged) he had not earned by being one of their own. Coming to the job as an outsider poisoned his relationship with the union representing patrol officers, who wanted leaders who came up through their ranks. He was an "FBI guy," a type disliked locally because the FBI investigates police corruption and civil rights violations. Reinforcing this point, during his term he launched internal investigations using listening devices and undercover officers as moles, attempting to root out corruption in one of his mobile units, the Special Operations Section.

Weis launched several modest but innovative initiatives, including more systematic crime analysis and the identification of crime hot spots; both ideas were late to come to Chicago. More boldly, he experimented with "call-ins" in which gang leaders were assembled and threatened with intensive police scrutiny unless they reined in their subordinates. A rigorous evaluation of this initiative found it led to very substantial declines in shootings within networks linking the young men (Papachristos and Kirk, 2015). The local reaction was he was "negotiating with gang-bangers." Weis did not care one way or another about stop & frisk and, more importantly, he effectively abandoned the department's CompStat management style (see below). He told me he would rather talk directly with individual commanders, plus having them drive downtown through Chicago traffic for regular meetings was a waste of their time. Pressure to complete contact cards slackened during his three-year term. Between February 2008 and February 2011, the number of stops dropped. They were down to about 28,000 per month during Weis' final year in charge, from an average of 38,000 per month during the last year of the Cline administration. In February 2011 his three-year contract as police Superintendent came to an end, and he was gone. A former Chicago superintendent, Terry Hillard, filled in for a few months until a new mayor could make his own pick for the office.

The Mayor, McCarthy, and Stop & Frisk

As is readily apparent in Figure 3-1, a regime change took charge in Chicago early in 2011. There was a new mayor—after 22 years!—and a new chief of police. In May 2011, the mayor's first month in office, police recorded less than 30,000 stops. Two years later, in May 2013, there were more than 64,000 stops.

The new Mayor, Rahm Emanuel, made crime a central issue during his campaign. He promised to put 1,000 more officers on the street, and to pick a new police chief who would make effective use of them. He had run against the "muddled" leadership of Weis, as well as a financial mess that proved real when he took over City Hall. Garry McCarthy came to Chicago from Newark, NJ, where he was chief of police, but he had spent most of his career with the New York City police department. There he was Deputy Commissioner for Operations and director of the department's CompStat management process. He was a fan of the "broken windows" policing strategy promoted by his Commissioner, William Bratton, whose enthusiasm for stop & frisk was noted in Chapter 1. Their general approach was to crack down relentlessly on minor offenses, such as curfew violations, loud music, public drinking, fare beating, jaywalking, vandalism, pot smoking and graffiti writing, in order to send a robust deterrent message to the community: law-breaking was unacceptable. When it came to finding guns and drugs, their favored tool was stop & frisk. Stops reached their crescendo in New York the year McCarthy made his move to Chicago.

McCarthy's numbers-driven orientation attracted Emanuel, who needed an efficient and effective response to crime. The city was broke. A collapse in tax revenue following the Great Recession had led Mayor Daley to begin cutting the size of the police department. It consumed about 38 percent of the city's corporate budget and, by 2010, Daley faced a $650 million deficit he could not fix with small efficiencies. By the time McCarthy arrived in Chicago in May 2011, the department had already shrunk by about 1,400 officers, and more might have to go. McCarthy needed a policing strategy that would do more with (possibly) even less, plus he needed to find the 1,000 replacement officers the new mayor had promised to put on the street. One thousand was a big number, and the only way to produce all of them was by sleight of hand. More than 500 officers were simply moved from one box to another on the organization chart. Previously they had been very much on the street, working in two special units (the Mobile Strike Force and the Targeted Response Unit) and roving around town in response to crime upticks. Under the new plan they were reassigned to regular patrol units working in the city's 25 police districts. Both special units had gotten into trouble during the Cline and Weis eras, for sins including excessive force, false and unlawful arrests, and robbing drug dealers. One of their number was tripped up after he tried to recruit an assassin to kill a fellow officer who he believed was cooperating with federal investigators looking into police corruption. These units would not be missed, politically (for more see Heinzmann, Lighty and Coen, 2007; Heinzmann and Fitzsimmons, 2007).

But in addition, McCarthy's insight was that district-based teams could be more effective than mobile units. As he told it to me, the roving squads he disbanded had no connection to the communities into which they were thrown. They showed up not knowing anybody or anything about the area, and they were only going to be there for a few days. The media used terms such as "commando-like" to describe their activities. The principal crime-fighting tactic at their disposal was to spread locals across the hoods of cars and search them for guns and drugs. Their only clues regarding who to sweep up were age, sex, and race. As McCarthy told *Chicago Magazine* in 2012, "With specialization, those guys have zero connection to the community. They offend a lot of people, because not everybody is a perp" (Isackson, 2012). By contrast, while working a steady beat in a district officers could learn who was up to what. They could learn the gang affiliations of neighborhood players and monitor the ebb and flow of young men just standing on their corners. In McCarthy's view, his mobile units had been doing dumb stops. Beat and district-based units could do smarter stops. He put it out to the press that the aggressive style of the roving units was driving a wedge between the police and minority communities, which was true as well. The mobile units came down hard on one side of the continuing tension between tough-nosed crime fighting and trust-building with the community. In an article titled "New police chief sets out to show he's not the old police chief," McCarthy was quoted as saying "We can reduce crime, we know how to reduce crime, and we can do it without the unintended consequences of 'heavy handed' policing that we've used over the last few years" (Dumke, 2011). What worked, in his view, was smart stop & frisk.

The Media Murder Mayor

An important force propelling crime and policing policy in Chicago is the media. In the city's very competitive media environment, the market-driven focus of news stories is driven almost inexorably toward a journalistic cliché, "if it bleeds, it leads." As we shall see, during 28 of the 48 months in 2012–2015 there were more local murder stories in the city's most important newspaper than there were actual murders. Students of the media credit it with creating a "scary world" for consumers through its selective attention to actual social conditions when crafting its messaging. Prolonged media exposure (which afflicts almost all Americans, for example) cultivates an assumption that the real world mirrors media accounts (Gerbner and Gross, 1976). This in turn has consequences. Research finds upward shifts in the urgency of discussions of crime trends lead to increases in public support for tough crime policies (Ramirez, 2013). Stop & frisk would certainly fall in the tough category. This attention activates attentive politicians and can ultimately affect both policy and personnel decisions. During a period in 2010 when the media was coming down hard on him, police Superintendent Jody Weis pointed out "overall crime" was going down, not up. He blamed "the 24-hour news cycle" for creating an impression violence was out of hand (Dumke, 2012). But he could not counter the power of the press—they could always find a number going up—and mayoral candidate Rahm Emanuel decided to add a promise to dump Weis to his campaign platform.

Why is media coverage of crime important? As Superintendent Weis learned, the media play an important role in *setting the agenda* for public discussion and shaping many of the issues that politicians debate. When news coverage appears, and the media raises questions that demand an answer, attention to the topic by politicians follows (Walgrave, et al., 2017). In turn, forcing political leaders to take stances on issues injects tactical political positioning, partisanship, and ideology into the discussion. Because prominent politicians command the attention of journalists, their pronouncements then become part of the story as well. Media coverage may also *affect the opinions* of the general public. The media "primes" their audience, letting them know what issues are important by featuring them prominently and frequently. They also try to frame issues so that they make sense for their audience, and they often do so by bringing their impact close to home.

Scholars have dug into the links between crime, media coverage, the partisan stances of political leaders, and public opinion. In a literature review and empirical national study pulling these strands together, Shi, Lu and Pickett (2020) concluded:

a. Media coverage does not closely follow the crime rate. Changes in the violent crime rate are not significantly associated with changes in the amount of news devoted to crime.
b. Changes in newspaper and television coverage are both linked to the public salience of crime. In their study, salience was measured by whether survey respondent identified crime as the country's most important problem. They found media coverage does not mirror crime, but it strongly influences public opinion.
c. Political rhetoric (measured by Presidential references to crime and criminals) also affects the salience of crime. The injection of leadership and partisanship into public discussions raised the profile of crime in the eyes of the public.

Another frequent research hypothesis is that, because media outlets of all kinds typically exaggerate both the frequency and severity of crime, they lead audiences to believe crime is increasing and becoming more violent. Research on this proposition reports mixed findings and is continuing. This potentially negative spin could be doubly important because, virtually across the board, negative media coverage of issues has greater impact on people's views than does positive coverage.

Into the twenty-first century, all these observations were at play in Chicago. Media coverage of crime was often unrelated to actual crime trends, and both were accompanied by a great deal of political rhetoric. It may have made a difference when the head of the powerful Chicago Teachers Union proclaimed, regarding Mayor Rahm Emanuel, "Look at the murder rate in this city. He's murdering schools. He's murdering jobs. He's murdering housing. I don't know what else to call him. He's the murder mayor" (Ford and Parker, 2013). This was a headline because Karen Lewis was fresh from thumping the mayor after leading her teachers through a successful seven-day strike.

To illustrate the local link between crime and media coverage I turned to one of the two principal newspapers in the Chicago area, the *Chicago Tribune*. Unlike its rival, the *Chicago Sun Times*, the content of the *Tribune* is paired with a search engine that can distinguish articles about crime in Chicago from the name of the newspaper. The searches covered the period from 2012 to 2015. I extracted coverage counts using online tools retrieving Chicago-oriented stories mentioning the search terms "murder," "shooting," homicide," and "killing." Minor variants in these terms were recovered as well. The results were then edited by hand, deleting irrelevant references to these terms (e.g., the local basketball team was not shooting well during this period). While there are many media outlets in today's world, research suggests newspapers may still be a good place to look for local media influence. A Pew Research Center (2011) study of what people look for among their diverse local media outlets found crime ranked as the number one issue they sought information about, and newspapers were the number one place (by a smaller margin) where they looked for it. However, I am also using the coverage of crime in this paper as a proxy for media attention in general over this period, a common practice.

Figure 3-2 contrasts monthly counts of the number of violent crime stories reported in the *Chicago Tribune* with monthly reports of homicide. Crime and media crime coverage were often vaguely related to one another; the overall correlation between the two was a virtually non-existent –.03. This was partly due to the extreme disjuncture between crime and coverage during 2013—we shall see more of the "media crisis of 2013" later. However, during 2014–2015 the correlation was only +.19, hardly strong, and news coverage frequently outpaced the murder count. During 2012 the media–murder

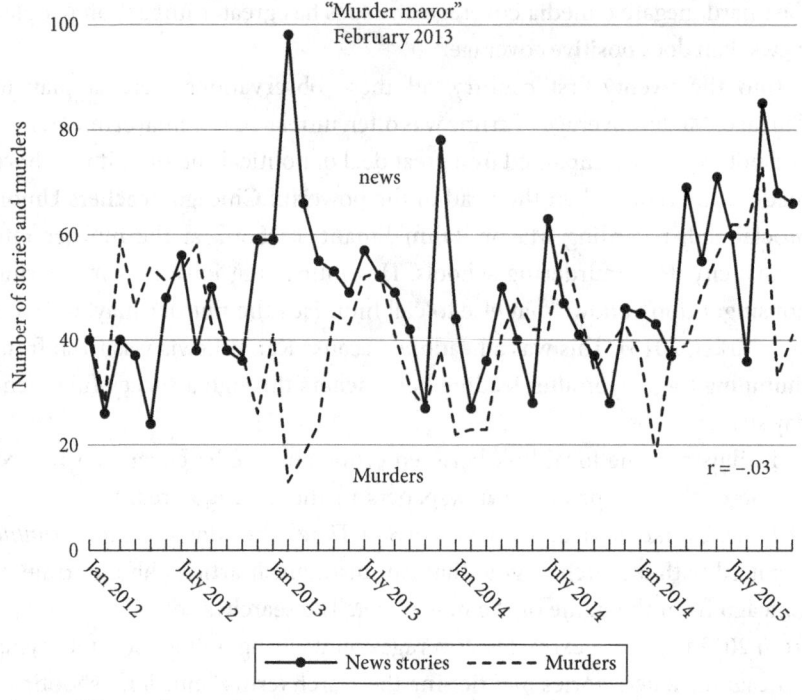

Source: Chicago tribune archive

Figure 3-2   Murders and Media Murder Coverage

correlation was –.07. But however inaccurate the media may be, there was a steady drumbeat of 30 to 60 local murder stories each month in just one daily newspaper. This extensive coverage of crime is a reality political and police leaders cannot ignore.

The Media Crisis of 2013

Figure 3-2 points to 2013 as an example of a "media storm." Following Walgrave, et al. (2017), these are periods marked an explosive increase in media attention. They found media storms influence the agendas of politicians, kicking issues into a higher gear than usual. "In storm mode, the media agenda matters more for the governmental agenda" (Walgrave, et al., 2017, p. 550). At the beginning of 2013 the city was coming off a bad year. Early on, shootings were up over the 2012 total by 11 percent, and murders by 17 percent. But 2013 became a highly divergent year. Crime went one way, while crime coverage went another. Reporting on the topic spiked in the unlikely month of February 2013, a month when little of consequence usually happens in Chicago due to the winter weather. There were 98 murder stories, seven times the 13 murders taking place that month, and February was the all-time low for this entire period. Compared to 2012, during the first six months of 2013 the number of murders was down by 27 percent, and the number of shootings was down by 25 percent. Later in the year media coverage receded as the murder count rose.

The political damage of the early-2013 media storm had been done, however. Taking charge of the situation, by May 2013 the Mayor had linked his fate to successes on the crime suppression front. "I know what my responsibilities are, and my responsibility is to make sure we are driving down the rate of shootings and homicides and overall crime. That's happening and that's day in and day out" (Pearson and Heinzmann, 2013). His poll numbers were not looking good. A May 2013 survey found more than one-half of African American and Latino registered voters said they were dissatisfied with his efforts to curb crime. Compared to a *Chicago Tribune* poll a year earlier, the percentage of African American voters dissatisfied with his performance in responding to crime was up by 10 percentage points, and among Latino voters disapproval of his anti-crime strategies had grown by nearly 20 percentage points (Pearson and Heinzmann, 2013). This was important. The mayor had won office handily because of a strong wave of support in Chicago's African American community, and Hispanic candidates led the charge against him in both 2011 and again in 2015.

On July 7, 2013, the *Tribune* reported their new online shooting database recorded more than 1,000 victims during the first six months of the year. Following the media's "bring it close to home rule," they wrote their data represent ". . . the inexorable toll of violence: Neighborhoods weary of yellow crime tape. Children who learn to duck when they hear a pop. Mothers terrified they might lose yet another child." Just days later, the Mayor indicated he had "absolute confidence" in [police Superintendent] Garry McCarthy, but "the progress that Chicago's police superintendent is making in combating gang violence is not good enough" (Spielman, 2013). McCarthy responded separately that he was "absolutely positive" he continued to "enjoy the mayor's confidence." But it was reported (according to "a city hall insider"), "Emanuel told his police chief that the department had better not allow a repeat performance of 2012 or McCarthy's days in Chicago would be numbered" (Bernstein and Isackson, 2014).

The apparent story in Chicago became a national one as well. In January 2013 the *New York Times* mapped social inequalities in the distribution of the city's homicide, headlining it, "In a Soaring Homicide Rate, a Divide in Chicago" (Davey, 2013). The story did not note that the number of homicides had actually dropped throughout the second half of 2012. In June 2013 the popular web news analysis source *Salon* proclaimed, "Rahm Emanuel is losing control of his city," and continued, "his disapproval rating soars, he's getting tagged with names like the 'murder mayor'" (Guarino, 2013). On July 8, the *Christian Science Monitor* (2013) reported "Chicago erupts in gun violence: 74 people shot, 12 killed over July 4 weekend." The article quoted an alderman, who explained, "There is a failure to police the streets." At the end of July 2013, three local members of Congress and the Congressional Black caucus held a National Emergency Summit on Urban Violence to respond to gun violence in Chicago and other cities. This kind of national attention to Chicago's apparent violence problem was unwelcome news to the mayor, who continued to harbor national political ambitions (for more on the political fate of Rahm Emmanuel see Lydersen, 2013).

The year concluded with another media spike, one which did follow a late-fall surge in killings. It included the *Chicago Tribune*'s endorsement of stop & frisk. Their editorial of December 29, 2013 demanded, "Defy the odds. Push the body count lower in 2014 and beyond." The paper went on to note:

> There's a decade's worth of evidence that a policing strategy applied here in various forms since 2003 reliably suppresses annual Chicago murder tolls that previously had totaled 600 or more for 36 consecutive years. Even one killing is too many. But putting more "cops on the dots"—that is, intensifying the police presence where violence occurred is likely to occur—saves lives by the hundreds. We applaud the steady progress (Chicago Tribune, 2013b).

CompStat: The Room Where It Happened

In an organization as large and decentralized as the CPD, calling for more aggressive street policing is one thing, but making it happen in a focused and effective way is another. The mechanism for translating the priority police leaders placed on stop & frisk down to the street level was CompStat. CompStat is a data-driven management strategy using crime and police activity data to hold field commanders accountable for successes in the areas they oversee. Chicago inaugurated its version of CompStat in early 2000. The various Superintendents since have used CompStat in different ways, including largely dispensing with it during most of the Jody Weis years. Beginning in 2011, as a new administration began to impose its priorities on the department, CompStat meetings were resurrected as the theater in which the shift toward stop & frisk was played out. The department's 100+ top leaders were the audience for this show; the director of the play was the new Police Superintendent.

CompStat-style management aims to maximize the effectiveness of three of the pillars of police crime prevention. These are timely and accurate intelligence, rapid deployment, and employing effective tactics at high-crime hotspots. Police need to be in the right places at the right time, managers must show agility in moving them around locally in response to changing crime patterns, and officers need to be smart about what they do while they are there. A fourth pillar driving the first three is relentless management follow up. How good was the intelligence? As an example, Chicago's traditional street gangs have broken into hundreds of discrete and sometimes competing factions, and commanders are expected to sniff out where their rivalries are likely to break out into active shooting. How well were officers briefed and deployed? Were they being sent promptly to conduct "directed missions" at newly emerging hotspots, or were they just being told at roll call to "stay alert?" Were they responding effectively to the priority crimes drawing them there, or were they just driving around hoping to spot something? Finally, rapid data analysis is a key element of the CompStat model. It is necessary for identifying spikes in crime at specific times and locations, and for monitoring the efforts of the districts and units responsible for responding to them. Eventually, the data might document that some of these efforts were effective at reducing crime.

The Chicago version of CompStat is held in a very large and uncomfortable room with terrible acoustics. The front of the room is dominated by huge LCD screens, which are used to display maps and statistical summaries. The commander of the unit under review stands on a raised podium in front of the screens, facing the front row of a panel of the department's top executives. Other senior leaders and unit commanders always attend, and frequently 65 to 70 of them form the rest of the audience. On the management side, the meeting agenda and review materials are prepared by a headquarters bureau that pours over unit reports and statistics. They highlight areas of concern the leadership should concentrate on. Wily unit commanders identify a member or two of their staff with analytic skills they can informally assign to doing the same, to help prepare them for their session. One of them (in his off hours he was an attorney) told me it was like preparing his commander "for the bar exam." A way to impress Superintendent Cline when he directed these sessions was to identify a local crime trend his analytic staff had overlooked. The questioning covers the key concerns of most big-city police departments: spikes in burglary and auto theft, robbery, shootings, and homicides. Commanders are often quizzed individually about each recent killing, and what was still left undone in its investigation. They also face detailed questions about gang conflicts in their area, and what they have been doing about specific narcotics hotspots. There will also be a review of arrests and gun seizures made by district officers. The department's analytic staff will have analyzed the data on all these issues, and commanders who do not evidence a similarly detailed knowledge of what is happening in their district will be called out for it.

As I noted, the new Police Superintendent was the director of CompStat activities in New York City. CompStat had been in operation there for more than a decade, and by the time he arrived in Chicago the New York Rules were well known. Superintendent Cline went to New York to observe CompStat in action, as did many other police leaders.[1] The sessions were tough, and the commanders under review were made to squirm. As Garry McCarthy described it, "When I was a commander in New York, it was full contact, and if you weren't careful, you could lose an eye" (Bernstein and Isackson, 2014). But in Chicago he started slowly, knowing that after the Weis years his commanders were not accustomed to being micro-managed from headquarters. A reporter sitting in an early CompStat session quoted him as proclaiming, "I'm not hearing a sense of urgency. I'm not satisfied with the answers I am hearing. This isn't going to go on like this, folks, of that I can assure you" (Levine, 2011).

As 2011 ended the meetings took on a more hard-nosed tone. Attending in October 2011, a police blogger reported:

> You really should go to one or two of these meetings. It's painful to watch: to watch the sup [Superintendent] twist the screws, and to watch the bosses squirm beneath them. But some of it really is justified. You have district

commanders who have NO idea who was shot, what gang they're in/were in, and what the motivation was. How can you command a district and even TRY to deal with what's going on when you have no idea who the players are and why they're shooting each other?

Armed with their data, the leadership turned up the pressure. The statistics were said to make or break a career. "The only evaluation is the numbers, says a veteran sergeant. God forbid your crime is up. If you have a 20 percent reduction this month, you'd better have a 21 percent reduction the next month" (Bernstein and Isackson, 2014). Evidencing "bad numbers" was a bad idea.

At first, Chicago's CompStat meetings tended to remain true to one mantra of its adherents: the focus should be on outcomes, with no points given for trying hard but failing. It was about the crime. But at the end of 2012 the city's numbers were not looking good. Murders were up 17 percent, and—as we saw earlier—there was both media and political pressure to do better. The 2012 stop & frisk numbers looked just like the Cline years, and this did not appear to do the job. There were 65 more killings than during Cline's last full year in office. McCarthy called it "a tragic number" and vowed things would be different in 2013 (Bernstein and Isackson, 2014). But city leaders took another drubbing from the media early in 2013, and police headquarters felt the pressure to "do something" about this trend. It was during 2013 that stop & frisk became a central issue addressed during CompStat sessions and became Chicago's primary crime prevention strategy. Much of the pressure at the meetings shifted from outcomes to activity. The number of stops grew by almost 200,000 during 2013 alone and hit a then-record high in March.

The line of pressure created by CompStat went from police headquarters to the commanders, and from them down to their line officers. Holding commanders accountable for their stops was intended to translate through them to their sergeants and street cops. This officer's blog post is an account of a meeting in January 2013:

Attended a compost [sic] meeting and this is exactly true. He yells over and over that its quality over quantity he's looking for, but then berates a commander over having low contact cards, arrests, anov's etc. He contradicts himself within 5 minutes and not one goldstar has the balls to speak up for themselves or each other.

The story was the same at a May 2013 meeting:

Went to one compstat meeting and he belittled this commander so bad that the entire room just felt so sorry for the guy. I'll never look at that commander the same again. He sat back down with his tail between his legs. It was tough to witness a grown man get cut down so bad. The guy is still a commander, but my outlook on him is totally different. All the respect is gone. All b/c of the supt. That's our leadership. Cut down publicly until the bosses cower into having no opposing voice or ideas.

By 2013, officers were reporting to me they were called in and questioned by their lieutenant if they returned at the end of a shift without any completed stop & frisk forms. Making numerous stops was widely understood to be the department's policy, which is a key difference between cops making stops and stop & frisk as an organizational strategy. As McCarthy announced at a 2013 CompStat meeting, when he "peppered a deputy chief with questions" regarding his crime trends, "Everything will improve if we just get out of the cars and put our hands on people" (Gorner, 2013).

It seemed to work for a while. Shootings and killings went down in 2013, homicides by 27 percent. But 2014 did not go as well, and by its conclusion shootings were up by 22 percent. In July 2014 alone, 63 accounts of local violent crime appeared in the *Chicago Tribune*. Commanders with static or declining stop numbers risked incurring McCarthy's wrath in front of their peers. The weekly CompStat sessions sometimes became shouting matches as he turned up the heat, exhorting the audience to produce ever greater numbers of stops. At one meeting I saw him throw a fist full of paperwork into the air and stomp from the room. In the view of many close observers—including me—the pressure to further increase the number of stop & frisks had become almost pathological. One of McCarthy's closest advisors in the department drew me aside to note the current level of stop & frisk was "not politically sustainable" in the neighborhoods. In his view, stops had become McCarthy's obsession. And this pressure was continuing to translate down to the districts. Another blogging observer stated:

His obsession with them, calling out bosses at Compstat about them, and having the bosses, basically, demand them from the troops is all on Garry's hands. Come in for a week straight with a mover, 5 parkers and an arrest/ day and they're [district managers] saying, "but you didn't have any contact cards."

As one veteran officer explained to a local journalist, "If you're out there, there's always people to stop." The number of stops went up by only 20,000 during 2014, but they shifted location. The number of stops of White and Latino subjects went down from their 2013 totals but stops of African Americans rose by eight percent, from an already large base.

The use of contact cards dropped a bit during 2015, although they continued to be more tightly focused than ever on African American neighborhoods. During the year, 71 percent of those stopped were Black. The card count continued to be a focus at CompStat meetings, and district commanders continued to feel pressure to have their officers make stops and fill the cards out. An October 2015 blog comment:

> Even though we are under the microscope more than ever he still expects people to be stopped because everyone is suspicious, right? This is what politicians want. Every day the bosses say we need more contact cards as though they grow on trees. It's easy for them to do this because they are not on the hook. Their names aren't on them. It all falls on the lowly patrolmen.

Are Stops a Response to Crime?

In research, there is a lot of debate over the possible linkages between stop & frisk and crime. Stops can go up as a policy response to rising crime. Alternately, crime may go down because stops went up. This is consistent with a deterrence perspective on stops. Chapter 7 discusses these up-and-down patterns in causal terms, when it examines the impact of stops on crime. But both views see the two as linked empirically, either positively correlated (higher crime encourages more stops) or negatively correlated (more stops deter crime). Among researchers, the correlation often apparent between them is seen as an impediment to teasing out their causal relationship using statistics.

But life is complicated when the third factor—politics and policy preferences—intervenes in the stop count. Over the months depicted in Figure 3-3, stops and crime sometimes went together, and sometimes they did not. The chart presents population-based rates for stops and shootings, using a somewhat different arithmetic for each so they fit on the same page. As an example of the problem this solves, in March 2013, there were 73,000 stops and 138 shootings. However, the issue is the correspondence between

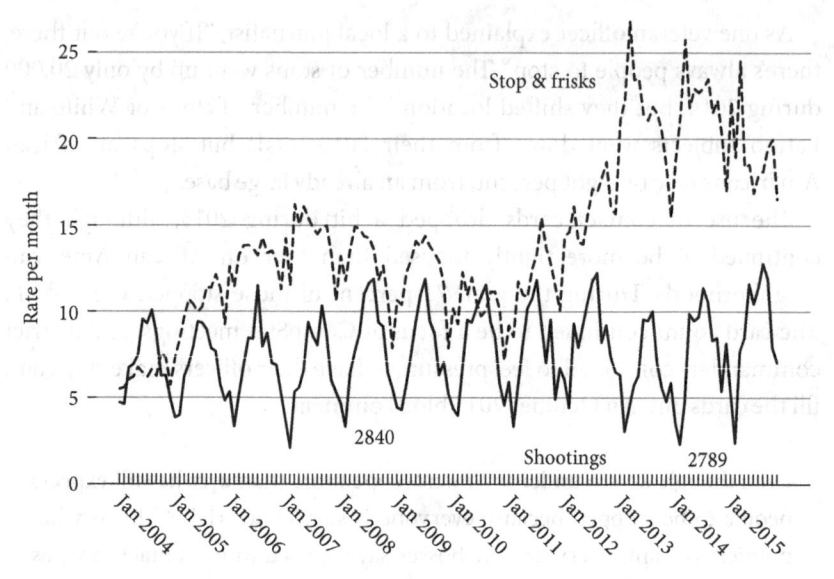

Figure 3-3 Stops and Shootings 2004–2015

the two *trends*: do they rise and fall together, or is the rise in one associated with a fall in the other?

The answer to both questions is no. A great deal of the apparent covariation between shootings (depicted in the chart) and stops was because they shared seasonal effects. They both went up and down with the temperature. Statistically removing the effect of season on stops and shootings ("de-seasoning" the data), they were not really correlated at all; the overall correlation between the two was −.05. For murders it was +.03. It is also apparent that after 2011, with a new mayor and police chief, stops marched in a decidedly in different direction, while—in broad scope—shooting patterns remained about the same. I placed the yearly count of shootings on the chart for two almost identical years, 2008 (2,840 shootings) and 2014 (2,789 shootings). There were 300,000 more stops in 2014 than there were in 2008.

Chapter 7 addresses the relationship between violent crime and stops in much more detail. There is more discussion of whether stops cause crime, or crime causes stops. It also includes several more years of data. It moves forward into a period when gun crime went up and down even more dramatically and when there was a significant shift in the city's stop & frisk policies. The chapter concludes Chicago's stop & frisk had a modest crime-reduction effect, one hard to spot by staring at charts. Over time, cities have many moving parts, and stops and crime are just two of them. In big picture, stop & frisk waxed and waned while the gun crime count marched to a *relatively* steady beat.

Here we have seen some of the organizational dynamics behind stop & frisk. Through early 2008, CompStat was in the hands of a detective who embraced data-driven policing. The number of stops grew during his regime, but at the meetings he usually focused on investigations and the clearance rate, the details of inter-gang conflicts, and high-quality arrests. He wanted clearances. His successor's internal organizational and external political problems diverted his attention and stop & frisk was not a strategy he was accustomed to. Then, during the period 2011–2015, Chicago police reported making more than 2,758,000 stops. Headquarters and city hall were reacting to short-term, often month-by-month fluctuations in crime. Violence was sometimes up and sometimes down, but the continuous media, political, and mayoral pressure on the department was always to keep the numbers lower. Longer term, police practices reflected the policy preferences of city leaders and pressure from the political environment. Chicago CompStat restarted under a new administration in 2011, still based on the premise that commanders were responsible for knowing their crime patterns and devising local strategies for dealing with them. The role of the meetings was to test their managerial awareness of problems and to assess the effectiveness of their team in coming come up with effective strategies. But in time the focus shifted. Activity measures replaced outcome measures, and the required solution to the city's violence problem was dictated from headquarters. No commander wants to be embarrassed by performing poorly in front of his superiors and his own management staff at CompStat, and increasingly the shouting focused on the volume of stop & frisks. CompStat abandoned the principle that local solutions to local crime problems could involve diverse tactics. Rather, there was a relentless and single-minded focus on stop & frisks. Internally, stops became the measure that mattered.

Were Stops on the Dots?

We saw in Chapter 2 that well-organized departments can make aggressive use of crime patterns to deploy their officers. A review of police research released in 2017 (Weisburd and Majmundar, 2018) concluded that focusing resources on hot spots (it was often vague about what "resources" meant when recommending policy) is potentially the most effective thing police can do when it comes to reducing crime. Police can hope to address a substantial proportion of all crime in a city by focusing on a small number of high crime places. This is true, and it has consequences. In Chicago, it meant largely unwarranted stops of innocent people piled up quickly in poorer and largely African American neighborhoods. There, stop & frisk contributed to an already heavy concentration of aggressive policing activity. Together, in just the span if 2013 to 2015, police stop & frisks, plus citations, arrests, vehicle impoundments, and orders to move along in Chicago's African American neighborhoods vastly outnumbered the total number of people living there.

Figure 3-4 examines the link between tract stop rates and street crime during 2015. The latter is a measure of crime used here because it was the prime target of aggressive stop & frisks. More than 32,000 serious street crimes were reported in Chicago during 2015 alone. What they had in common was that they occurred in public places: in parks or parking lots, along the city's lakeshore, on streets or sidewalks, in front yards, and the like. About three-quarters of street crimes involved assaults—fights, beatings, and attacks with all manner of weapons, some involving injuries and others not. About 11 percent of street assaults involved a gun, four percent a knife, and eight percent some other weapon. More than one in five street crimes were

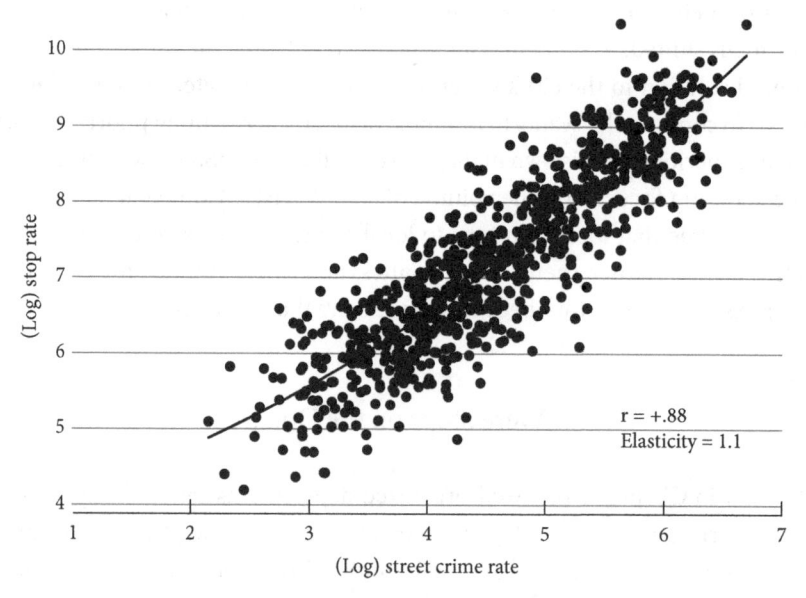

Figure 3-4 Street Crime and Stops by Tract

robberies, which involve taking people's money or goods using force or the threat of force. Two-thirds of all the city's robberies during 2015 occurred on the street, and one-half of all assaults. The remaining street crimes were about equally divided among murders and sexual assaults. About 70 percent of Chicago's murders took place on the street, but only 11 percent of rapes. Overall, one-half of all the city's crimes involving a gun took place on the street.

Compared to many other offenses, street crime should be counted among the responsibilities of the police. Decades ago, sociologist Arthur Stinchcombe (1963) reminded us that when it comes to crimes taking place in private spaces, or at least out of the public eye, police will inevitably be reactive, arriving only after the fact and when they are summoned. They can do their paperwork, and officers may be successful in catching someone if the parties involved can identify who did it. This might have some deterrent value for those offenders in the future, but they have already done their worst. Street crimes, on the other hand, are potentially "on-view," which is how Chicago police classify offenses they themselves witness. There can also be more bystanders and potential witnesses who could help identify suspects if something should occur. But most importantly, the presence of police will certainly be noted when potential offenders are on the prowl. In short, street crimes are most likely to be deterred from happening in the first place, with a sufficient density of policing.

An important point is that street crimes are not found everywhere; instead, they are concentrated geographically. Across the city's 788 census tracts, the top 10 percent of tracts (about 80 of them) were home to 30 percent of all 2015 street crimes. The top 120 of 788 tracts accounted for over 40 percent of the total. Between being carried out in public places and enough of them being concentrated in a few areas, it could be practical to target them; therefore, street crimes should be among the offenses most amenable to deterrence by visible and well-managed police activity.

It is apparent in Figure 3-4 that stops were very largely on the street-crime dots, in this case during 2015. The figure compares stop rates and street crime rates (per 10,000 residents) for each of the city's 788 inhabited census tracts. The two went together strongly: they were correlated +.88. Statistically, a one percent up-or-down difference in the rate of street crime from place to place in the city was associated with a 1.1 percent difference in the level of stops. This is an almost perfect "elasticity"—an economist's term for the extent to which one thing leads to another. There was even a slight tendency for higher-crime tracts to attract additional enforcement efforts; this is signaled by the upward-sloping curve describing the relationship between the two. Looking at the sheer number of stops, five percent of all stops during 2015 (about 27,000 of them) took place in the lowest-crime 20 percent of tracts during 2015, while almost 50 percent of all stops (274,000) were concentrated in the highest-crime 20 percent of tracts.

Effective implementation of stop & frisk is often described as "putting cops on the dots." But because about 7,000 Chicago officers typically work in assigned districts dividing up the entire city, it was not so much that cops were on the dots. Chicago police are actually not apportioned well with respect to violent crime, largely because of the interference of aldermen and City Hall in personnel decisions. As a result, district staffing levels are not clearly coordinated with the level of crime. In 2010, Superintendent Jody Weis floated a plan to reallocate officers, but city council resistance just added to his political woes. Over the years, repeated efforts by department planners to rebalance officer assignments based on crime or workload numbers were stymied at the political level by White aldermen. So, rather than cops themselves, their stops were on the dots. There were plenty of officers elsewhere, but gun violence was lower, and their priority was not stop & frisk.

Stop & Frisk and the African American Community

The persistent concentration of crime presented problems as well as opportunities for mounting a focused stop & frisk regime. Research on the distribution of stop & frisk has documented huge racial disparities in how it usually operates. In New York City, the rate at which African Americans were stopped (which controls for the size of the potential target population) expanded exponentially as the city's policy took hold. In 2002, African American New Yorkers were stopped at a rate of 200 per 100,000 residents; by its peak in 2011 this number rose to 1,500 per 100,000. This was 7.5 times the rate at which Whites were stopped. By contrast, White stop rates rose hardly at all over the entire period. The stop rate for Hispanics (in New York City they originate primarily in Puerto Rico, the Caribbean islands, and Central America) was 4.5 times the White stop rate during 2011.

The general pattern was no different in Chicago. Figure 3-5 charts the rise in stop & frisk rates, separately by race. African Americans were always over-represented, but it is apparent the post-election runup in stops under

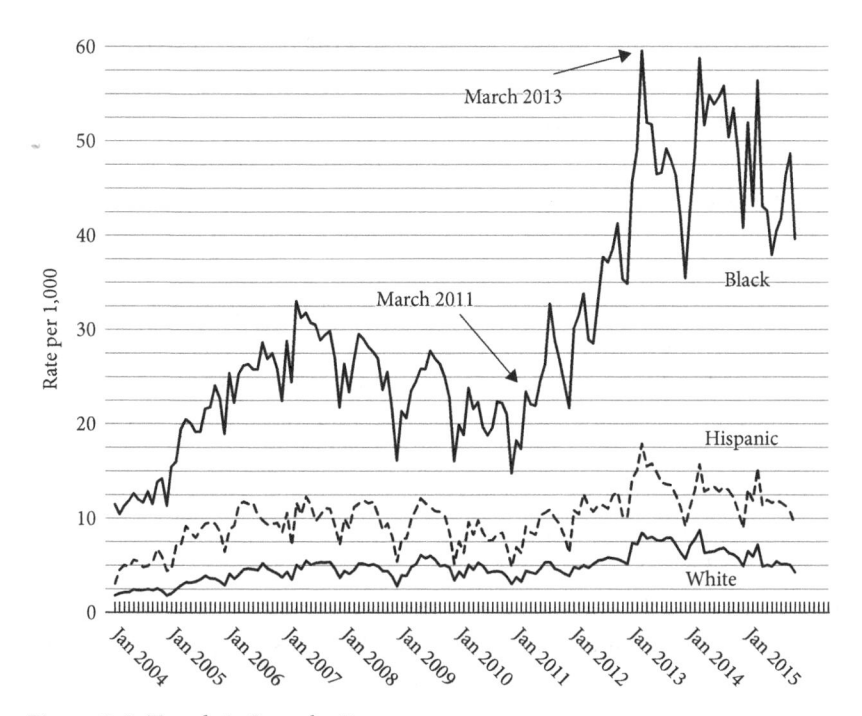

Figure 3-5 Trends in Stops by Race

Mayor Emanuel's new administration was focused on the African American community. Figure 3-5 presents stop rates (per 1,000 residents) to account for the differential size of the three population groups, plus the growth of the city's Latino population and a drop in the African American population over the period. During the peak of Philip Cline's tenure (2003–2007) the average monthly African American stop rate was 33 per thousand, 2.5 times the Hispanic rate (12 per 1,000) and more than six times the stop rate (five per 1,000) for White Chicagoans. These ratios had not changed much by the nadir of the Weis administration, which was December 2010, but the drop in the African American stop rate accounted for most of the overall decline in stop & frisk during his time on the job.

Then came the tidal wave of stops we saw earlier. From the trough to the peak in March 2013, stops of African Americans rose by 400 percent. More than 73,000 people were stopped then, and more than 50,000 of them were Black. The peak year for stops was 2014, however. We saw earlier more than 718,000 stops were recorded then, 72 percent of whom were of African Americans. During 2014 just nine percent of stops involved Whites.

Before looking at more implications of these trends, it is important to recall again Chicago stops were only documented if nothing came of the investigation. During 2014, there were 718,000 unwarranted stops, 516,000 of whom were African Americans who ended up having had no reason to be stopped— except, perhaps, to send their community a message. Looking at it geographically, during 2015 the average stop rate in predominately White census tracts was 660 per 10,000 residents. In predominately African American areas the average was almost *nine times* higher, about 6,000 per 10,000. Note how close the latter two numbers were, with a denominator for the rate including men, women, and children of all ages. The stop rate in heavily Hispanic areas was 2.2 times the stop rate in predominately White tracts, but it was still only 25 percent of the rate in African American neighborhoods.

The police argued they were just directing stops at where the crime was, and in Chicago's highly segregated neighborhoods it meant they often only encountered racial minorities. Digging deeper, it is the case that race—plus household poverty, residential evictions, commercial abandonment, ill health, and a long list of other social inequities—is strongly correlated with both stops and crime. The correlation between street crime and poverty in 2015 was +.65, and. between percent African American and the street crime rate it was +.75. It is fruitless to attempt to untangle the various social and economic factors describing where—and perhaps why—stops were concentrated where they were, from this mass of highly inter-correlated data. In truth, all of these (and many other) neighborhood characteristics really represent a single underlying dimension, the fate of the poorest, (largely) African American Chicagoans in the twenty-first century.

Equally troubling, this single underlying dimension of inequality expands beyond stop & frisks, crime, economics, and demography to encompass many aspects of policing and its impact on neighborhood residents. The concentration of stop & frisks is just one of these. Table 3-1 reports the distribution of a broad range of encounters between police and the public, classified by the predominate racial composition of four clusters of census tracts (across the top of the table). I geocoded them all from individual records. The rows sum to 100 percent, and the data are for the period of 2013–2015. *Traffic stops* were reported by officers over the radio to the 911 center, while I identified *car tows* in a massive city traffic citation database. For many Chicagoans, having their car towed and impounded, plus facing the stiff fines and mounting fees going with it, can be a financial catastrophe (Ramos, 2019). It is also a very big business; more than 100,000 cars were towed away

Table 3-1 Police Encounters by Race 2013–2015

Encounter	Percentage of encounters by predominate race of the area			
	Black	Hispanic	Diverse	White
Traffic stops	58	14	16	12
Cars towed	34	15	25	26
ANOVs issued	51	12	18	19
Minor arrests	66	13	15	6
Search warrants	73	12	12	3
Dispersals	71	15	12	2
Stop & frisks	62	14	16	8
Total encounters	58	13	18	12
Street crime	57	14	18	11
Population	27	22	25	26

Rows sum to 100%

Measures aggregated from individual administrative records

each year during this three-year period. *ANOVs* (Administrative Notice of Violation) are citations issued in lieu of arrest for a variety of infractions, including public drinking, minor drug possession, and eating on a bus. About 360,000 ANOVs were issued during 2013–2015. The *minor arrests* category included simple drug possession (later mostly de-criminalized), disorderly conduct, gambling, vandalism, liquor law violations, prostitution, and various municipal ordinance violations not subject to a jail sentence. During 2013–2015 there were about 158,000 minor arrests. *Search warrants* are often made by special teams knocking on doors and (too often) crash through them, in order to make surprise apprehensions of wanted persons. There were about 1,700–2,000 warrant arrests per year, and they can be dangerous encounters for everyone involved. Finally, Chicago police are empowered to inform groups of persons "engaged in gang loitering" that they must move on, and they can be arrested if they do not do so promptly. During 2013–2015 there were more than 57,000 of these dispersals (there is more on this in Chapter 7). As in Chapter 2 (which examined differential trends in crime over time), all these administrative records were aggregated into the four census clusters described in Table 3-1.

Of this list, only car tows were distributed relatively widely across the city. Parking tickets (not shown here) also bedeviled residents all over town. Both are revenue items for the city. Otherwise, with 62 percent of stops concentrated in primarily African American neighborhoods, stop & frisks proved to be distributed like many other activities of a department conducting aggressive proactive policing. Anywhere between a majority and almost three-quarters of the traffic stops, citations, and other encounters listed in Table 3-1 were concentrated in African American areas. At the top were search warrants and orders (usually directed at gatherings of young men) to disperse. The distribution of stop & frisks closely resembled traffic stops, with about six-in-10 involving African American neighborhoods.

In sum, so many of these encounters with the police were piling up together that they threatened to dominate daily life. During 2013–2015, the encounters listed in Table 3-1 totaled 2,131,000 in African American neighborhoods alone. The population of these tracts totaled 731,00. Over this three-year span there were three times as many police enforcement actions as there were people.

The Dynamics of Stop & Frisk

This chapter focused on the organizational dynamics lying behind stop & frisk in Chicago. Over the past two decades, stop & frisk has become a central tool in the policing kitbag. During this period, politicians, journalists, and many segments of society have accepted the idea policing is no longer supposed to be just reactive. Rather than waiting to be called for help, police are expected to stop crime before it occurs. The police have by-and-large accepted this responsibility, which is one reason why they tout not just the arrests they make and criminals they send away, but also the number of stops they make. The aggressiveness with which they pursue deterring crime from happening has become one of their performance measures.

The Chicago story digs into how this happened. Through early 2008 the police department was headed by a detective who embraced data-driven policing. The systematic recording and use of stop & frisk data for management purposes grew during his regime, but his CompStat sessions focused on traditional investigative practices and arrests. His successor was diverted by internal and external political problems. Stop & frisk was not a strategy he was accustomed to, and he was not impressed enough by CompStat to continue using it manage operations. CompStat restarted under a new administration—one that began using the meetings to test the managerial effectiveness of unit commanders at coming up with effective strategies. But in time the focus shifted. Many of the widely touted benefits of CompStat-style management faded as stop & frisk counts replaced outcome measures. This further move toward stop & frisk also fit the experience and strategic preferences of the leadership. Under pressure from the mayor and the media/political environment, decisions at police headquarters were driven by short-term, often month-by-month, fluctuations in crime. Stops were a policy they could fine-tune in response, and they became the measure that mattered.

This shift in orientation had both internal and external consequences. Internally, the resources it required were squeezed out of alternative strategic initiatives, including the department's historic commitment to community policing. Under the McCarthy regime there was a dramatic downsizing of the district staff committed to community policing. The headquarters unit overseeing it was shut down, and management oversight of what remained was shuffled several levels down in the bureaucracy. I sat with district commanders at the 2013 meeting at which this move was announced internally, and they clearly saw it as making the reduction in community policing resources their problem. Their job grew harder in 2015, when the community policing budget was cut again, down to 0.3 percent of the department total. "Everybody practices community policing" the mayor announced during his successful campaign for reelection. During this period no one was focused on the key issue identified in Chapter 2, the collapse of the department's ability to solve violent crimes. The traditional model of policing—responding to crimes and deterring them effectively by determined detective work drawing upon community cooperation—had largely ceased to function when it came to gun violence. Tackling the apparent emergence of a "no snitching" culture which discouraged this collaboration was complicated. Stops were a solution in their hands.

Externally, the intersecting spatial and racial dynamics of stop & frisk generated a huge burden of unwarranted stops in Chicago's African American community. This was generally understood, but it was still astonishing when the data revealed that from 2013 to 2015 there were, on average, more enforcement encounters than there were people living there, each year. These sometimes confrontational but always punitive interventions into community life exposed residents to a deeply flawed criminal justice system, in massive numbers. That substantially less than one-half of the African Americans interviewed during 2015 had much trust in the police, and one-half of the African Americans who were stopped that year thought they were badly treated (Chapter 4), should not be a surprise.

4

What Happens During Stop & Frisk?

This chapter examines some of the personal consequences of stop & frisk. A stop & frisk strategy presumes a relentless focus on presumably hot people concentrated in crime hotspots that increases the risk involved in carrying drugs or weapons. Concentrated stop & frisk presumably increases the perception among potential offenders and the general public alike that they face a high risk of being apprehended if they commit a crime or are inclined to do so, and this reduces offending.

But "the general public" is a big target, and almost all of them are *not* up to no good. The very large number of unwarranted stops resulting from a strategy of sending a general deterrent message risks the large-scale accumulation of a variety of human costs of stop & frisk against which we must weigh the presumed benefits of a widespread stop policy. The previous chapter presented police administrative data on the growth and distribution of recorded stops. However, the official data were silent regarding what transpired out in the field, at the other end of those encounters. Some of what happens needs to be counted as costs. Administrative records do not tell us anything about how professionally officers approached and then eventually released the individuals they targeted, how they responded to the reactions of those they targeted, and how respectful they were of their subject's legal rights. These questions are doubly important because most were innocent stops. They were a burden imposed upon people who could not avoid them, even though the stops turned out to be unwarranted. Stopping them was just policy. This chapter reports that a survey of city residents found almost 30 percent of all adult Chicagoans described being stopped in a year, but more than 75 percent of those who were stopped faced no subsequent official action. How *they* were treated was one of the consequences of stop & frisk.

The answer to the opening question is that a great deal happened during Chicago stop & frisks. Virtually everyone was questioned and asked if they carried any identification papers. Fewer were searched, mostly African Americans. About 36 percent of African Americans reported being searched, compared to 29 percent of Hispanics and just nine percent of Whites.

Stop & Frisk and the Politics of Crime in Chicago. Wesley G. Skogan, Oxford University Press.
© Oxford University Press 2023. DOI: 10.1093/oso/9780197675052.003.0004

It was Black respondents (19 percent) and Hispanics (21 percent) who were handcuffed while they were being questioned but then were released. About 35 percent of African Americans and 30 percent of Hispanic respondents reported they were subjected to force of some sort, including verbal threats, the display of weapons, and physical force; for White residents the comparable figure was 14 percent. Overall, 77 percent of Chicago stops were innocent stops & frisks, and 23 percent led to enforcement action.

All these experiences had further consequences. This chapter includes Chicagoans' assessments of the fairness and respectfulness with which they were treated. Research indicates that confidence in the police is created in part by fair treatment (Maguire, Lowrey and Johnson, 2017; Tyler, Fagan and Geller, 2014). Especially in high-stop neighborhoods, many people form opinions assessments of the police based on their own experience, including if police have good intentions and are to be trusted. This chapter examines what Chicagoans thought about their police, and how the targets of stop & frisk rated their experiences on four dimensions forming the "pillars of procedural justice"—voice, neutrality, respect, and impartiality.

The Frequency of Stops

One purpose of the survey was to examine the frequency with which individual Chicagoans are stopped by the police. This cannot be found in administrative records. Department reports record the number of stops but, because some people are stopped multiple times, official data are an uncertain guide to individual experiences with the police. Only the aggregate rate at which stops take place can be discerned. During their interview, respondents were first presented with questions regarding crime and disorder in their neighborhood, fear of crime, and their participation in community activities. Further questions gathered their general assessments of Chicago police on several dimensions. These questions served as cues, to encourage respondents to be thinking about the police. Only then did the survey turn to their personal experiences. Respondents were presented with multiple, specific verbal cues to aid them in thinking about their involvement in police-initiated encounters. They were first asked if they had *ever* been involved in a vehicle stop. This was followed by a similar question about having ever been stopped "when you were out walking, or shopping, or just standing around?" There were also open-ended questions about being stopped in other circumstances or for other reasons. In response to the "have you ever . . ." questions, *72 percent* of everyone interviewed recalled being stopped at some time by Chicago police. Among African Americans the total was 79 percent. These were large numbers, but not of much use here. The time period "ever" is long for older residents, and much shorter for the 16- and 17-year-olds. It can also conjure up reports of long-ago and perhaps hazily recalled incidents among those with more life experience, and it also risks overlooking forgotten events from the distant past.

To address this, follow-up probes were used next to determine which of their encounters occurred in the past 12 months. A 12-month recall period was used to estimate a yearly stop rate, and to give respondents of all ages an equal span of time to consider. In addition, respondents' ability to recall in detail what happened during encounters should be greater if they focus only on relatively recent events. If respondents recalled being involved in more than one police-initiated encounter during the past year, they were eventually asked which was the most recent of those events. This was significant—almost 30 percent of those who recalled being stopped in the past 12 months reported being stopped more than once during the period. In this circumstance, they were asked in detail about the *most recent* of the multiple contacts, which provides a reasonably random selection from among them. Incident details were gathered in follow-up questions about what happened during their only, or most recent, encounter, if it had occurred in the past year. The interviews were conducted continuously during 2015, so those occurring early in the year referred to events happening during the latter part of 2014, while interviews conducted later mostly referred to 2015 events. These turned out to be the peak years for stop & frisk in Chicago.

Knowing who had been stopped, asking detailed follow-up questions enabled us to examine the frequency and character two categories of police-initiated stops: stop & frisks and enforcement stops. "Enforcement stop" is the term used here for encounters resulting in someone being arrested, receiving a ticket, or being taken to a police station. In Chicago many enforcement encounters were traffic-related; only six percent of respondents reported being cited, arrested, or taken to a station after being stopped while on foot. Chicago police can issue civil ordinance violation tickets (called "Administrative Notices of Violation, or "ANOVs") for offenses such as public drinking, public urination, smoking or eating on a bus, riding a bicycle on the sidewalk, littering and (before it was legalized) minor marijuana possession. Previously these were arrest-worthy offenses. Across all enforcement stops, 97 percent of respondents received a ticket, 13 percent reported being arrested, and 19 percent said they were taken to a police station for further processing (all three things could have happened, and sometimes did).

However, if at the conclusion of their encounter with the police those we interviewed were not cited or formally sanctioned, and instead were free to walk away, the encounter is categorized as an innocent or unwarranted stop. Occasionally these stops will also be described as "investigative" stops, to parallel the "Investigative Stop Report" forms officers filled out documenting them. The vast majority of respondents falling in this category were questioned and asked for their identification. Many also reported being searched, threatened, handcuffed, and roughed up or even injured—particularly if they were African Americans or Hispanics. A majority of innocent stop & frisks (56 percent) took place near respondents' homes, in contrast to only 36 percent of enforcement stops.

The survey also quizzed respondents regarding 10 different reasons why they may have contacted the police themselves during the past year. For example, they were asked, "In the past 12 months, did you report a traffic accident or medical emergency to the Chicago police, or did you not report a traffic accident or medical emergency to the Chicago police?" In all, 40 percent of respondents described a recent citizen-initiated contact—a very large fraction of the population.

Who Was Targeted?

As in many American cities, the frequency and social distribution of stop & frisks in Chicago was a subject of political contention. When this survey was completed, the Chicago police became engulfed in a tremendous scandal over charges they had been concealing a horrific act of brutality to protect themselves and the political ambitions of the city's mayor. The resulting firestorm of criticism led to the creation of a special commission to investigate the situation and recommend changes to the city's policies and practices. It also sparked a federal investigation. Based on administrative records, the Police Accountability Task Force's 200-page report released in May 2016 observed that in the summer of 2014 (they were given just a little data) the Chicago police stopped more than 250,000 people. As a rate per 10,000 residents this was more than four times the comparable rate for New York City at the peak of its stop & frisk era (Police Accountability Task Force, 2016,

p. 36). This was taken by many as a very large and politically unacceptable number. Chapter 6 reports in detail on the Laquan McDonald incident and the cascade of events that followed.

Another focus of attention among those concerned about police policy was the *distribution* of stops. For example, of the 250,000 stop & frisks recorded during the summer of 2014, 72 percent targeted African Americans, while 17 percent involved Hispanics and nine percent involved Whites (Police Accountability Task Force, 2016, p. 10). Based on other data, the Task Force report provided extensive documentation of similarly enormous racial disparities in the actions of Chicago police officers. These included whom they shot (74 percent African Americans) and whom they downed with Tasers (76 percent African Americans). There was an extensive analysis of racial disparities in traffic stops (72 percent African American) and arrests for loitering (82 percent African American) (Police Accountability Task Force, 2016, pp. 35–47). Less than one-third of the city's population was African American, in contrast. There seemed to be little time left for any extra attention to the city's Hispanic population. They make up about one-third of the city's population, but on many measures their experiences did not differ notably from those of Whites.

The survey was designed to capture many of the experiences concerning the Task Force and others in the city. It was completed just as the scandal broke, so it and accompanying media coverage of police-community relations could not have affected the survey's findings. Unlike studies based on administrative forms, it does not "double count" individuals who are stopped more than once; as we will see, this is quite common. The survey gathered reports of encounters directly from individual citizens, and these can be related to other analytic variables and to their assessments of how they were treated. Figure 4-1 examines the social distribution of stop & frisk and enforcement encounters described in the survey. It categorizes Chicagoans by age ("young" is age 16–34), sex, and race (persons of other races are excluded, as they were too few for this detailed analysis). The bars in the chart each represent more than 90 respondents, with nine of the 12 lying in the 100+ range. It reports the percentage of respondents in each age-sex-race category who were stopped during the past year, dividing stops between enforcement and investigative encounters. A version of this figure appeared in the final report of the Police Accountability Task Force, in which I participated.

Several points are illustrated in Figure 4-1. First, in Chicago, being stopped for investigative purposes was the predominant experience residents had

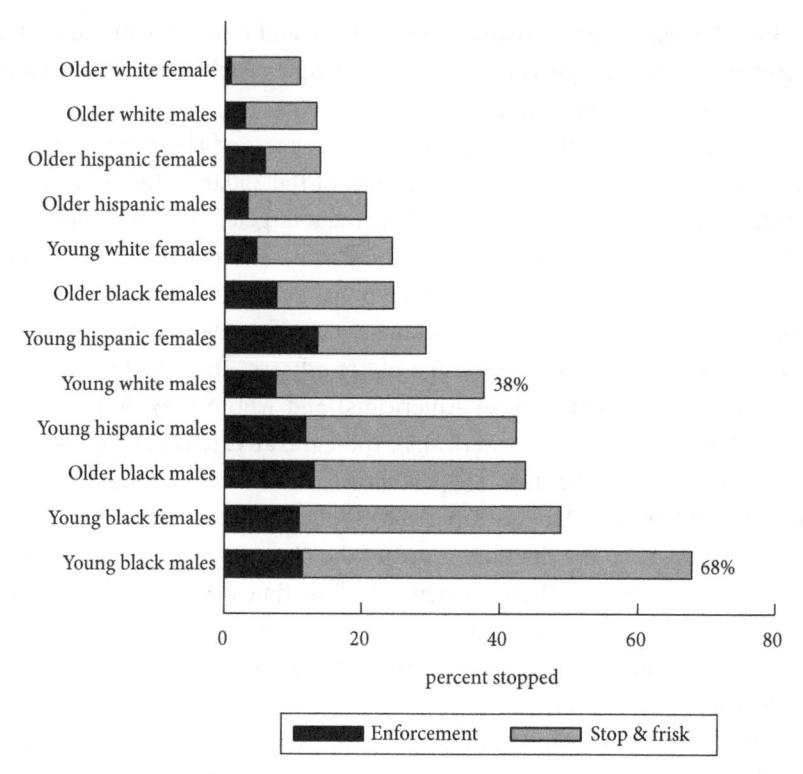

Figure 4-1 Stops by Age, Race, and Sex

with the police. Every group mainly reported being stopped for questioning rather than being ticketed or arrested. The least-often stopped group (11 percent in a year) was older White females, and they were six times more likely to be stopped for questioning rather than for an actionable offense. Among young African American males, 17 percent of those stopped were arrested or ticketed while 83 percent were involved in an innocent stop & frisk. Overall (the bars do not represent equal numbers of people), 22 percent of all Chicagoans aged 16 and older reported being caught up in an investigative stop and seven percent were formally sanctioned by ticketing or arrest, a 3-to-1 ratio. The wide net being cast by Chicago's stop & frisk strategy was one of its most surprising features.

It is difficult to judge whether 29 percent stopped or 22 reporting a stop & frisk are high or low numbers, compared to other places and times. Every study of the topic estimating the prevalence of stops using surveys has used a different questionnaire strategy or examined only specific sub-populations, such as young people. Police records recount stops, not the number of individuals stopped, so they are not very comparable. As we will see later in this chapter, a significant number of people questioned in the survey described being stopped repeatedly even within a twelve-month period. They would contribute disproportionately to the number of stops recorded in administrative records.

Second, police–citizen encounters in Chicago varied widely in frequency. Among young people, men, and African Americans, being stopped was a common rather than an exceptional circumstance. Statistically, age was the largest determinant of being stopped; note being classified as "young" describes six of the seven most-stopped groups. Overall, 31 percent of those interviewed who were under age 35 (the "Millennials" in this sample) were caught up in stop & frisk, as were 23 percent of Chicagoans aged 35–50. Race came next in terms of predicting the probability of being stopped for questioning. About 30 percent of African American respondents were involved in stop & frisk, in contrast to 16 percent of Whites and 20 percent of Hispanics. Gender was the third best predictor of being stopped. In total, 18 percent of females and 28 percent of males recalled being stopped for questioning. In addition, lower income people and short-term residents of their neighborhood were more likely to be involved in stop & frisk encounters (this is not depicted in Figure 4-1).

Third, age, race, and sex conspired to create a huge stop rate among young African American men. As Figure 4-1 illustrates, in just one year 56 percent of young Black males reported being targeted by stop & frisk, and 68 percent were stopped overall. They were five times more likely to be stopped for investigation than to be formally sanctioned.

Since at least the 2000s a great deal of concern has been expressed about relations between the police and immigrant communities. Chicago is officially a "sanctuary city." In March 1985, then-Mayor Harold Washington halted the city's practice of questioning city job and license applicants about their citizenship, and he halted most cooperation between city agencies and federal immigration authorities. During this period—but not later, under the federal Trump administration—undocumented immigrants stopped by police for minor crimes should not have feared deportation. During 2015 there was a clear tendency for foreign-born Chicagoans, and especially non-citizens within this group, to avoid encounters with the police, either for enforcement or investigative reasons. Foreign-born respondents were only one-half as likely as native-born residents to be stopped. Among the foreign born, 17 percent of citizens but only 11 percent of non-citizens were stopped. This is consistent with the general tendency of newcomers to be circumspect regarding potential encounters with law enforcement officials, and a preference for "staying below the radar screen" (Skogan, 2009).

Rounding Up the Usual Suspects?

Were police in Chicago often just "rounding up the usual suspects?" In the popular film *Casablanca*, Captain Renault (played by Claude Rains) of the local police substituted frantic activity for actual police work when he ordered his officers to "round up the usual suspects" rather than investigate the killing of a German military officer by his friend, Rick (Humphrey Bogart). The organizational context of this study of stop & frisk made such often unproductive but activity-producing roundups a distinct possibility. At the department's CompStat management meetings the chief of police roared at commanders who failed to produce ever-increasing numbers of stops. This translated into continuous pressure at the district level to make stops for the purpose of stopping people and completing forms documenting contacts. Officers in many districts were exhorted at roll call to bring back stop reports. One officer reported being told to go to a park ". . . and get a couple of kid's names. I was compared to another officer who will fill out contact cards by the dozen daily." Another described his strategy: "We contact card the same piss bums and drunks week after week to keep the numbers up. I data warehouse checked one of our regular beggars and he has over 100 contacts this year."

In the survey, respondents describing a stop & frisk that occurred during the past 12 months were asked how frequently these kinds of incidents had happened to them in the past year. The numbers who were stopped are shown in Figure 4-2. African Americans proved to be the usual suspects most often. They reported experiencing an average of four of stops in the past year; for Hispanics, the stop average was 2.4; and among Whites, it was 2.3. These figures were calculated after applying a top 2.5 percent trim on accounts of how often respondents were stopped, to discount improbably large estimates. Figure 4-2 classifies the frequency with which these groups described being stopped, capping the top range at five stops or more. As it indicates, 40 percent of African Americans who had been stopped fell in this category, while only one-quarter were stopped only once in a year. Whites and Hispanics were about twice as likely to be stopped only once, and many

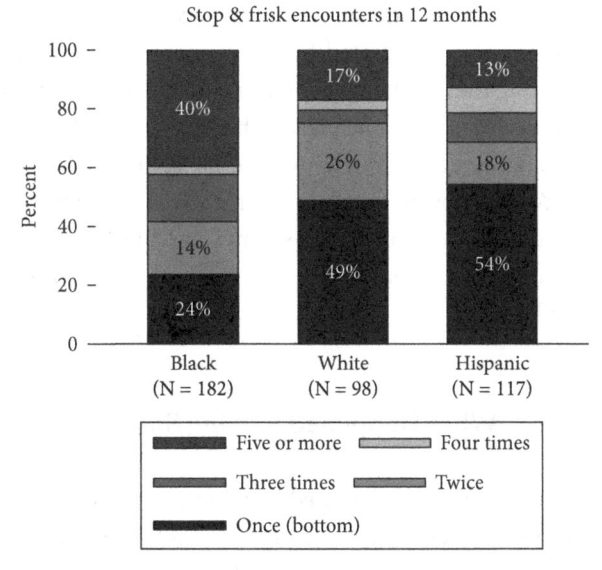

Figure 4-2 Frequency of Repeated Stops by Race

fewer were stopped extremely frequently. Other factors were related to roundups. In particular, older residents were not swept up as often as their younger cohorts. However, being an African American was the predominant predictor of being a usual suspect. Subjects of stop & frisk were also more likely to be *repeatedly* stopped than were targets of enforcement stops. About 60 percent of those reporting enforcement encounters were stopped only once in the year, while about 60 percent of stop & frisk subjects were stopped more than once.

A second consequence of the practice of rounding up the usual suspects is that African Americans most often faced the repeated indignity of being hassled, frequently searched, and (along with Latinos) most often handcuffed before being sent on their way. Some of the resentment and rage accumulating in minority communities may be attributed to this kind of systematic harassment. They may feel they and their rights are being violated. They were all innocent of any actionable offense, but they still were powerless to resist in the face of police power over them on the street.

Why would the police persist in these roundups? One reason may have been to reinforce their authority to do so among young men on the street. Another was the organizational imperative to produce an increasing number of stops for presentation at the department's CompStat sessions. This does not mean they are happy to do so. An experienced police Captain reported officers themselves were frustrated by the concentration of problems they were sent to, feeling they are being applied again and again as a Band-Aid on top of the same issues in the same places. She noted, "You don't even want to ask anyone questions because you know it's their 50th contact with the police over nothing. You don't want to talk to them and they have nothing to say to you." Why did officers continue to do so anyway? "It got so blatantly out of control. It wasn't arrests. It wasn't guns recovered. It was how many contact cards" (Mitchell, 2016).

What Happened During Stops?

As we have seen, most people stopped by Chicago police were not ticketed or arrested. Instead, a very large majority of street stops were investigative stop & frisks. These involved identity checks, questioning, and searches of vehicles and persons. Chicagoans also reported being on the receiving end of threats, handcuffing, and physical force during investigative stops, although in the end there was no reason to hold them. Facing these intrusive police actions was much more common among African Americans and Hispanics.

Figure 4-3 details some of the actions taken by the police during stop & frisks. As it documents, a big majority of non-White Chicagoans faced an identity check; police demanded identification from about three-quarters of the African Americans and Latinos who were stopped. For Whites, the comparable figure was 56 percent. During this period, stops were of particular concern to immigrant Chicagoans. Our sample of Hispanics was large enough to examine origin and citizenship issues within this group, which was one of the largest communities in the city. To summarize, police were clearly more likely to ask foreign-born Hispanics for identification, and they were particularly likely (85 percent) to ask for their papers when they encountered people who primarily spoke Spanish. Respondents were classified as Spanish-speaking if for our interview they had to be questioned in Spanish.

Searches were less common during stop & frisk encounters, but they were also disproportionate in their impact. More than 35 percent of African Americans reported they were searched; among Latinos the number was 25 percent, while for Whites it was nine percent. In addition to race, the correlates of being searched included age: Chicagoans aged 16–35 were most

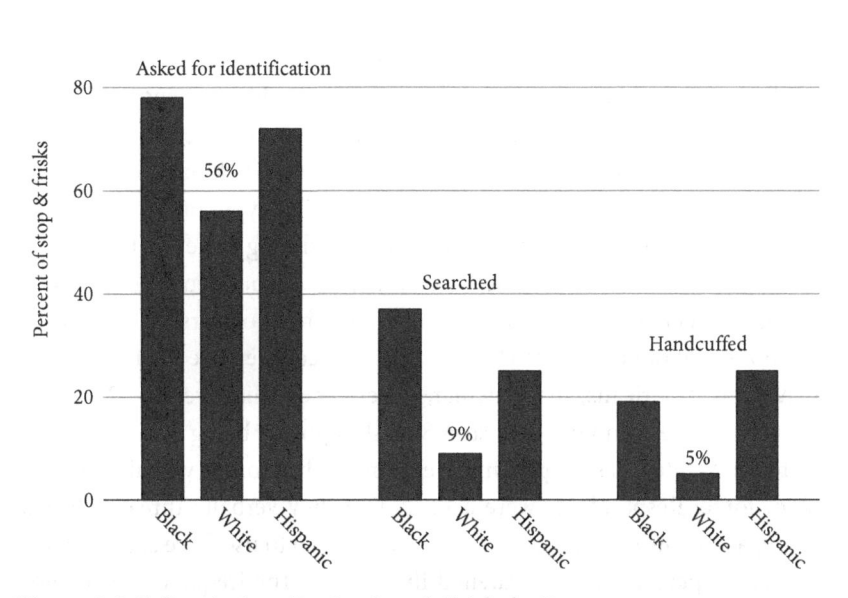

Figure 4-3 Police Actions During Stop & Frisks by Race

likely to be searched, as were lower-income and less educated people who were swept up in stop & frisk encounters. On the other hand, foreign-born and Spanish-speaking Hispanics—who might have found it harder to make their case—were not more likely to be searched.

A perhaps surprising fraction of African Americans (19 percent) and Hispanics (21 percent) were also handcuffed in the course of being questioned, but then eventually released. For Whites the figure was five percent. In principle, handcuffing could have been precautionary, or in response to anticipated or actual violent action by the citizens involved. The survey did not probe this point, but because in the end none of the people represented in Figure 4-3 were arrested, they certainly were not doing much that was provocative. In addition to race, handcuffing was more common for younger and male subjects, low-income people, and respondents without much formal education.

Respondents who had been stopped were questioned in some detail about any police use of force during the encounter. Their responses can be classified along a commonly used "force continuum" developed by policing scholar David Klinger (Klinger, 1995). Early research on use of force often treated it as a dichotomous, "yes-or-no" feature of encounters. Focusing mainly on personal injury, these studies tended to conclude police use of force during encounters was rare. Beginning in the early 2000s, researchers began to cast a wider net. First, they recognized there was a broader spectrum of "nonlethal" force applications in play. Later they incorporated elements of police intimidation tactics into the concept (for more see Hickman, Piquero and Garner, 2008). Recognizing there are many possible types of force an officer can apply, it is most useful to think of it on a sliding scale. At the bottom of Klinger's continuum lie shouted commands. Respondents caught up in stop & frisk encounters were asked, "Did they shout or curse at you, or did they not shout or curse at you?" Overall, 23 percent reported being shouted at. African Americans, in particular, experienced this; overall, 32 percent of African American targets of stop & frisk reported being shouted at. The figure for Whites was 10 percent. Next on the list comes verbal threats of use of force. Respondents were asked, "Did they verbally threaten to use force against you, or did they not verbally threaten to use force against you?" In total, 13 percent were threatened in this way. The frequency of weapon threats was measured by responses to two questions: "Did they verbally threaten to use a weapon, or did they not verbally threaten to use a weapon?" and "Did they take out a weapon, such as a gun, a club, or a Taser, or did they not take out a weapon?" Officers were described as taking out a weapon in 10 percent of stop & frisks and threatening to in another six percent; those are combined here. Finally, the use of physical force was indicated by positive responses to the question "Were you pushed, grabbed, kicked or hit, or were you not pushed, grabbed, kicked or hit?" In total, 13 percent of those caught up in stop & frisks were pushed or shoved.

Figure 4-4 arranges these descriptions of use of force in order, from shouting commands at the bottom to the use of physical force at the top. Each respondent was placed in their highest position on the force continuum, based on their description of what happened at the scene. For example, while 32 percent of Black respondents reported being shouted at, shouting was the worst thing that happened to only nine percent of them, and the value is illustrated in the figure. The overall height of each bar illustrates the proportion of each group subjected to any kind of force. Figure 4-4 illustrates the large racial disparities in the use of force during innocent stop & frisks. At the top end, the use of physical force was particularly disparate. During stop & frisks, 14 percent of African Americans and 20 percent of Hispanics reported being shoved or pushed around, in contrast to seven percent of Whites. Eleven

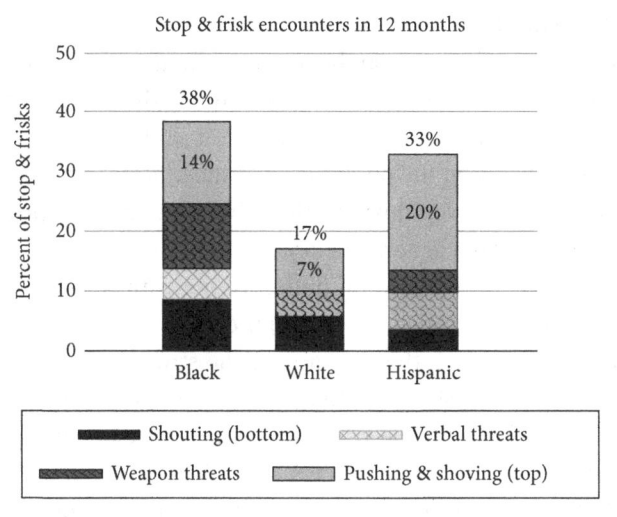

Figure 4-4 Use of Force by Race

percent of African Americans reported a weapon threat; among Hispanics it was four percent, and for Whites it was zero. Overall (examining the total height of the bars), during stop & frisks, African Americans (at 38 percent) and Hispanics (33 percent) were about twice as likely as Whites (17 percent) to have been subjected to some form of force before being released. (It is important to note that two percent of those stopped for anything reported being injured in some way during a stop & frisk, a figure too small to be visible in Figure 4-4 or to do much analysis of.)

In addition to race, other factors were implicated in what happened during stops. Across all groups, women and higher-income respondents were less likely to be subjected to the use of force, while young people were much more frequently roughed up at the top of the continuum. An important protective factor was social class. Flagged either by income or education, better-off Chicagoans who were stopped were less likely to be searched or handcuffed, or to fall anywhere on the use-of-force continuum. Few college graduates were subjected to any significant force or were handcuffed.

How Were They Treated?

In describing what happened during stop & frisks, a perhaps equally important issue is how well officers *handle* stops and the residue of experience that they leave on those who are caught up in them. While there are many dimensions along which researchers assess the *quality* of police–citizen contacts, perhaps the most well understood are those recommended by "procedural justice" theory. Procedural justice is a set of principles regarding the relationship between the public and the state.[1] Research indicates it is a primary contributor to legitimacy—the belief an authority's power is right and proper. While it is a general theory, a significant amount of research on procedural justice has focused on police. Along with schoolteachers, they are the agents of government with whom ordinary people have the most contact, and about which they often have the strongest views. Procedural justice moves to center stage the concern about the ways police (and other authority figures) treat people with whom they come in contact. Research has identified some key components of police–citizen interactions that seem particularly important to those who are involved. These include not displaying bias or favoritism, listening to what people have to say rather than cutting them short, and showing them a bit of respect rather than silencing them by intimidation and fear. We know from this research that the public is concerned about the fairness and evenhandedness of police decisions, and also hope officers abide by the laws and rules governing the exercise of their powers.

When he arrived in Chicago in mid- 2011, new Police Superintendent Garry McCarthy included among his priorities a call for department members to act in accord with the principles of procedural justice. Both in the training academy and in general orders describing the department's standards for their behavior, Chicago officers were reminded they were to attend to the fundamental dimensions of procedural justice. McCarthy's new departmental order announced this commitment:

> All interactions with members of the public will be conducted with the upmost respect and courtesy and be based on the concepts of Procedural Justice and Legitimacy. During each interaction, Department members will strive to attain the highest degree of ethical behavior and professional conduct at all times.

The order specifically listed the concepts of voice, neutrality, respect, and trustworthiness as making up the components of procedural justice.

Why focus on procedural justice? Many of the reasons for doing so have been summarized by Tom Tyler and Tracey Meares (2019). Research promises important "wins" for policing adhering to the standards of procedural justice. For example, it finds that the public will be more supportive of the police, more compliant with their requests, and more willing to defer to them in moments of crisis when they believe them to be procedurally just. There is also suggestive evidence that beliefs about procedural justice are linked to voluntary cooperation with law enforcement, greater willingness to report crimes and to provide police with tips, and to step forward as witnesses.

In addition, when they view the police as acting justly, people may come to believe police have a rightful monopoly over the use of force, thus reinforcing the legitimacy of the state. By many definitions, trust is a core component of legitimacy. For example, Tyler (2006) sees legitimacy as a combination of trust and a duty to obey legal authorities. Trust reflects a belief in officers' benevolent intentions (this is dubbed "motive-based trust"), while a duty to obey reflects the belief that police have the authority to dictate appropriate behavior (see also Jackson and Gau, 2016). Among immigrants, fair treatment by police also increases their sense of (new) national identity. There is intriguing but still developing evidence that just treatment by police helps neighborhoods build their own crime-prevention capacity (Sargeant, Wickes and Mazerolle, 2013). All these research findings have been used to support efforts encouraging police agencies and their officers to attend more carefully to the manner in which they deal with the public.

However, police casting a wide net and intervening in the lives of a broad spectrum of citizens to announce their presence and signal they are to be feared, could easily undermine any belief that police motives are to be trusted. Claims stops initiated in response to truly suspicious behavior, which is one basis of their legality, lose credibility when tens of thousands of unwarranted stops are conducted each month. From the point of view of many of the citizens involved, these stops could seem illegitimate. Even in crime hotspots, most people—most of the time—are just going about their daily lives. One of the negative features of stop & frisk is that doing nothing wrong will not protect them against being swept up by the police. Instead, they may feel besieged, even in their own neighborhoods. In their experience, being stopped, and stopped repeatedly, is demeaning, and it certainly can signal that people like themselves are not respected.

A high-volume stop strategy like the one adopted in Chicago also may not command careful management of the quality of stops. Procedural justice theory emphasizes the importance of officers letting citizens speak up, listening to what the public has to say, carefully explaining their actions, and being respectful and polite (Van Craen, 2016). At a minimum this involves taking their time. But, based on this survey, too often stops in Chicago more resembled "confront and command" policing, rather than procedurally just policing. Being stopped is also potentially dangerous—among all but White Chicagoans, more than 30 percent of our respondents reported being threatened or worse by the police during stop & frisks. Tyler and Huo's (2002) original formulation of motive-based trust involved the belief that police are doing their best for the people with whom they are dealing. Stop & frisks of innocent parties do not send this message. A crime prevention strategy based on generating large numbers of unwarranted stops to promote deterrence may ultimately undermine the legitimacy of the police, and perhaps the state.

Measuring Procedural Justice

The Chicago community survey was designed to measure key components of procedural justice theory. In broad scope, many elements of the theory fall into two categories: perceptions of the *quality of treatment* people receive by the police and the *quality of police decision-making*. Here we will examine two aspects of quality of treatment—respect and fairness—and two aspects of quality of decision-making—neutrality and voice. In the community survey, everyone who had been stopped in the past year was asked to rate their recent experience on multiple questions addressing each of those dimensions. The resulting data were organized to address the frequency and impact of procedurally just stops compared to those rated nearer the other end of the spectrum.

Respect. Respect encompasses treating people with dignity, acting politely, and granting them some of the routine signs of respect we grant others every day. Respect is a status signal. People—and especially young people—are constantly gauging their self-worth by the respect they garner, and police are one of the messengers of their standing in society (Slocum and Wiley, 2018). Disrespectful treatment sends the message that individuals, or the groups they are identified with, are not valued by the powerful. Stops police might make to demonstrate their control of the street and their ability to command obedience could fall in a category of encounters not likely to score high on the respect dimension. In the survey, respect was measured by responses to questions like "How respectful were the police to you?" and "To what extent did the police respect your rights as a human being?"

Figure 4-5 illustrates responses to one of the questions focusing on respect for rights. It charts positive responses lying above the mid-points. In this instance, just about one-half of all respondents agreed that officers respected people's rights "a lot" or "a great deal." However, as Figure 4-5 indicates, it was white Chicagoans (more than 70 percent of them) who drove this total, reporting police respected their rights. African Americans fell behind them by about 20 percentage points.

Fairness. Fairness is another aspect of procedural justice. Fairness encompasses attention to rules about process and the consistency of their application. Fairness should be embedded in the law and the policies of any police department; the survey tells us something about the actual implementation of these rules. Fairness was measured by responses to "How fairly were you treated by the police?" and "Taking everything the police did into account, how satisfied are you with how fairly you were treated by the police during this contact?" Their replies could range from extremely to not at all fairly or satisfied. Figure 4-5 describes responses to the first, fair treatment

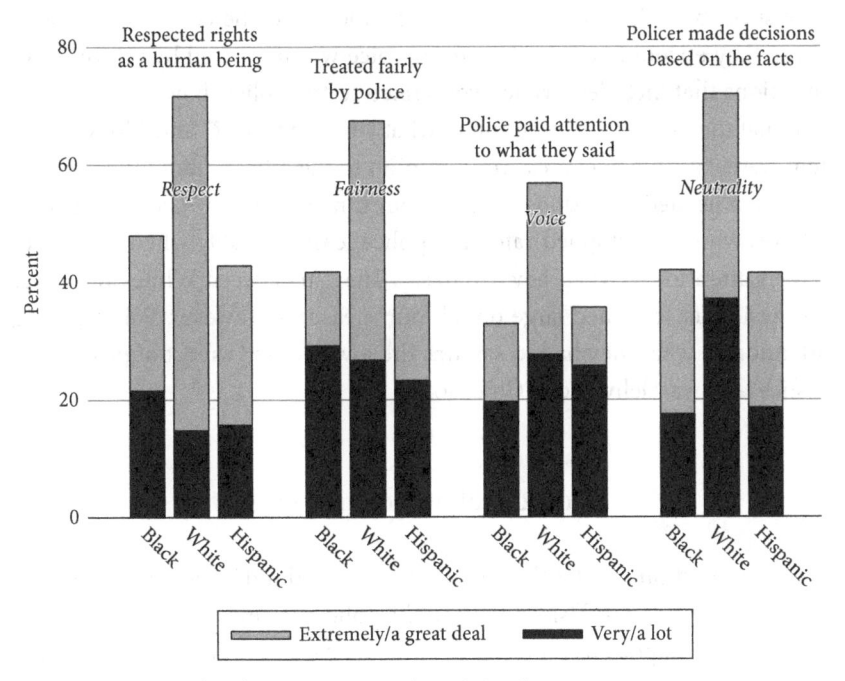

Figure 4-5 Procedural Justice During Stop & Frisks

question. In the example, only 12 percent of African Americans thought police were extremely fair to them, and only 14 percent of Hispanics.

Neutrality. Neutrality encompasses believing decisions made by the police were objective, and that they were stopping people for legitimate reasons. Neutral decisions are impartial and fact-based. In the survey, neutrality was measured by questions such as "How many of the facts needed to make good decisions do you think the police actually got?" and "To what extent do you believe the police made their decisions based on the facts?" Figure 4-5 illustrates that Whites were again more positive, with about 70 percent indicating the officers confronting them made fact-based decisions on what to do.

Voice. The voice dimension involves giving citizens an opportunity to describe their situation and tell their side of the story while officers are deciding what to do. Giving people a chance to speak signals that their concerns are being taken into account. Studies of crime victims have documented the importance of voice in their satisfaction with police service, and "listening" is a routine component in officer training on how to handle crime victims. The importance of voice has been demonstrated outside of surveys. For example, in observational studies of on-street encounters, McCluskey (2003) and Dai, Frank and Sun (2011) both found opportunities for voice and expressions of respect by police while making stops increased the cooperativeness of those they encountered. In the survey voice was measured by responses to questions that included "When you talked to the police, how satisfied were you that the police paid attention to what you had to say?" and "To what extent were you able to express your opinion to the officers about the incident and what needed to be done?" Of the four dimensions of procedural justice, Whites who were stopped rated the police least favorably when it came to paying attention to what they had to say. The gap between Whites and other city residents remained large on all four measures, however. Police paying attention to what they had to say was the lowest-rated aspect of procedural justice, as it was delivered in Chicago.

Procedural Justice and Trust

The next question, what is the impact of the procedural justice experiences of the subjects of stop & frisk on trust in the police? In research, trust is viewed as one of the important products of policing, caused to an important extent by the quality of the service police deliver and the reputation they develop in the community. Trust is said to involve evaluations of the "intentions and capabilities" of the police (Jackson and Gau, 2016, p. 53). It is evidenced when citizens believe police try to do the right thing, acting on behalf of the best interests of the people they encounter. In this view, people will trust police if they are seen as embodying the norms and values of the community and when they think police are sincere and well-meaning. Trust is sometimes labeled "motive-based trust" because it is a belief regarding the intentions of the police, that "their heart is in the right place" and they mean well even if they do not always succeed. Trust creates expectations about the future behavior of the police. When confidence in the typical and anticipated behavior of the police is strong, trust can help sustain public support should there be an occasional breech and police do not manage to live up to expectations, including their own (Tyler and Huo, 2002). Trust is also seen as a key component of legitimacy, one of the bedrock concepts in democratic theory. In Tom Tyler's (2004) view, trust is one of the most crucial components of procedural justice theory because it underlies legitimacy—which he defines as the obligation to obey police and the law. The more people trust the police, the more likely they are to support them and act in accordance with their requests. On the other hand, well-publicized cases of corruption, abuse of people's rights, and other scandals can damage the reputation of the police and undermine trust.

Trust in police serving in their neighborhood was measured by the questions summarized in Table 4-1. One component of this measure refers to Constitutional policing (protecting basic rights) while others

Table 4-1 Measures of Trust in Chicago Police

How likely is it that people's basic rights will be well protected by the Chicago police?

How likely is it that the leaders of the Chicago police will make decisions that are good for everyone in the city?

How sincere are police working in this neighborhood about trying to help people with their problems?

How honest are police working in this neighborhood?

How much of the time can the police be trusted to make decisions that are right for the people in this neighborhood?

---

reference "helping" people and making decisions "right for the people." These referenced trust as the belief that police are motivated by community concerns. An opposing view might emphasize police inattentiveness and indifference. As for honesty, research conducted in shady places finds perceived corruption and self-reports of having to pay bribes are related to measures of confidence in the police (see Peacock, 2021). Note that by one account (based on federal indictments) Chicago is the most corrupt big city in the United States, and Illinois the third-most corrupt state in the nation (Simpson, et. al., 2020). For these respondents—including separately by race—perceived honesty clustered tightly with other indicators of trust. Responses to these questions were all measured by five-point response scales centered around mixed or neutral categories. They were highly correlated (an average of +.59) and single-factored, so they were combined to form one measure.

Figure 4-6 illustrates the impact of our respondents' judgments about their personal experiences on their trust in the police, controlling statistically for the other factors on a long list of additional factors. Across all 1,450 respondents, the average trust score was 3.28, just above a middling score of 3.0 on a one-to-five scale. To highlight the contributions of procedural justice to levels of trust, Figure 4-6 subtracts the mean from this score. As a result,

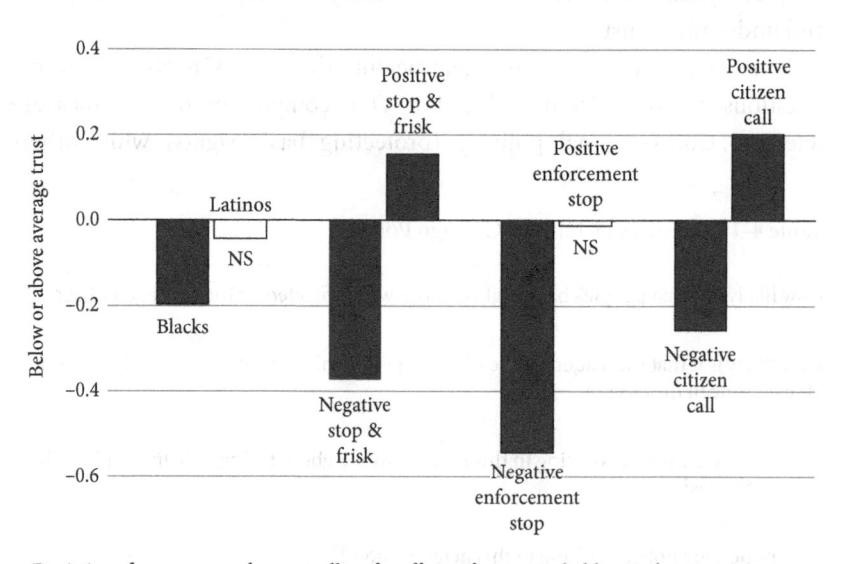

Deviations from average also controlling for effects of young and old age, education, ownership, income, gender, length of residence, foreign born, kids at home, area poverty and recorded crime, and use of force during the encounter

Figure 4-6 The Impact of Encounters on Trust in Police

Figure 4-6 illustrates differences *above or below the city average* associated with citizens' reports of their recent experience with the Chicago police. It includes the independent influence of race—the views of African Americans and Hispanics in contrast to those of Whites—to serve as a benchmark against which to judge the importance of recent experience.[2]

While the focus here is on procedural justice during stop & frisk encounters, Figure 4-6 expands the scope of popular experience with the police to encompass other contacts with the Chicago police as well. The community survey asked about citizen-initiated encounters, as well as police-originated ones, and about one-quarter of the respondents who were stopped by police were ticketed or arrested and therefore classed as subjects of enforcement stops rather than Chicago-style stop & frisks. Respondents with something to tell us about any of those experiences were questioned. In total, 13 percent of respondents (about 190 of them) recounted recent experiences with both citizen-initiated *and* police-initiated encounters, further highlighting the importance of taking reports of all these contacts into account. In total, *57 percent* of those we interviewed (825 respondents) reported one or another of these contacts with Chicago police in a single year. Improving the quality of stops could have a quick impact on much of the city.

The findings highlight the persistent impact of *quality* of the experience on police–citizen encounters of all kinds. Figure 4-6 divides respondents into "positive" and "negative" groups based on responses to the procedural justice measures described above. Based on their own ratings, 42 percent of the 317 respondents involved in a stop & frisk fell in the bad experience category and 58 percent reported a good experience. Looking in detail, the biggest concerns among those caught up in a stop & frisk included not being treated very respectfully and that the officers they encountered did not pay attention to what they had to say.

In every case, the bars in Figure 4-6 contrast positive and negative experiences with respondents who recalled *no* encounters with police in the past year. The analysis included all the encounters described here, plus the list of control factors documented in the figure. Together, respondents' contacts with police and the many control factors accounted for 58 percent of the variance in trust. These data suggest stop & frisks significantly undermined trust in the police when respondents judged them to be outside the bounds set by procedural justice theory. The negative influence of poorly received stop & frisks was roughly twice the magnitude of remaining Black–White differences in trust in police. But, notably, stop & frisks approaching the standards suggested by procedural justice theory actually *contributed* to trust, rather than undermining it, but only by about one-half as much as poorly rated stops subtracted from trust. In this multivariate analysis, the views of Hispanic respondents did not vary significantly from the city-wide average.

By contrast, the net impact of enforcement stops was decidedly negative. Among the 98 respondents who described coming away with a ticket or being taken away under arrest, having a good experience did not have a statistically significant impact on their trust in the police (this bar is labeled "NS" in Figure 4-6). This was in part because there many fewer of them, and about two-thirds of enforcement encounters were poorly rated. The targets of enforcement stops were most dissatisfied on the "voice" dimension of procedural justice—officers paying attention to their side of the story. On the other hand, reports of officers not treating them in a procedurally fair, respectful, and factually neutral way (which was much more common) had a very negative impact on trust. The impact of poorly received enforcement stops was more than twice as influential as remaining Black–White differences in trust, and larger than that of a negatively received stop & frisk.

Finally, 607 respondents reported recently contacting the police themselves about some matter. Two-thirds of them recalled a good experience, and this contributed to trust. Respondents recalling a positive experience were most likely to report they were treated respectfully by responding officers, and the police decided what to do based on the facts (neutrality). Those reporting a generally poor experience were least satisfied with officers paying attention to what they had to say. As Figure 4-6 illustrates, differences in trust associated with positive and negative respondent-initiated contacts were of roughly the same magnitude as the influence of stop & frisk.

The good news here is the perceived respect, fairness, neutrality, and attention Chicagoans felt they experienced at the hands of the police did play a role in shaping their trust in the police as an institution that protected their individual rights while serving neighborhood and community interests. This was true of both citizen-initiated encounters *and* during stop & frisks. Good police practice, efforts in line with department policy and the officers' training, made a substantial difference, one resembling the remaining effect (after many important controls) of race. This finding corresponds with other research. Good practice seems to cast a positive influence on people's views of the community engagement efforts of the police (Bradford, Jackson and Stanko, 2009), and a very sophisticated analysis by Thiago Oliveira and his colleagues (Oliveira, et al. 2021) found perceptions of their procedural fairness were *most* influenced by good police practice, which is also reported here.

The Costs of Stop & Frisk

In Chicago, being targeted by stop & frisk was not an extraordinary occurrence, but a common event. The survey described here found that unwarranted stop & frisks swept up 22 percent of the adult population in just one year. Almost 70 percent of young, male, African Americans reported being stopped in a year, and most of those were stop & frisks. African Americans and Hispanics were also the repeatedly targeted as "usual suspects." It is also important to note that being stopped is not the only way people experience policing. With stop rates at the high levels described here, word was certainly getting around within poor and minority neighborhoods concerning what was happening to resident's relatives, friends, and neighbors. People draw lessons concerning policing from what they see and hear, and not just from their own direct experiences (Antrobus, et al., 2015).

Also, when compared to Whites, the city's African American, Hispanic, and other minorities were more likely to be caught up in *abrasive* encounters with the police. Young Black males were five times more likely to be stopped and released than they were to be ticketed or arrested, the largest ratio of any major demographic group. They also reported being stopped most frequently during the year. Stop & frisks were not "quick and harmless" encounters. Being stopped was not just an inconvenience. When they were stopped, the city's racial minorities were more likely to be searched, handcuffed, and roughed up during investigative stops before they were let go. The force used was largely verbal, involving shouting and verbal threats—unless they targeted African Americans. Among Black Chicagoans, about one-half of the force employed by officers involved threatening them with a weapon or pushing them around. Among this group, staying out of trouble did not protect them from being stopped. They could not control their own fate, and that fate threatened to be risky.

The significance of *how* individuals are treated by the police, plus the fact it can be multiplied by *how often* they call or are stopped by them, reinforces the importance of the *distribution* of procedural justice in a Chicago which

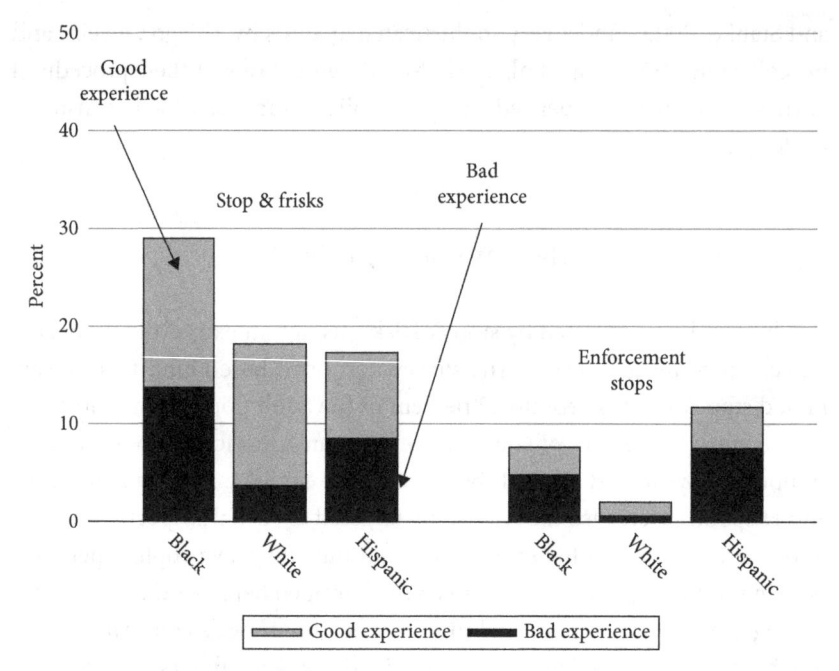

Figure 4-7 Frequency and Character of Encounters by Race

is deeply divided along racial lines. To illustrate this, Figure 4-7 brings both elements into relief. It illustrates the frequency *and* the character of Chicagoans' experience with the police during a period in which stop & frisk stood at a historic high. The height of each bar indicates the percentage of each group with a policing contact. Divisions within each bar classify the encounters as positive or negative based on their fit with procedural justice, using a generous standard when making this distinction.

During this period, almost 30 percent of African Americans surveyed were caught up in a stop & frisk. Almost one-half of the contacts reported by African American respondents were rated poorly, multiplying their overall importance. On the other hand, while lower in frequency, the experiences of Whites and Hispanics differed in character. Like African Americans, about one-half of Latino stop & frisks fell in the bad experience category. Good experiences are summarized on the top of each bar, to highlight their central role. In detail, the mix of experiences reported by Hispanics who were native born or citizens was more positive than those recalled by Latinos born elsewhere or who were not citizens. They were disproportionately represented in the bad experience category.

The role of nativity and citizenship was similar within the smaller number of enforcement stops reported by Hispanics in the survey. Foreign-born and non-citizen Hispanics were not ticketed or arrested often—as noted elsewhere their efforts to remain "below the radar screen" are well known. However, when stopped, it was foreign-born and non-citizen Hispanics who reported (mostly in a Spanish-language survey interview) they were not well treated. Almost two-thirds of all Latinos recalling an enforcement stop ended up in this category. Almost two-thirds of African Americans in the enforcement stop category also described encounters lying outside the procedural justice paradigm. Whites just had little to report. The overwhelmingly negative influence of enforcement stops on trust stems from the largely negative character of these encounters. There were not enough Chicagoans with a good enforcement experience to register statistically.

Stops influence people's judgments concerning the trustworthiness of the police generally. Why does all this matter? Popular opinion matters in part because widespread confidence in the police can make their work easier and more effective. Trust is threatened when police stop people but do not turn up any reason to hold them, and then stop them again. Trust is undermined by often demeaning, as well as unjustified, experiences. Stops sent the message their targets were not respected. People felt besieged, even in their own neighborhoods. Casting a broad net that scoops up large numbers of persons to no avail thus undermines public confidence in the police. The vast number of residents being stopped without any reason to be held—this totaled about 718,000 stops in 2014 and above 600,000 during 2015—could fairly be taken as evidence stops were not being initiated in response to reasonably suspicious behavior, which is the basis of their legality. In Chicago, residents who were caught up in stops often doubted officers' character, their sincerity and honesty, their interest in community concerns, and their ability to make making decisions right for people. Stop & frisks aligned with the principles of procedural justice made a difference, but only to those who were treated so.

Who Supports Stop & Frisk?

Contemporary research often focuses on negative assessments of law enforcement. Surveys have probed the extent, and consequences, of the view that police are unreliable when it comes to dealing fairly with the public or that they have been unable to prevent crime or maintain order (Doering,

2017). Studies of trust have concentrated on the origins of *distrust* of the police, including experiencing poorly conducted encounters and living in a high crime neighborhood. Carr, Napolitano and Keating's (2007) description of the experiences of poor African American youths in inner-city Philadelphia concluded that they were still more fearful of the police than they were of their potentially violent neighbors.

However, while crime and fear in the main may undermine confidence in the police, that reaction is not the whole story. Another result—some call it a "law-and-order backlash"—is to call for more aggressive policing. As policing scholar David Bayley and others have noted, "Many people believe strongly in being 'tough on crime' and not 'coddling criminals', and they are willing to excuse intrusive and punitive policing when they fear the crime is close at hand" (Bayley, Davis and Davis, 2015, p. 7). Academic research that has probed *support* for the police has included studies of public attitudes regarding their use of force (Johnson and Kuhns, 2009), racial profiling (Silver and Pickett, 2015), and searches (Peffley, Hurwitz and Sniderman, 1997). In a 1971 article, Richard Block addressed the links between fear of crime, support for the police, and feeling individually respected by the police—his measure of trust. Fear did not play a major role but feeling personal respect/ trust predicted supporting the expansion of police stop & frisk powers, as did opposition to the then-current expansion of civil liberties protections for criminal suspects (Block, 1971).

In every era in my experience the looming threat of a law-and-order backlash of significant magnitude has shaped the politics of policing and crime. It provides an upper limit to how far civic leaders are willing to go along a path of criminal justice reform. We have seen crime was rising as the survey was being conducted during 2015. Was there political space for a law-and-order backlash even in this progressive city?

When Chicagoans weighed the balance between being perhaps too-heavily policed and feeling that crime is close at hand, it turns out that a substantial fraction of them came down on the side of maintaining order. Civil libertarians downtown were concerned about unfairness, stressing the risks associated with communities being over-policed. But in the neighborhoods people were also concerned about being under-protected. Here we examine support for proposals to *increase* the discretionary reach of the police using stop & frisk. In Chicago, both fear of crime and trust in the police were involved in generating support for further empowering them to "fight crime."

The survey's measures of support for tougher law enforcement focused on the wisdom of granting the police more power in stop-and-search situations, rather than the possible punitiveness of other parts of the criminal justice system, such as sentencing. Chicagoans were asked what they thought about:

giving police more legal powers so they could effectively control crime;
   giving police the right to stop and question people whenever they need to; and
   giving police the power to do whatever they think is needed to fight crime.

In each instance, respondents were asked to rate these proposals as an excellent, good, fair, poor, or very poor idea. The average correlation between responses to the three options was +.65. A single underlying factor explained 86 percent of their total variance, so their ratings were combined to form a single measure of support for (further) empowering the Chicago police. Extreme support for a law-and-order agenda was far from being a majority opinion. About 30 percent of Chicagoans thought, on average, these proposals were at least a fair idea. However, here we focus on respondents who, averaging across the three questions, thought them to be a good or excellent ideas. They were the most strident supporters of unshackling the police, and they represented about 20 percent of all adults in the city.

It turns out that the dual, if often conflicting, concerns of Chicagoans regarding crime and the police go some distance toward understanding support for tougher stop & frisk policies in the city. The first concern is fear of crime. In the community survey, fear was measured by responses to questions regarding how "worried" respondents were about home burglary, robbery, and assaults in their neighborhood. Worry provides a flexible approach to measuring fear that encompasses a broad range of crime types and speaks to the impact of crime on people's emotional state. The average correlation between these ratings was +.67, so responses were combined to create a single "fear of crime" measure. In interviews, everyone expressed the most worry about residential burglary. Hispanics were particularly worried about burglary; more than 30 percent of those interviewed were either very or extremely concerned about break-ins. After burglary, African Americans were most worried about robbery, while Hispanics were concerned about assault. By contrast, less than 10 percent of Whites were worried about burglary, and many fewer expressed any concern about robbery or assault.

Overall, higher-income and more educated respondents were less fearful, while foreign-born and Spanish-speaking respondents and people living in poor, high-crime, and disorderly neighborhoods reported worrying more about crime.

The other concern of Chicagoans that underlay support for stop & frisk was trust in the police. We have seen that asking about trust brings the intentions and capabilities of police to the table, and many Chicagoans are dubious about them. Trust in police and fear of crime are described here as "conflicting" because in general they do not go together. In the survey they are negatively correlated –.21, and separately run counter to one another among White, African American, and Hispanic respondents. However, they do go together in the sense that support for tough crime policies turns out to require both *motivating* (why do this?) and *enabling* (why this course of action?) factors, and these are provided by fear of crime and trust in the Chicago police.

The dual effects of fear (a motivating factor) and trust in police (an enabling factor) can be seen in Figure 4-8. Chicagoans who voiced support for tougher stop & frisk policies measured high on fear *plus* they scored high on trust. Very few—nine percent—of respondents who felt safe and distrusted police supported further empowering them. High fear but low trust boosted this total to 17 percent, while low fear plus high trust raised it to 26 percent of Chicagoans. But the count among respondents reporting high levels of worry

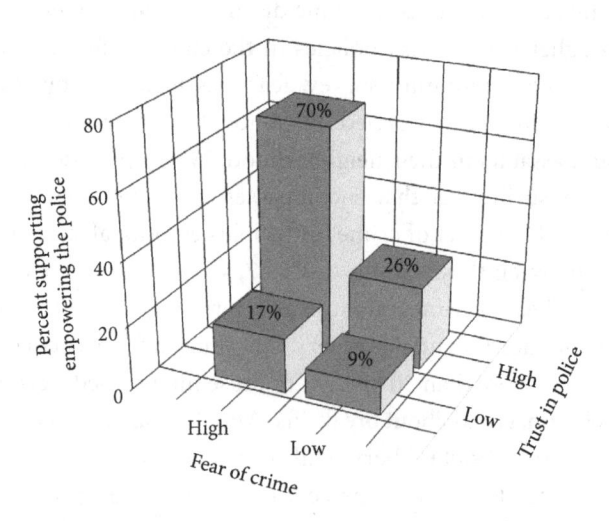

Figure 4-8 Trust, Fear, and Support for Tougher Stop & Frisk

about crime *and* who put their trust in police towered above the others—70 percent called for tougher stop & frisk.

Importantly, this was a very general finding. It was true separately for White, African American, and Latino respondents. Also, for all groups, trust in police was somewhat more important than fear in driving support for stop & frisk, as suggested in Figure 4-8. Respondents who supported tougher stop & frisk were also the most likely to think Chicago police were doing a good job in controlling crime, they believed police were providing good quality service to all residents of the city, they felt obligated to obey police commands, and they felt they and the police shared the same values regarding right and wrong. In all groups, supporters of stop & frisk were distinctively older and less educated. This familiar combination of pro-police demographics and beliefs is frequently taken as defining a law-and-order coalition. However, while support for tougher stop & frisk was definitely a form of "law-and-order backlash," it was hardly "White backlash." In Chicago, Whites were trusting but did not have a crime problem. African Americans were fearful of crime but did not trust the police, and they did not support further empowering them. It was the city's Hispanic residents who most often filled the fairly fearful *and* relatively trusting categories that provided the most support for stop & frisk.

5

Police Versus the Community?

The opinions police hold regarding the public is the other half of their two-sided relationship. Officers' views are important because the nature and organization of their work make the public heavily reliant on their motivations. They work far from the watchful eye of even of their most immediate supervisors. They are out in the field, often at night, heavily armed, and usually accompanied only by their longtime partners. Most of what we know about their activities comes from forms they choose to fill out and reports they occasionally make by radio (often using just a cryptic number) to a dispatcher. At the same time, the exercise of their sometimes life-taking powers is highly discretionary. The decision to initiate a stop & frisk, make a traffic stop, issue a ticket or make an arrest rather than issuing a stern warning, or to use force to accomplish any of these things, is in their hands. We expect them to use good judgment as well as "the letter of the law" to accomplish the goals we have for them (cf., Skogan and Meares, 2004).

Here we examine police views of the community, including how much they think the public likes *them*. Chicago police did not see much hope in this regard. There is a description of what officers think of the politicians and reporters who help hold them accountable for their performance, and a discussion of the roots of police isolation from the communities they serve. One source is the racial composition of the area where they work, a factor linked in striking fashion to their views of the people who live there and how they deserve to be treated. Officers who work in high intensity stop & frisk neighborhoods report other distinctive views. They feel the intensity of the workload, they report being isolated from the communities they serve, and they see their work world as a riskier place. The discussion is based on a survey of Chicago police officers conducted during 2013, while stop & frisk was in its prime. It was carried out independently, but with the general endorsement of the department. A total of 619 police officers and 95 sergeants were interviewed at the 22 district stations where they worked. A Data Appendix describes the survey; more details can be found in Skogan (2015).

Stop & Frisk and the Politics of Crime in Chicago. Wesley G. Skogan, Oxford University Press.
© Oxford University Press 2023. DOI: 10.1093/oso/9780197675052.003.0005

Police Views of the Community

One widely recognized feature of police work is the isolation of many officers from the wider community. It is often remarked that police are socially isolated. Early in their career they typically work midnights, and they develop strong bonds of friendship with others on the job. Like many cities, Chicago also has a strong "police family" tradition, and it is common to encounter the children and other relatives of long-serving officers in uniform. More significantly, many see their job as antithetical to developing strong community bonds. "You can't be the friend of the people and do your job," one officer remarked to me. On a day-to-day basis they can have an adversarial relationship with the subset of the public with whom they deal. They fear if they become familiar with people in the areas where they work, those residents will start to request special favors or take advantage of their acquaintance. They expect to be asked to ignore parking violations, and to do neighbors "a favor" if they seem to be alcohol impaired. Officers become cynics, believing everyone lies strategically, and are in it only for themselves. From this point of view, there is little role for other motives or sincerity in one's stated motives.

Many studies have also reported that police perceive members of the community as hostile, and they believe the public does not accord officers the support their dangerous and important job is due. William Westley (1970), the academic explorer who "discovered" police culture, devoted a chapter of his 1970 book on police violence to this point. It was titled "The Public as Enemy." As one Chicago officer noted on a police blog, "My advice is to avoid any interactions with the people or folks of our wonderful Illinois communities as much as possible. And don't spend your RDO's [regular days off] with anyone outside of your immediate family. Everyone else hates us."

In the survey, many Chicago officers expressed pessimism about the community's view of them. In response to a question aimed at gauging their isolation from the community, only 13 percent of officers indicated the public had a decent understanding of "what it really means to be a cop." Figure 5-1 presents their responses on a left-hand scale ranging up to 100 percent. This is to emphasize that, while they varied a bit in their views, only small numbers of officers thought the public understood them. Not shown in the chart is the most negative group, the more than 50 percent of officers who responded that the public understands the police "not at all." On the chart, only three percent thought the public understood them very or extremely

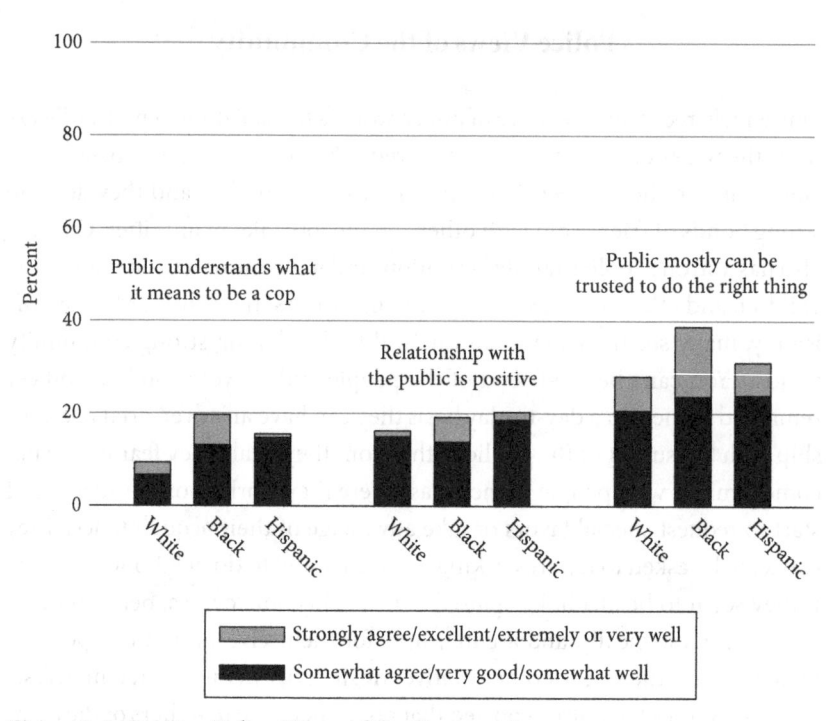

Figure 5-1   Positive Police Views of the Community

well. Another 10 percent thought the public had "somewhat" of an understanding of their work, and they are also included in Figure 5-1.

Officers were also asked how they would rate "the relationship between the police and the people of Chicago." Overall, only 18 percent indicated this relationship was either excellent or good; those proportions are also illustrated in Figure 5-1. Another 35 percent thought police–community relations were poor or very poor; the remaining 46 percent put it at "fair."

Officers were somewhat more positive in response to a measure of a concept examined in detail in the previous chapter—trust. From the point of view of the public, trust is evidenced when officers treat citizens as if they will "do the right thing" instead of always assuming the worst about their intentions. The officer survey reversed this, asking officers about their trust in the public. In discussions at the Chicago Police Training Academy, I have watched trainers warn how suspicion, distrust, and even paranoia can come to dominate the views of new police officers. "The rose-colored glasses come off," a trainer observed, meaning officers come to focus on the potentially dark side of every situation. Suspicion can come to dominate their personal lives. In an example that trainers frequently used, risk management shapes where officers choose to sit in restaurants (in the rear, their back to the wall), not just how they interact with citizens on the street. Trainees were enjoined to not let mistrust and suspicion contaminate their family lives. The trainers also noted that distrust generates emotional and physical stresses on the job. In the survey, about 30 percent of officers endorsed the view that the public, "mostly can be trusted to do the right thing." Few strongly agreed with this (the lighter section of the bars); about 20 percent took the more middling position, agreeing "somewhat." On the other hand, probably only a few officers would rate the situation in Chicago as badly as this police blogger:

> I have started bringing my lunch from home. Every place I enter I can see the hate in everyone's faces. I have gotten paranoid about people doing things to my food. I am halfway through with my career and am thinking of getting an entry level position in some other town. This is all I ever wanted to do, and I can't anymore.

Views of Community Institutions

The survey also included questions directed separately at two key community institutions providing public and democratic oversight of the police: the news media and political leaders. Politicians and the media potentially could have been viewed differently by the officers, but they were not. Chicago officers looked down on both in almost equal measure, and cynicism was strongly in fashion. Their cynicism extends past individuals to include institutions, and they are as skeptical of them as they are of residents.

As Figure 5-2 illustrates, officers voiced disdain for politicians. Politicians are commonly viewed as pandering to public opinion rather than remaining resolutely in the corner of officers. Figure 5-2 is organized so that higher bars indicate more *dissatisfaction* on every measure. When asked if "police officers could do a better job if politicians weren't always getting in the way," 75 percent of those interviewed agreed, most strongly so.

Journalists fared no better. In the police blogging world, a leading local newspaper—the *Chicago Sun Times*—is known as the "Slum Times." The *Chicago Tribune* is tagged the "Fibune," and the police union has an official policy of not responding to their requests for interviews. When asked to rate

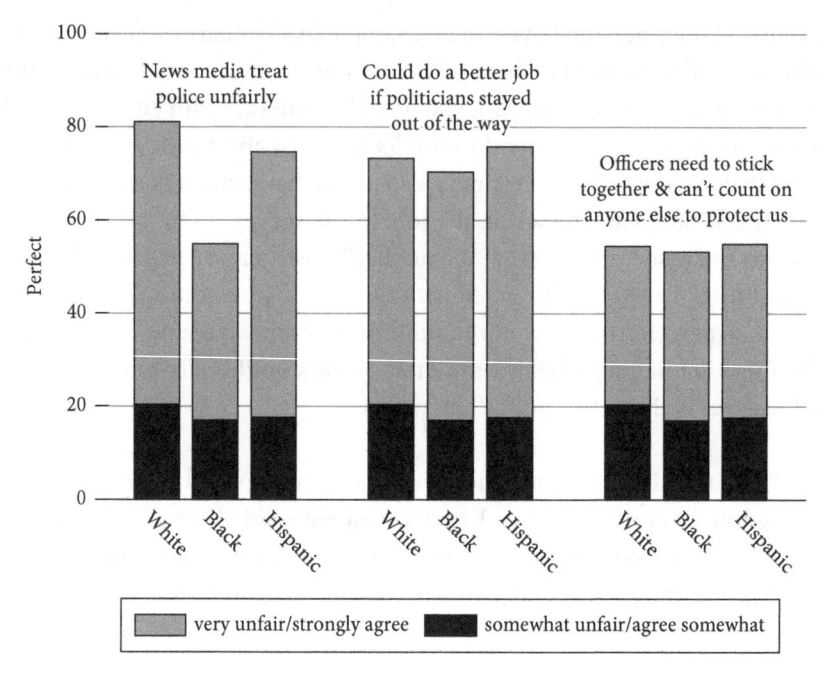

Figure 5-2 Negative Police Views of Accountability

"How fairly or unfairly do you think the news media treat the CPD?" about 70 percent rated the media as somewhat or very unfair.

To whom can they turn for support? Chicago officers feel misunderstood by the public, with whom they believe they have a largely negative relationship, and they do not get supportive coverage in the media or from craven politicians. Standing alone, without understanding or support, and without reasonable oversight, they look to themselves for validation. As one police blogger lamented, "Blue shirts only have each other." Solidarity, which is evidenced by strong bonds of mutual support among police officers, is a commonly encountered aspect of police culture. Officers tend to look out for one another and believe that they must be prepared to follow each other without hesitation into grave danger. Solidarity is described as having many benefits for the police. "Strong bonds between officers offer reassurance that the other officers will 'pull their weight' in police work; they will defend, back up and assist their colleagues when confronted by external threats; and they will maintain secrecy in the face of internal and external investigations (Goldsmith, 1990, pp. 93–94). Solidarity also helps ensure officers will not "snitch" on their fellow officers internally, and they will stand shoulder-to-shoulder against the external world. The "code of silence" which insulates police from outside forces also serves to keep bad news from traveling upward in the organization and protects officers from the wrath of their superiors.

As Figure 5-2 suggests, Chicago is a fairly high-solidarity, we-versus-they department. More than one-half of those interviewed agreed, "Officers need to stick together because we can't count on anyone else to protect us if we get in trouble." Thirty percent of them indicated they strongly agreed with this view. This and the other charts in this section also illustrate the point that—in addition to their general negativity—there was not much variance within the ranks in officers' views of the community and its institutions. Across these and many similar measures the Chicago police were exceedingly *uniform* (so to speak) in their views. The charts presented here illustrate the very small role played by race in creating divisions within the ranks. Officers' views were generally negative, and they were mostly "blue" in color. More generally, officers' views were overwhelmingly unrelated to many other conventional demographic measures that are often used to describe "who thinks what?" For example, their responses were unrelated to education. Chicago has a well-educated police department. Due in part to its generous tuition support for officers returning to school during their off hours, fully 63 percent of the officers surveyed reported having a college degree, and 16 percent a graduate degree. (Nationwide, almost 50 percent of police officers have a college diploma, including 16 percent with an advanced degree.) In Chicago, a four-year degree is required to be promoted to sergeant. Many degrees are earned via online programs, which are vastly easier to integrate into officers' work schedules. However, the views of college graduates generally were the same as those of their less formally educated counterparts. Likewise, police opinions were unrelated to any military service, or working in special district tactical units.

This uniformity extended even to gender, a social cleavage historically dividing policing. Women have made up about one-quarter of the CPD employees for decades, and they contributed 25 percent of our district officer interviews. In the 1970s, the entry of growing numbers of women into the ranks was a source of widespread discussion and some discord. In those days women did not patrol the streets. They were assigned as matrons in the lockup or to the Youth Division, where they babysat for crime victims, searched female suspects, and assisted with juvenile offenders (Martin, 1982). In Chicago, their regulation uniform included a tight pencil skirt. By

2008, however, Chicago was ranked near the top of the nation in the percentage of sworn females, tied for third place with Washington, DC, and just a percentage point or two below the top-ranked city, Detroit (Langdon, 2010). The views female officers reported in the officer survey were usually indistinguishable from those of their male counterparts.

As Figures 5-1 and 5-2 indicated, there was only a small association between race and officers' views of the public. In 2013, 24 percent of CPD employees were African Americans, and they made up 21 percent of district respondents. African American officers were slightly more likely than others to report that the public can be trusted, and they were a bit more likely—but still not very likely—to think they were getting a fair shake from the media. In fact, in a detailed multivariate analysis, only age stood out as a watershed factor. Across many of their views of the community, younger officers felt more isolated and cynical than their peers. They also they felt the pull of solidarity with their fellow officers most strongly. Looking at the data, the turning point seems to come as they approach the age of 40. It is likely that by then factors other than "the job" begin to shape their lives. These include getting married; having families; settling in among neighbors; worrying about their children; and becoming involved in school, church, and community affairs. These kinds of maturational experiences have powerful effects on most people and could serve to reshape the views of officers as well.

However, the general uniformity among officers' views—a largely negative one—suggests powerful social, political, and organizational forces structure the policing profession. These include their internal police culture and the external law-and-order political environment characterizing many cities. These factors are seen by many close observers as transcending the personal identities of officers. The race and gender composition of the force might be peripheral to many of the policing issues concerning the public. Research on what police *do* often finds it reflects these same, homogenizing forces. Police encounters with the public and their varied outcomes often show few differences associated with the race of officers (for example, see Terrill, et al., 2018, a rare eight-agency study). A study of 383 Chicago officers involved in shooting civilians found their racial profile very closely matched their numbers in the force; for example, 53 percent of all officers were White, while 51 percent of shooters were White (Sekhon, 2017). Complaints levied against officers often show the same uniformity. Instead, how police behave on the street is extremely situational. It is strongly (perhaps mostly) driven by how the civilians involved initially respond to an encounter. Terrill, et al.

(2018) report subjects of stops who are young, male, and drunk seem to attract a distinctive amount of trouble. Encounters can be also shaped by the crime context of the neighborhood in which they occur, although estimates of neighborhood effects vary (for a review see Shjarback, 2018).

Many advocates of police reform focus on hiring and the composition of the force, but it is not clear that this is among the most significant lever for improving their actual relationship with the public. Instead, when recommending how to improve the quality of policing, many police researchers would focus first on leadership, the quality of officer training, agency commitment to procedural justice, efforts by supervisors in the field, clear and vigorously pursued use of force policies, body cameras, and even access to non-lethal weapons. Most of the things on this list could be more important than officer race and gender. The external *legitimacy* impact of the visual composition of the force might be a different matter. Some public relations wins could be associated with a more racially representative policing corps, and it could broaden access by under-represented residents to what is a good public sector job. But in the end, the evidence shows that the measured quality of street policing does not seem to be much affected by either the race or gender of officers (cf., Skogan, 2018).

Which Communities Do They Serve?

The complexity of focusing on officer race is further illustrated by examining the effects of the *context* within which they work. Research has documented the many ways in which police work is contextual. Importantly, context frames the *risks* they face during their shift. Analyses of violence against police officers find that it clusters in areas sharing concentrated disadvantage, family disruption, a youthful population, residential instability, commercial settings, dilapidated buildings, active drug markets, public drinking, and many 911 calls (cf., Gibbs, et al., 2018; Caplan, et al., 2014). Tough neighborhoods provide frequent opportunities for acrimony. More officers patrol there, and they typically make more stops. When officers typify neighborhoods as troublesome, they are more likely to stereotype residents as uncooperative, hostile, and crime prone, and therefore approach residents with suspicion, behave more aggressively, and act more punitively (Smith, 1986). Studies indicate police verbal and physical abuse, unjustified street stops, and corruption are more prevalent in disadvantaged and high-crime areas. However, in socially disorganized neighborhoods, residents can lack the capacity to mobilize against police mistreatment, whereas residents of more affluent communities often have connections to local elites who can be mobilized to hold officers accountable, if they need to (Weitzer, Tuch and Skogan, 2008). Steve Herbert (1998) described how Los Angeles officers distinguish between "pro-police" and "anti-police" areas of the city, a division based on residents' support for them and their likelihood of posing a threat to working officers. Given their general views, officers are unlikely to see this support everywhere. Finally, race can make a difference. A study of policing in a few matched neighborhoods found officers reported better relationships with residents of the White community in the study (Stein and Griffith, 2017). Along these lines, Weitzer, Tuch and Skogan (2008) report community groups are more likely to be supportive of the police in predominately White areas.

In July 2016, when things were tough following the release of a damning video documenting police use of fatal force (see Chapter 6), a blogging Chicago officer described the mobilization of one Chicago community, Garfield Ridge, in their support:

> With blue ribbons on trees and blue light bulbs, porch after porch in Garfield Ridge illuminated in the color of law enforcement, a way for residents to say to police, "We're leaving the light on for you." "It sends a message home. It's such a quick indicator, a very simple action, but there's a lot of meaning behind it. And we certainly hope it catches on," says Al T_ of Garfield Ridge. He is among many in the community bathing their porches in blue. The campaign was organized by residents of this southwest side neighborhood where many cops live. At a community meeting Monday night there were prayers for the safety of officers. "We just want to show them that, hey, you know what, in all the troubled times that are going on in the country and in Chicago, that, hey, we've got your back. We support you," says resident Al C__.

Garfield Ridge presents an illustrative case of one of the key elements of procedural justice theory: "moral alignment." Also referred to as "value alignment," or "shared values," studies of the public's views of police find those who feel aligned with the police—that is, who feel they and the police share core values—see themselves and the police as being on the same team. An important reason people trust them is that they feel the police represent the things they believe in, ethically and normatively, and that—as best they can—police are reflecting the community's moral values (Hough, et al., 2013). Moral alignment strengthens the instrumental and emotional connections between the public. And, when both sides share it, value alignment can form a basis for solidarity, mutual respect, and cooperation between police and the public (Jackson, et al., 2012b). As in Garfield Ridge, studies of the public find citizens who feel aligned with the police—who feel they and the police share core values—accept their leadership and cooperate with them more readily. Police will "have their back," as resident Al C__ noted.

From their side, police believe that when "the good people" of the community share their values, officers may be able to rely on them for support. Such value agreement would generally mean the public is seen as respecting order and stability, and supportive of the police in maintaining those conditions. It provides them some moral authority and is a source of deference to the police. Moral alignment turned out to play a central role in officers' views. It was strongly related to measures of some of the most fundamental aspects of policing, including several aspects of police culture. Officer support for many of the policies and practices that have been on the police reform agenda was also strongly linked to their perceived value alignment with the public. The survey also revealed that the extent of this alignment depended on the racial composition of the neighborhood to which they were assigned.

The extent of value congruence between officers and the communities where they work was measured by combining responses to three statements: "Generally speaking, most people are on the side of the law when it comes to what is right and wrong," "The public and the police generally have the same sense of right and wrong," and "As a police officer I feel I represent the values of the public in the areas where I work." Officers were asked to indicate the extent to which they agreed or disagreed with each. Responses to the three questions were correlated +.40. Overall, about two-thirds of the officers agreed (either somewhat or strongly) that most people are on the side of the law. Fewer strongly believed that the public and the police shared the same sense of right and wrong; on the other hand, almost 30 percent disagreed with this view. Again, older officers stood out as thinking they had supporters in the community.

Moral alignment turned out to be a strong predictor of officers' views of the community. Among all officers, the correlation between scales measuring trust in citizens and value alignment was +.58, which is strong for survey data. That correlation ranged only between +.55 and +.65 when calculated separately for White, African American, and Latino officers—the link was strong among all three groups. Officers also did not differ much in terms of value alignment by race. White officers were a little less likely to see themselves sharing values with the community, while African American officers were a little more likely to see a value congruence between them and the neighborhoods they served. However, it turned out solidarity with the community really varied not by race, but by the type of neighborhood they were working in. This could be examined because the survey captured the police beat or the sector of the district in which each respondent spent most of their duty time. Their workplace could be matched to other data, including local crime and a demographic description of residents of the area.

To summarize the findings, officers of all races were more likely to see themselves as aligned with the White community, and, for Latino officers, the Hispanic community as well. Officers of all races assigned to disproportionately African American beats were less likely to view themselves as sharing the values of those they policed.

Figure 5-3 illustrates how this works. It presents the statistical relationship between beat racial composition (ranging from zero to virtually 100 percent) and officers' perceived alignment with the community, by race of officer. For example, the topmost regression lines describe the relationship between the

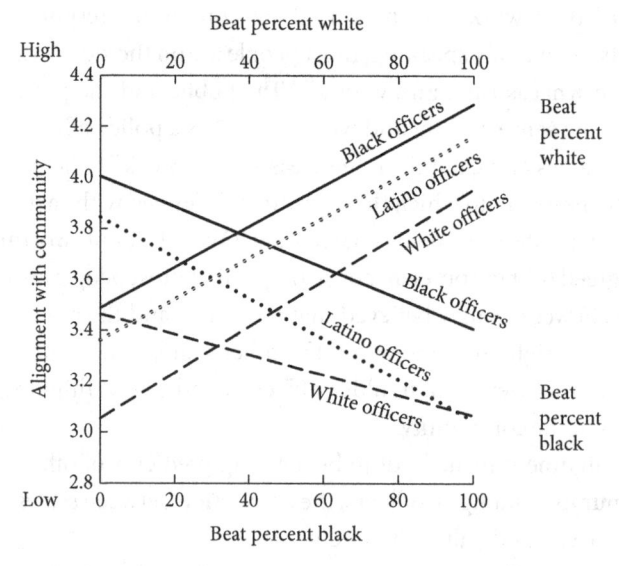

Figure 5-3 Officer Race, Beat Race, and Value Alignment

percentage of the population in each officers' assigned beat who are White and their sense of value alignment. These were calculated separately by officer race. (The hundreds of data points they are based on are not displayed here.) Value alignment rises (and this is statistically significant) with a concentration of White residents, and it does so for African Americans, White, and Hispanic officers. By contrast, the bottom-most lines in Figure 5-3 illustrate the (significant) statistical link between the concentration of African American residents and officers' perceived value alignment with the community. The two groups of lines march in decidedly different directions (and because there are many predominately Hispanic beats, they are not a mechanical reflection of each other). Officers of all backgrounds did not see themselves in league with the community where the community is largely African American. Among Latino officers, if the line linking their views and the percentage of their beats that were Hispanic were depicted in Figure 5-3, it would slope sharply upward and closely resemble others in the uppermost group. White and Black officers were not strongly affected by the Hispanic composition of their workplace. Serving African American communities was another matter.

What About Procedural Justice?

As we saw in the last chapter, procedural justice is a theory about the relationship between the public and the state, here represented by the Chicago police. Most procedural justice research has focused on the consumer end of the relationship, but some has involved the police.

Procedural justice is viewed favorably in policing circles, including by the chiefs and mayors I have introduced to the perspective. "Common sense in handling people" is how many of them interpret it, and "something good cops have always done." The field of procedural justice is one in which the translation of research into actual policy has been quite direct (Skogan, 2018). However, as David Bayley noted, mindfulness is not always a priority among officers on the street. "Many police officers believe respect comes from a display of authority. They believe that they are the best judges of people who are deserving of soft or hard treatment, and they resent having their decisions challenged" (Bayley, Davis and Davis, 2015, p. 7). As is too often the case, slippage can appear between well-sounding policies made at the top of police departments and their reception by the rank-and-file.

The stationhouse survey offered officers a chance to react to statements regarding the core elements of procedural justice, to judge their level of support for the idea. By 2013, when the survey was conducted, the department was already far along in training all employees in its concepts. Following the distinction between quality of treatment and quality of police decision-making introduced in the last chapter, officers were asked several questions about each subdimension of those two aspects of procedural justice. For example, *respect* was measured by responses to statements like, "People should be treated with respect regardless of their respect for the police." Just over one-half of Chicago officers supported this view. The principle of *neutrality* encourages officers to explain the basis of their actions and decisions to citizens they encounter. This might include describing why they were stopped or questioned, or why they received a ticket rather than perhaps "deserving" a warning. In the survey there was widespread support for the view "It is necessary to give everyone a good reason why they are being stopped, even if it is not required." About 72 percent of the officers surveyed agreed strongly or at least somewhat with this view, with one-half of the total agreeing strongly. There was broad but somewhat weaker support for the idea that "If people ask why they are being treated like they are, it is necessary to stop and explain." Support for the principle of *voice* was measured by responses to statements like, "Officers need to show an interest in what people have to say, even if it not going to change anything." Overall, about 70 percent of officers agreed to some extent with this idea. *Trust* was the most difficult idea for offices to support. Trust is evidenced when officers treat citizens as if they can "to do the right thing," instead of always assuming the worst about their intentions. However, just 30 percent of officers agreed with the statement "Citizens mostly can be trusted to do the right thing." Few—overall nine percent of officers—agreed strongly with this idea.

As Figure 5-4 illustrates, minority officers were more likely to endorse these principles, often by 10 to 20 percentage points among African Americans and slightly less by Hispanic officers. Figure 5-4 describes responses to the sample questions from the four dimensions discussed above. More of the variation was in the *extent* of their enthusiasm for each principle, which is reflected in the lighter-colored bars recording those who agreed "very much." Officers of all stripes expressed the most enthusiasm for the principles of neutrality (giving reasons) and voice (showing interest in what people have to say). In the procedural justice training sessions I attended, the trainers frequently reminded officers of the safety benefits of adopting their recommended

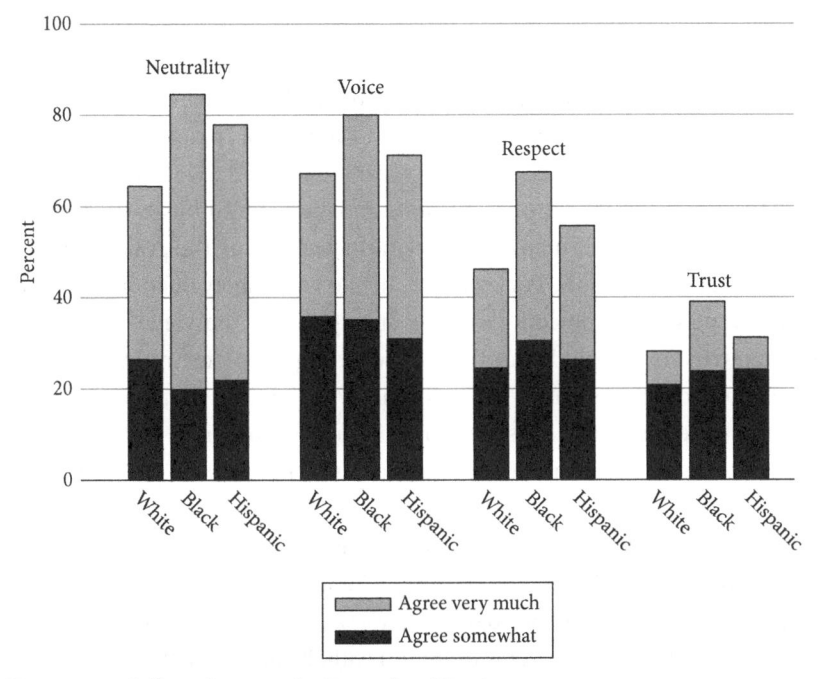

Figure 5-4 Officer Support for Procedural Justice

approaches to dealing with the public. Both listening to people's stories and patiently explaining the situation to them were identified as practical things officers could do to get through their day more safely. In procedural justice theory neutrality and voice are both aspects of fairness in decision making, so support for them could be important. For example, fairness in decision-making facilitates the public's acceptance of unfavorable outcomes, like receiving a speeding ticket, because it was awarded in a fair manner.

When it came to quality of treatment, while officers were less likely to be supportive of displaying respect for the citizens they encounter. Less than one-half endorsed this principle. This is not surprising. The concept of respect has had to swim upstream against a countercurrent in police thinking, which is that respect needs to be visibly *earned* (Pickett and Nix, 2019). One way to do this is to be deferential to officers and obey all their commands promptly. It is possible among officers to hear dark discussions of the need for some "attitude adjustment" among those who do not toe the line. Troublingly, observational studies of field encounters reveal police are more likely to be actively disrespected by suspects during encounters in poor neighborhoods, possibly sparking escalating trouble (McCluskey, Mastrofski and Parks, 1999). There is ample evidence that where police view residents as troublemakers, they are more likely to act defensively and aggressively, not a good combination (Weitzer, Tuch and Skogan, 2008). Finally, support for trust was distinctively tepid. Among the 30 percent of officers who endorsed the idea, most fell in the "agree somewhat" response category, and few were enthusiastic. This is in line with the results of many surveys conducted among the police: granting trust is hard to swallow. For example, in the training evaluation described next, 57 percent of officers *disagreed* strongly with the view "Police have enough trust in the public for them to work together effectively." This is, of course, a bedrock assumption of community policing. A trainer interviewed during procedural justice sessions in Chicago reported trust was also a difficult topic for his fellow trainers to address. As he put it:

> We've been taught to trust nobody, to show less emotion.... We come to see everything as bullshit—going to another domestic, going to a beat meeting, going to training. We come to see people as assholes. But in reality, there's a big population we never come in contact with. It's the rest of the world.

Our evaluation of this training program found it had the smallest and least-enduring impact on trust, in contrast to three other dimensions of procedural justice (Skogan, Van Craen and Hennessy, 2015).

Officer support for procedural justice also proved to be linked to neighborhood context. As in Figure 5-3, Figure 5-5 links officers' views to the racial composition of the area to which they were assigned. The procedural justice measure on the left combined responses to the four questions described above, which were correlated an average of +.35. Again, officers of all backgrounds serving in predominately White areas were more likely to endorse procedural justice as a workable tactic. On the other hand, officers working in predominately African American beats were less likely to be supportive. For example, among White officers working in predominately (above 80 percent) White beats, 60 percent thought "citizens mostly can be trusted." In predominately African American beats (again, above 80 percent) that number dropped to 11 percent. Among Black officers working in predominately African American beats trust stood at 35 percent; in largely White areas that number rose to over 90 percent. Like feeling in synch with neighborhood residents, support for the principles of stop & frisk was highly depended on who "the community" was.[1]

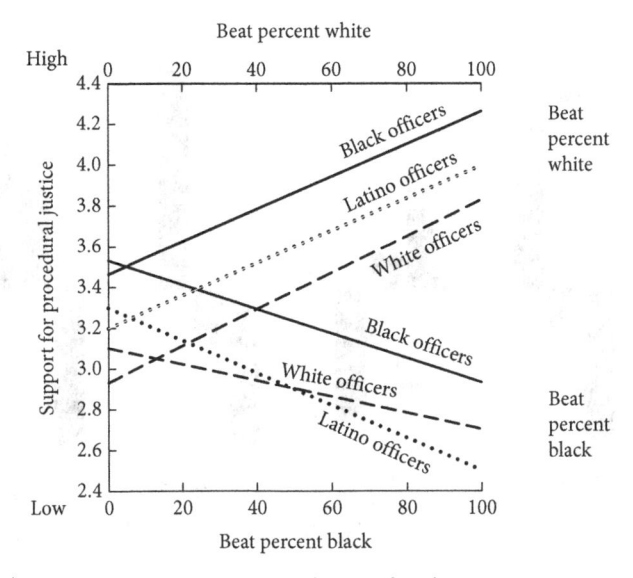

Figure 5-5 Officer Race, Beat Race, and Procedural Justice

The Cops Who Make Stops

A final question is, what do we know of officers who do the work of stop & frisk? Most stops are conducted by just a fraction of the force. Allocating stops during the period of the officer survey to the city's 269 police beats revealed 80 percent of stops were conducted in only 25 percent of beats. By contrast, only nine percent of stop & frisks were conducted in the sleepiest 25 percent of beats. Because of the wide discretion they enjoyed in choosing whom to target and how to treat residents they approached, it is the experiences and views of officers serving in the high intensity beats that are particularly relevant to Chicago's stop & frisks. They and their work environment shape both the experiences of the subjects of most stops and the relationship between police and the local community.

Figure 5-6 summarizes reports by officers working in low (the quiet 25 percent of beats), middling (the middle 50 percent of beats), and high intensity areas, measured by stop & frisk rates per 10,000 residents. In the stationhouse survey, 159 responding officers worked in the highest-activity areas, 390 in the broad middle, and 70 in the lowest-stop beats. Figure 5-6 first examines their perceptions of the risks of "the job." As noted earlier, violence against police officers—like serious violence against everyone else—is

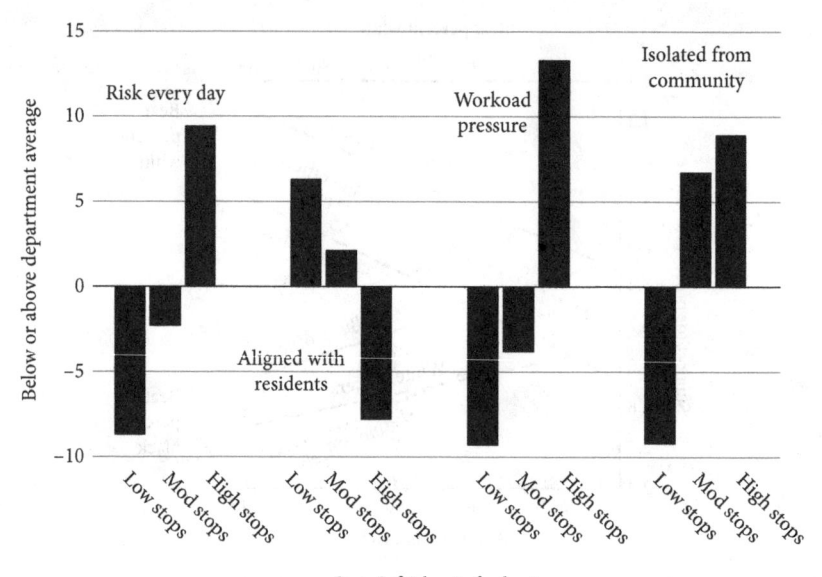

Figure 5-6 Beat Stop Rates and Officer Attitudes

heavily concentrated, and the large number of stops this attracts creates in turn more opportunities for things to go badly. Risk to themselves is perhaps the most important dimension on which officers typify the places where they are assigned. To measure this, officers were asked to rate how concerned they were about "getting home safely at the end of the day," and how concerned their family and friends were for their safety "due to the risks of working in this area." Looking at officers who averaged either very or extremely concerned illustrates the very large contextual effect of working in high-intensity beats. Compared to the department as a whole (the "zero" line in the chart, after subtracting the department average), officers working in high-stop areas were almost 10 percentage points more likely to rate their risk as substantial. By contrast, working in Chicago's lowest-stop areas, looked a lot safer to the officers assigned there.

Another practical consequence of working in high-intensity beats was the workload. This was measured by questions regarding the extent of "pressure to make arrests," "keeping up" their "count of citations and contact cards," and "keeping constantly on the run to deal with calls pending and other demands." At the time of the survey (it was conducted during 2013), tremendous pressure was being exerted at CompStat (see Chapter 3) to keep "the numbers" flowing in these areas. The survey illustrates that line officers were feeling the heat in high intensity neighborhoods. At the same time, officers in busy areas felt themselves more isolated from the communities they served. We saw the extent of the social and political isolation reported by Chicago officers earlier, in Figure 5-1 and Figure 5-2. Their ratings of "the relationship between police and the people of Chicago," and how well the public understands "what it really means to be a cop," were generally pessimistic. We see here it was only in the sleepiest areas that officers were relatively more optimistic than most about their relationship with the community. This extent of this isolation can also be seen in the distribution of the measure of value alignment between officer and neighbors described in Figure 5-3. Officers' beliefs that they shared a sense of right and wrong with the community, and that most people on their beat "are on the side of the law," took a turn for the worse in high stop beats.

Police Views of the Public

The stationhouse survey found most Chicago officers felt misunderstood and they were pessimistic regarding what the community thought of them. Overall, Chicago officers judged police–community relations to be bad. They looked down on both politicians and the media, who were another of their problems, and felt blue shirts only had each other. More than one-half agreed they could not count on anyone else to protect them.

A closer examination revealed the importance of *where they worked* in shaping officers' views of the community and their job. The racial composition of the area was one of those dimensions. White, Hispanic, and African American officers alike were likely to see their views of right and wrong aligned with residents largely White neighborhoods. They were all "blue" in their response to neighborhood conditions. Hispanic officers also saw themselves in sync with residents of predominately Latino beats. White and African American officers were neutral in this regard. Importantly, community context also affected whether officers felt acting in accordance with the principles of procedural justice could work. Again, this seemed a standard for policing that was more relevant in predominately White neighborhoods. Finally, these and other reports of officers' views and experiences diverged significantly among those assigned to high-intensity stop & frisk beats. They felt overworked and more at risk, two of the banes of police work. They also perceived themselves as most estranged from the community and the least likely to have anything in common with residents. The wedge between police and the community in Chicago was largest in the places where these potentially abrasive encounters between them were concentrated.

6

The Collapse of Stop & Frisk

By 2013, stop & frisk had become Chicago's primary violence prevention strategy. From the top down, the organization stressed making stops and conducting searches. The weekly CompStat management sessions at which the chief grilled his unit commanders became shouting sessions as he turned up the pressure, challenging them to lay hands on people and produce ever greater levels of activity. The peak years for stops were 2014 and 2015. Gun violence spiked notably during August 2015 despite police pressure on the street. Aldermen were complaining and calling for new police leadership. There was frustration at police headquarters, which was facing criticism from the media for both the gun violence and the stops.

Then, in a dramatic moment, it was revealed that Chicago police and top leaders at City Hall had been hiding dramatic visual evidence regarding the killing of a young man by one of its officers in October 2014. The department itself, including middle managers and executives, engineered a cover-up of the incident. The top brass assembled to view a dashboard video of the shooting, and no one objected. In the political scandal following the video's release in November 2015, senior officials were fired or driven from office, agencies were folded and replaced with new ones, marchers occupied the city's major shopping streets, the FBI began investigating the police department, the involved officer was charged with murder while others were indicted for conspiring in the coverup, and the mayor cried at his podium in the city council chamber. Longer term, he declined to try for reelection and was replaced by an African American reformer.

These events and more that swirled around in the moment had both immediate and long-term consequences. Among them was the collapse of stop & frisk as the city's principal strategy for deterring crime. Between the end of 2015 and February 2016 stops dropped by more than 80 percent. Importantly, they *stayed* down. This chapter describes the collapse of stop & frisk, but this is only the beginning of the detective work required to understand its significance. How did it come about? What does it reveal regarding the forces shaping policing policy in the city? What were its consequences?

Stop & Frisk and the Politics of Crime in Chicago. Wesley G. Skogan, Oxford University Press.
© Oxford University Press 2023. DOI: 10.1093/oso/9780197675052.003.0006

In largest scope, this chapter describes the *policy community* surrounding policing in Chicago, and how it reacted to crisis. This policy community shapes policing, including by deciding what department budgets are going to be, who will lead them, the terms of their politically sensitive policies, and what tools of their trade officers will carry. Many interested actors are involved in policing policy. The CPD's political environment is populated by politicians and their donors, leaders of local criminal justice agencies, reporters and their editors, community organizations, business owners' associations, consulting firms, foundations and think tanks, government reform activists, federal funders, civil libertarians, academics, pension-cost watchdogs, sworn and civilian police unions, and vendors hawking their wares (e.g., body camera distributors). Some were already actively engaged in reshaping the city's stop & frisk regime, and the crisis of late 2015 brought others out of the woodwork. This chapter reviews the forces swirling around the police department during this period and their impact on stop & frisk, while the next chapter addresses the role the collapse of stop & frisk may have played in the ensuing Great Crime Spike of 2016.

Stop & Frisk Falls of a Cliff

As we saw in Chapter 3, the period of 2014–2015 represented peak stop & frisk in Chicago. The stop rate was about three times as high as New York City's maximum, taking the size of the two cities into account. During 2015, Chicago police recorded more than 529,000 stops, registering 40,000 to 49,000 stops per month from March to October. Then came the crisis, and the collapse.

Figure 6-1 charts the course of its decline. The data presented there are comparable over time. In October 2015 there were 47,000 comparable stops. Stops dropped to 25,000 in December, and to just 5,500 in February of the following year. They began to stabilize by March 2016 at a about 10,000 per month.

The right-hand panel of Figure 6-1 describes this sharp decline separately for Whites African American, and Hispanic subjects of stops. Everyone felt the collapse in similar degree. In the immediate period, stops of Whites dropped by 78 percent; for African Americans they were down by 76 percent, and among Hispanics stops were down by 72 percent. As Figure 6-1

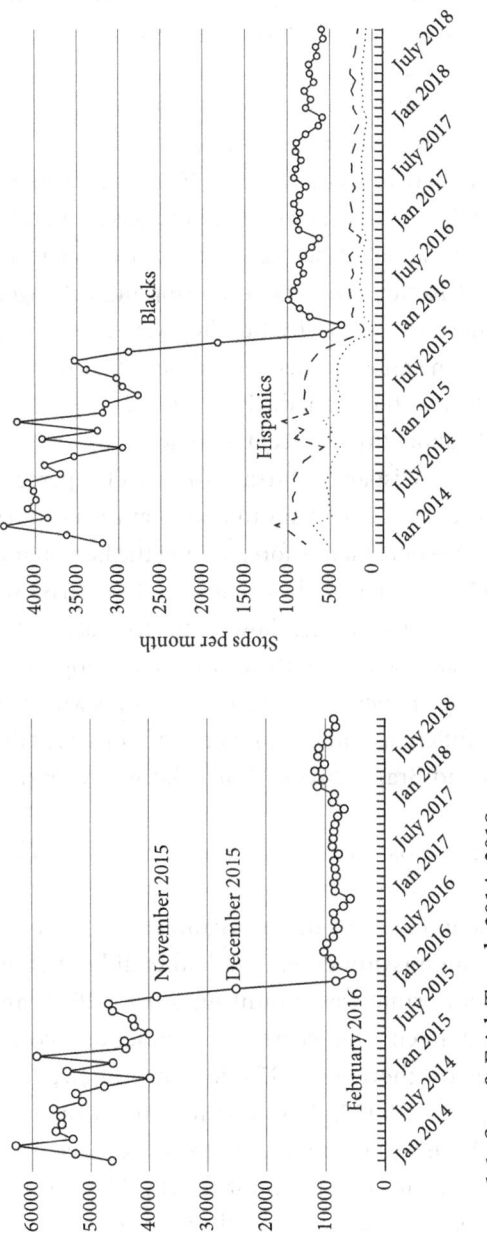

Figure 6-1 Stop & Frisk Trends 2014–2018

documents, the resulting new normal was distributed in about the same way as it was under the old stop & frisk regime, but it involved significantly fewer people. While there were 529,000 unwarranted stops of adults during 2015, there were just 97,000 in 2016.

Geographically, the collapse of stop & frisk occurred virtually across the board. Of the city's 788 census tracts, stops declined in 787 of them. Tract-level stops were down between 80 and almost 100 percent almost everywhere. However, following the collapse, any remaining stops were still concentrated in roughly the same locations as before. Across census tracts the correlation between 2015 and 2016 stop rates was +.85. Stop rates changed the least in predominately White areas of the city, but they were already quite low there, and in several White neighborhoods stops dropped to zero. The upshot of these changes was to shift the racial distribution of stops slightly. In contrast to 2015, during 2016 about three percent more were African Americans, and four percent more were Hispanic. During 2016, just 0.1 percent of stops involved White subjects. It is important to note that each of these categories included *many* fewer people than before, muting the human impact of these shifts. However, in New York City the collapse of stop & frisk was associated with a very different pattern. There, following the federal court ruling greatly restraining the practice, the race of the census tracts stops occurred in was no longer was a strong predictor of the race of persons who continued to be stopped, and racial differences in the outcomes of stops went down substantially (MacDonald and Braga, 2019). Things did not work out that way in Chicago.

Finally, one of the most interesting and perhaps significant features of the 2015–2016 collapse of stop & frisk is that stops *stayed down*. It was not the momentary result of an organizational or political shock; there was no ensuing mission creep; old habits did not take hold again. Even though violent crime was mounting during 2016, and remained uncomfortably high in ensuing years, the number of recorded stops did not rebound. In 2016, there were 97,000 stops, in 2017 it was 99,000, and 2018 there were 118,000. This was not much of a change, when contrasted with the 629,000 innocent stops recorded in 2014. Many explanations were advanced to account for the 2016 drop in stops and its consequences—some analytic and others politically expedient—and these claims will be examined. Explaining what *kept* stops low needs to be part of the story.

Were There Dark Stops?

A possible reason for the dramatically lower number of stops in 2016 and later is that officers may have resorted more frequently to initiating what are known locally as "dark stops." These can be difficult to document. One attorney representing individuals in a federal class-action suit claimed the number of dark stops could have been "substantial," as several of his clients reported they had not seen the officers who stopped them filling out any forms. Attorneys for a few individuals alleged they were *not* stopped, yet records in the Illinois Secretary of State's office indicated their client's names had been checked against the wanted persons database (Hoerner, 2016). I doubt there were many dark stops prior to 2016. Then there was unremitting pressure from district management to produce reports of activity, in response to demands emanating from headquarters for more "numbers." At the same time, there was little incentive for officers to hew closely to the legal requirements for stops because no one was really monitoring what they wrote in the box on their contact cards as the reason for the stop or what happened.

After, the incentive for recording innocent stops that did not produce an arrest or a citation may have changed. In interviews I watched for hints that dark stops were occurring. Dark stops might be found in up-ticks in citizens' complaints about being needlessly singled out or treated unfairly. However, between 2015 and 2018, complaints by the public alleging excessive force or unlawful searches trended steadily downward. Complaints concerning searches totaled 724 in 2015, then dropped (along with the number of stops) to 304 during 2016 and only 173 in 2017.[1] There were problems galore with the city's complaint process, but (as we will see) the old head of the agency was fired at the end of 2015 and a larger staff and revamped procedures were in place by mid-2017. There certainly were stories covered by the media describing stops that did not seem to appear in police data systems. However, I did not turn up clues that dark stops had suddenly become a widespread practice. If they were occurring in a large enough volume to compensate for the decline in recorded stops (down by almost 500,000 compared to 2014) the numbers involved would have to be very large, perhaps 40,000 per month! In a leaky organization like the CPD, this would be hard to miss. That said, due to the highly discretionary nature of street stops and the low visibility of decisions to record or not record them, the possibility that dark stops will take place at some scale always remains a concern.

The City Noticed

The attentive public certainly noticed that stop & frisk had been virtually suspended. There was much debate regarding "the end of stop & frisk" as the magnitude of the decline became apparent during 2016. As early as January 13, 2016, a prominent online news outlet headlined, "Police officers are making drastically fewer investigative stops and confiscating fewer guns as murders and shootings have increased so far this year" (Konkol, 2016). The story, attributed to "sources," revealed details regarding a decline in stops, gun arrests, and gun confiscations by the police. This kind of information was typically supplied to reporters only in response to detailed Freedom of Information Act (FOIA) requests. This process can be arduous. Activist groups tell me they must "FOIA everything" to spring loose the data they need, and often it takes follow-up contacts and revisions of the initial request to pry needed information out of the department. This story emerged just three weeks into the new year, so the "sources" leaking these surprisingly timely statistics were clearly one or more disgruntled insiders choosing provocative material to dribble out.

Journalists continued to revisit the stop & frisk story for much of the year. By March the headline was "Chicago Police Stops Down By 90 Percent as Gun Violence Skyrockets." In July a story leader was "Chicago Sets Aside Stop-And-Frisk as Deterrence Strategy, Police Data Show" (Mitchell, 2016). In November, the Chicago Tribune noted "key measures of police activity appear to back up concerns that cops have pulled back on their aggressiveness. While arrests have generally been on the decline in recent years, they have dropped sharply . . ." "Even worse, the records show, street stops over that same period have plunged . . ." (Gorner, 2016).

Stop & Frisk and a Political Cascade

The events swirling around the city during late 2015 constituted what political scientists call a "political cascade." The term "cascade" is metaphorical, evoking a pent-up body of water suddenly bursting forth and sweeping away barriers standing in its way. Cascades build up slowly but break quickly, they are often triggered by unanticipated events, they can grow in apparent strength and brush aside new obstacles as they gain traction, and they may leave a changed policy terrain in their wake.

Chicago's trigger event was the release of video evidence of a "bad" police-involved shooting. The video created a media storm leading policymakers to flail about for palatable descriptions of what happened and craft somber responses. However, the event alone was not enough to explain the collapse of stop & frisk. There had been shootings before, and some damning videos had previously circulated. But in this instance, there was already wide awareness among insiders that there was a problem, and some key players in the policing policy community had already succeeded in laying the groundwork for significant changes in the city's stop & frisk practices. Some of these changes were scheduled to take effect on January 1, 2016, bracketing almost exactly the collapse of stop & frisk. In its turn, the media firestorm wrought further havoc within the city's political class. Two consequential investigations were launched within days of the release of the video. Even more immediate were the marches and protest rallies beginning on the day of the video's release and continuing through the Christmas shopping season and into the next summer. Opinion polling rapidly identified a broad shift downward in public support for the political class, and new awareness among White residents of the depth of the city's policing problems.

The Triggering Event

The event focusing attention on the Chicago police was the public release of a video depicting the fatal shooting of a young man, Laquan McDonald. He was wandering alone in a circle in the middle of a late-night-quiet street, mumbling and waving a knife, but already surrounded by several police officers. They were giving him ample distance while waiting for someone to answer their call and bring them a taser, which was probably a good strategy. Then, a newly arriving officer leapt from of his squad car, and within six seconds emptied his service weapon, shooting Laquan McDonald 16 times at close range.

The shooting itself was not the crucial incident. It took place on October 20, 2014, but the crisis it sparked gestated for more than a year. The event shaking the city was instead an emerging phenomenon in American policing, one known as "the release of the tape." The shooting scene was surrounded by patrol cars, and enough dashboard cameras were working (some had been sabotaged) that the entire sequence of events surrounding the event was on record, clearly and completely. A large component of the eventual scandal was what happened, and what did not happen, during the 13-month quiet period that followed.

Next in the sequence of events during 2014–2015 was an investigation by the Chicago police. A shooting-scene inquiry was conducted by the city's external Independent Police Review Authority (IPRA), and reports were written. But before those inquiries began, officers who had been at the scene gathered for a meeting led by a senior department manager, so that they could coordinate their testimony. They had time to do this because the city's contract with the police union gave them breathing room before they had to answer questions, including time to consult with their union's attorneys. They came up with a scenario placing the shooting within department guidelines. McDonald was menacing the officers surrounding him. He was advancing and brandishing his knife. He was getting back up after he was shot. The police shooter—on the scene, recall, for six seconds—testified he was backpedaling as best he could but feared for his life. The testimony later gathered by department investigators was reassuringly consistent, and it looked like a "good shooting." The IPRA received its copy of the video just four days after the event and did nothing visible with it. A conference room full of top department leaders met to view the tape themselves, reports in hand, and "everyone agreed" (testified a lieutenant later, under oath) the shooting was justified. All the necessary reports were approved without an objection.

There remained the problem of the video. Insiders knew it was a problem. E-mails released later documented that City Hall staff members were coordinating their counter-story. There was an election looming in just four months, and the mayor was facing serious opposition. It is a custom in Chicago to sue the city when police shoot someone under murky circumstances, and the recording would certainly be demanded as evidence. It was rumored the attorney for the McDonald family already had an underground copy. So, the city's attorney went directly to their home. He arranged an enormous hush-money payment to the McDonald family before a lawsuit could be filed, in part to continue to conceal legally admissible direct evidence regarding the killing. In a 2018 interview, the Police Superintendent at the time, Garry McCarthy, described what happened:

> The cover-up happened with (Chicago Corporation Counsel and Mayor Rahm Emanuel's senior legal advisor) Steve Patton. He orchestrated the cover-up. When he saw the video he said, "This is a case of murder." He

lied to the City Council to get the pay-out. In his testimony in April 2015, he made the case to give the family $5 million dollars with the condition of not releasing the video. That happened when the mayor was in the runoff. It was Rahm's way of stealing the election. (Hartman, 2018)

The video remained under wraps for 13 months following the shooting, and the mayor was indeed re-elected. The word was out in informed circles of its existence, but the city continued to fight a pitched battle to prevent its public release. In mid-November 2015 (after the election), a judge ordered the release of the video following a FOIA hearing sought by a local journalist. The city was given a few days to plead with religious leaders and community activists to tone down the demonstrations and marches that were sure to follow, and to prepare its public relations strategy. The video was finally released on November 24, 2015. The result was a media firestorm. The video played repeatedly on local and national television news programs. Individual images filled the newspapers. The horror of the event was on display, and it was difficult to discern on its face why McDonald had been shot. The scandal grew as reporters and activists poured through investigative reports filed by the police, while at the same time watching the video replaying on their screen. As two journalists put it, the account of the incident in reports by officers at the scene was "strikingly at odds with the video evidence" (Gorner and Nickels, 2016). McDonald was not brandishing his knife; he was not waving it wildly; he had not turned toward the officers, he was walking away from the police; the police shooter was edging forward toward him rather than moving back; and McDonald did not live long enough to try to get back up (Zorn, 2018). The county medical examiner's autopsy report did not support the latter claim, either.

Investigations continued of the department's handling of the incident. In a few months three officers who had been at the scene were taken off the street, and in June 2017 (32 months after the incident) they were charged with conspiracy, official misconduct, and obstruction of justice. A broader-ranging investigation by the city's Inspector General identified 16 officers involved in aspects of the coverup. He recommended 11 of them be fired for actions including making false statements and fabricating details of the event. However, in the end, only one person was convicted of anything. All other criminal indictments of participating officers were eventually dismissed. The two senior police leaders the Inspector General recommended be fired chose instead to retire rather than face internal charges, including the Chief of Detectives. Later, when four more officers were being fired by the department, the civilian body which reviews serious allegations of misconduct ruled their testimony was "demonstrable false," as evidenced by their stories' conflict with the video. The police shooter himself was sentenced to almost seven years in prison. He was the first Chicago police officer to be convicted of an on-duty murder in more than 30 years. As for immediate reform, the department hired a new public relations director.

The scandal following the murder of Laquan McDonald reverberated through Chicago government and politics for years. It had all the elements of a classic Chicago story. Payoffs were arranged. False testimony was organized. Insiders knew what was going on but kept it quiet. A culture of silence shrouded the role of the police department. The video was buried until after the next election, so no one would face public accountability. For more than a year, everyone inside spread patently false accounts of what happened and used the city's resources to stonewall outsiders trying to use legal channels to find out what did happen. But this time the incident was both horrible and eventually on full view, in a gripping video.

Cracks Open in the Establishment

There quickly followed a significant collapse of the political establishment. The cascade of events following the McDonald revelations included firings and forced resignations. Within a few months the sitting prosecutor was abandoned by her party and defeated for re-nomination by a reformer, and candidates emerged to run against the incumbent mayor.

Police Chief Fired. In the political scandal that followed it was clear either the police chief or his boss, the mayor of Chicago, would have to go. One week after the release of the video, the mayor fired his Superintendent. In a statement, the mayor pointed to "the undeniable fact that the public trust in the leadership of the department has been shaken and eroded" (Korecki, 2015).

The Superintendent was already in trouble with a significant faction in the City Council. In mid-October the bulk of the Council's Black Caucus demanded he be fired. They were concerned about a retiring high-ranking African American being replaced by a Hispanic. They also felt they were getting insufficient respect from the Superintendent. They charged he was not responding to their phone calls or consulting with them regarding staffing changes in police districts in their wards. On the day the video appeared the

Caucus renewed their demand that he resign. At their press conference one member lamented the Council had been misled regarding the video:

> We were told there was an active investigation. And we were led to believe there was something fuzzy or something questionable that could be interpreted a different way than it was . . . We were misled. We were misled in terms of whether or not this particular tape showed some grey area where it needed to be investigated for all this period of time. (Spielman, 2015)

At that moment the mayor's office announced that he "fully supported" his police Superintendent. He remained firm in his resolve for almost a week. However, the furor erupting in Chicago was being directed in almost equal measure against the police and the mayor, so he eventually took a page out of the standard mayor's crisis playbook. He first asked the Superintendent to resign, and when McCarthy refused to do so, the mayor fired him. In local terms, the chief of police was "thrown under a bus." The former Superintendent remained uncharacteristically low-profile following his dismissal, but—as we will see—he resurfaced later, seeking revenge.

Head of Civilian Review Fired. The head of the city's external review agency, IPRA, Scott Ando, was the next to roll. Eleven days after the release of the video he resigned, and his chief legal counsel and head investigator were both fired. The agency had long been branded as ineffectual by its critics. It was created in 2007 to replace the agency previously charged with investigating complaints involving serious misconduct, use of excessive force, and all police-involved shootings. It had found few of those to be troubling. Between 2007 and mid-2015, IPRA investigated more than 400 fatal and non-fatal police-involved shootings but found only two allegations against police officers to be credible. In June 2015 the headline of a report on IPRA read, "Chicago tops in fatal police shootings among big U.S. cities" (Better Government Association, 2015).

On the day the old administrator was fired the mayor introduced his replacement, Sharon Fairley. She came from the office of the city's Inspector General (where she was First Deputy and General Counsel), and previously had served as a prosecutor for the state attorney general and in the federal courts. By early January she announced a series of reforms, including involving more lawyers in investigations and doing community outreach to encourage more people to come forward with their stories. She promised to "meet" with an agency investigator who had been fired, he claimed, because he submitted reports finding officers at fault in excessive force incidents. When he was fired, the agency press release described him as "the only supervisor at IPRA who resists making requested changes as directed by management in order to reflect the correct finding with respect to officer-involved shootings" (Mitchell, 2015). Importantly for those concerned about transparency, the new administrator promised the agency would begin releasing more details regarding current cases. Past practice had been to shut out the public until cases were closed, and they were often by then forgotten because the review process could take years. At a press conference she noted, "I think that position is now untenable in the world that we live in" (Quig, 2016). She lasted almost two years before stepping down to run unsuccessfully for Illinois Attorney General.

Prosecutor Booted Out. Four months after the release of the video, the county prosecutor in charge of bringing criminal charges against any of the officers involved in the case was defeated for re-nomination as her party's candidate in the upcoming general election. The primary election she lost was widely viewed as a referendum on the continuing scandal and the perceived indifference of the political establishment to the case before it became a *cause célèbre*. She charged the officer with murder, but not until after the judge ordered city officials to release the video and just hours before it appeared. Her defense was that the investigation was "complex and meticulous." There is no question that the mix of multiple collaborating witnesses, high-ranking involvement, falsification of evidence, and obstruction of justice made this case a minefield. But it was wrapped up in just three days once the judge had ruled. Her leading opponent charged that "she waited until her hand was forced by intense political and media pressure surrounding the release of this painful video. She waited even after City Hall was prepared to pay the McDonald family $5 million in damages" (NBC5 Chicago, 2015). A powerful local labor leader added that the case had "become a national symbol of the failed policies of our criminal justice system" (Dardick, 2015). Her opponent, a political insider who positioned herself as a reformer, had strong establishment backing. The local Democratic party abandoned their own incumbent and endorsed a vocal critic instead.

Police Chief Runs for Mayor. By September 2017, the former Police Superintendent was back in the headlines, running against the mayor who had fired him. An "exploratory committee" was formed to conclude that he should run and could win in 2019, and they did. Garry McCarthy was unable to raise much campaign money, so his strategy hinged on holding

Mayor Rahm Emanuel to only 35–40 percent of the vote during the primary election while he came in second. This was a much smaller vote share than Emanuel had garnered in the last primary. McCarthy conceded the mayor would have a formidable campaign war chest, as he was backed by the city's big money interests. However, his theory of the campaign was no one actually *liked* Emanuel in light of emerging revelations of how City Hall was being run. (He was not wrong; see a following discussion on public opinion during this period.) Instead, McCarthy thought he could build a coalition of high-turnout voters among the city's 12,500 police officers and their families, firefighters, and other city workers—and especially *retired* city workers, who felt the city was pulling their health care and other retirement benefits out from under them (which was partly true).

As for his policing policies, he promised to "stop the political manipulation and micro-management of the Police Department. That means creating an achievement-based organization run by professionals and not dictating policies from City Hall. We cannot have legitimate policing under an illegitimate government" (Ruthhart and Pratt, 2018). McCarthy's story of what had transpired between him and City Hall during the dark days of 2015 shifted a bit with time. It became one in which his hands were tied by mayoral interference, the prosecutor's endless investigation, and the police department's established disciplinary procedures.

His was not a law-and-order campaign. On occasion, candidate McCarthy denounced what he dubbed "soft-touch policing policy." Also, the city was on its way to more than 650 murders, following a horrific 769 killings in 2016, and this would not hurt his chances. However, his campaign focused largely on corruption and skullduggery in high places. "We need new leadership and we're going to get it and it's obvious that the people of Chicago are tired of bullying politics and pay-to-play and failed leadership," he argued at a campaign stop. It is important in this regard that the city's population at the time was closely balanced among three major groups, with White residents representing about 32 percent of the population, Hispanics 29 percent, and African Americans 30 percent. One of the few positives of Chicago's otherwise dysfunctional political system is that this population split meant it was necessary to assemble a coalition of voters with lots of representation from more than one of these groups in order to win citywide office. There is not much political space for a backlash White candidate, for example. Even this former police chief was careful not to let his candidacy for mayor be painted into that small, losing corner. Nonetheless, one of the city's most popular and powerful African American politicians dismissed him as "a racist bully boy" (Velasquez, 2016). He ran but did not win, finishing 10th in a field of 14 candidates.

Community Push-Back

Community mobilization around the McDonald shooting and its cover-up began almost immediately, and it grew into a larger political debate about control of the police and even whether Chicago should have a police department at all. The "abolitionist" view that the resources of the criminal justice system should be diverted in their entirety to community development emerged but did not get very far during the timeframe of this book. It gained greater local attention after the 2019 election of several democratic socialist aldermen in Chicago and following events in Minneapolis and other cities in 2020.

Demonstrations broke out almost immediately following the release of the McDonald shooting video in late November 2015. That night hundreds of protesters paraded through downtown Chicago, chanting "16 shots" and calling for the resignation of the mayor and the dismissal of the police Superintendent. Hundreds of protesters marched on a police district station on the west side of Chicago, blocking traffic for hours. At the station, they taunted officers lined up outside, accusing them of waiting for a chance to open fire. Protesters grabbed police bicycles while chanting "don't shoot," and threw water bottles at officers who attempted to detain a demonstrator.

The next major actions focused on the city's leading shopping area, promising to disrupt the Christmas shopping season. "Black Friday," one of the nation's premier shopping days, fell on November 26, just two days after the release of the video. The irony that demonstrations were beginning on Black Friday was lost on no one. On the day, protesters numbering (it was claimed) in the thousands crowded into the Michigan Avenue commercial district to promote a shopping boycott and block entrances to stores. Their chant was "16 shots and you can't shop." News reports described the protesters as "largely peaceful, but angry." The *Chicago Tribune* reported foot traffic on the street was greatly reduced, and "their goal of forcing retailers to suffer economic pain on what's historically the busiest shopping day of the year was a success, according to unhappy store staff and managers who said Black Friday sales on the Magnificent Mile were 25 percent to 50 percent below projections" (Janssen, 2015). Major stores closed early in the face of protests, some locked down by their security staff. On December 1 came the first of a series of organized marches down the same street, aimed at continuing the disruption of Christmas shopping. Prominent African American politicians and the president of the teacher's union headed the most organized efforts. On December 8, hundreds of protesters marched through streets closer to the city center, blocking traffic and chanting, and on December 9, hundreds again marched up Michigan Avenue, stopping at intersections to disrupt traffic. December 24 was declared "Black Christmas" and there were more (if smaller) protests in the area. By the end of the month demonstrators had closed Michigan Avenue six times.

Protests continued throughout 2016. Through the winter and spring demonstrators gathered frequently outside Chicago Police Headquarters, demanding to be heard at monthly meetings of the Police Board. In July alone there were five consecutive days of demonstrations in the downtown area protesting violence against African Americans. The events of the month included sit-ins, rallies around the city's federal office building plaza, and marches shutting down traffic during the rush hour. Marchers blocked access to stores and at one point attempted to storm a major downtown festival. At the same time, protesters occupied lanes of one of the city's busiest expressways, clogging rush hour traffic. Later in the month demonstrators—singing, chanting, and reciting poems—chained their bodies together and blocked the entrance to a police department building. There were marches around the mayor's home as well, something that never happened during the Daley administrations.

At the same time, the city's African American politicians were under mounting pressure from their constituents to do something in response to widespread accusations of police abuse in the city's neighborhoods. As I noted earlier, even before the video was released, a coalition of African American city council members had called for the Superintendent's firing. The entire city council was feeling the heat. In mid-December 2015, virtually every member attended a 10-hour session at which high-ranking officials within the police department were quizzed about what went wrong with the Laquan McDonald case. At the meeting, the head of the police union held the aldermen and their rhetoric responsible for collapsing police morale, which he believed to be the lowest he had seen in his years at the department. The aldermen were not pleased at being indicted, and heated words were exchanged. Outside of the meeting, protesters chanted "16 shots and a cover up!" In January, on Martin Luther King Jr.'s birthday, a Black youth group led a symbolic funeral procession delivering coffins to African American aldermen whose decisions they deemed harmful to Black lives, which mattered.

Of course, the city was not standing still during all of this. In July 2016, officers fired at a stolen car driven by Paul O'Neal, and then killed him after he crashed the car and attempted to run away. The events were captured on dashboard cameras, and activists accused the police of murdering O'Neal. After reviewing the video, the (new) Superintendent stripped three of the officers involved of their police powers for violating department policy regarding firing at passing vehicles. In November, Joshua Beal was killed in an incident involving an off-duty police officer and a uniformed sergeant. It was a "road rage" incident sparked by an African American funeral caravan navigating through a largely White Chicago neighborhood. Thirteen shots were fired during this murky episode. The next day an ugly confrontation erupted when Black Lives Matter demonstrators gathered at the scene and were met by hundreds of residents waving "Blue Lives Matter" signs.

In all, during 2016, Chicago police killed 11 people, and shot another 14 non-fatally. Two of the 25 persons shot were White.

Investigations Were Launched

Was Chicago ready for reform? This was yet to be seen, but almost immediately two major investigations of police policies and practices were launched. The first was hatched in-house, by City Hall. In an immediate response to the tumult surrounding the Laquan McDonald revelations on November 24, the mayor adopted a time-tested formula for defusing scandals and making them go away. He created a special commission to study the situation in detail and present a report, sometime in the future. His Police Accountability Task Force (PATF) was the first of the post-McDonald investigations, and it quickly focused on the nature and quality of police–public encounters. A different and probably more significant investigation began just a few weeks later. It was conducted by the Civil Rights Division of the U.S. Department of Justice, by a team armed with investigators from the FBI, federal prosecutors, and experienced police consultants. It focused largely on organizational and management issues, including supervision, training, agency policies, and officer mental health. This provided a useful counterpart to the Task Force's emphasis on citizens' experiences with the police, and it produced a checklist of expensive new investments the city needed to make in many aspects of policing.

There have been numerous local commissions and investigations in the past. In 1993, the local arm of the federal Civil Rights Commission produced a data-driven report documenting inequalities in the distribution of police manpower across the city's neighborhoods (Illinois Advisory Commission, 1993). However, White aldermen would not countenance the redistribution of their officers to other districts, so the report was stillborn. In 1997, Mayor Richard M. Daley appointed a special commission to fend off any consequences of the indictment of a group of officers on charges of conspiracy, racketeering, and extortion. The ensuing report reviewed a litany of past scandals leading up to the latest, one involving a group of crooked police officers dubbed "The Austin Seven" (Commission on Police Integrity, 1997). The Seven's sins included murder for hire, extortion from tavern owners, kickbacks from vendors, bribing judges, drug sales, robbing drug dealers, and protecting gambling rings. The report included a great deal of information about many sordid matters but did not point a finger at anyone in particular. It concluded with a call for better police hiring and training, and reforms for the department's internal affairs bureau and disciplinary system. The report was duly received and filed away.

Next up was a report prepared for the next mayor *pro bono* by the managing partner of a global law firm based in Chicago (Safer, 2014). He was asked to conduct an independent review and assessment of what the CPD was doing to address police misconduct. He promptly produced a report, *Preventing and Disciplining Police Misconduct* (Safer, 2014). The written report was cryptic regarding *why* it had been commissioned, but it referred to the large number of citizen complaints being made each year and concluded that "work remains to be done" regarding the fairness and effectiveness with which they were processed. There was a veiled discussion of the "code of silence" making misconduct investigations by (and of) the department difficult to conduct. The report presented a comprehensive list of recommendations but acknowledged many were unlikely to be implemented; for example, "we recommend that any officer found to have deliberately concealed or failed to disclose information about a fellow officer's . . . acts of misconduct be dismissed" (Safer, 2014, p. 23). It was a fine report, and readers would learn a great deal about how difficult it is to impose discipline on the Chicago police, but it also was filed away without any concrete response.

With this history, it was easy to anticipate that a new study of the police and their problems would be, at best, a waste of time. So pervasive was the cynicism of the moment that, when the Police Accountability Task Force was announced, an editorial in the *Chicago Tribune* responded "A Task Force to Study the Police? Please Say You're Kidding." It concluded the new panel was among "the most ineffective, least inventive, most timid and deeply insincere solutions on the table" (McQueary, 2015). More charitably, the news pages of the *Tribune* reported the mayor was using the Task Force to buy time while exploring other options. Events were certainly cascading around him, but whatever his motive, on this occasion the strategy did not work. The mayor's new Police Accountability Task Force quickly went rogue. It captured control of its membership, raised independent funding, hired a staff, garnered a broad range of community support, boosted its media presence, and quickly produced a damming report it did not clear first with City Hall. The Department of Justice's investigation also got off the ground quickly. Initially the mayor tried to fend it off, and later he attempted to negotiate a deal with the incoming Trump administration to make its recommendations non-binding and avoid any independent monitoring. Those efforts failed as well. The mayor found he had to reinvent himself as a bit of a reformer because his other escape routes were closed.

The Police Accountability Task Force

Despite the lessons of local history, the new Task Force organizer sensed that, unlike the past, *this* time Chicago *might* be ready for reform. The panel was headed by Lori Lightfoot, a partner in a large, downtown law firm who earlier served as a federal prosecutor. At the time of the McDonald scandal, she was the head of the Chicago Police Board, a statutory volunteer civilian oversight body that reviews appeals in serious police disciplinary cases. She was determined to conduct an analytic, data-driven investigation that would incorporate community concerns and document the organization's shortcomings in indisputable fashion. This was not going to be cheap, but the Task Force had no staff or budget, and it had neither the legal authority nor an administrative infrastructure to receive external funding. The five newly appointed members of the Task Force conferred, and on December 7, 2015 (they were moving fast) they presented the mayor with an outline of the issues they intended to address. They also requested authorization to hire staff and presented the budget they needed to support their work. The silence at City Hall was telling. It quickly became clear the *creation* of the Task Force was the solution to the mayor's problem, but it was not to be a source of new issues for him to confront.

At this point the Task Force went rogue. To pursue its own agenda and distribute a final report it controlled they needed money. So, on January 5, 2016, Lightfoot attended an extraordinary meeting of the directors of all the major foundations in the city. I was there as part of a team from the largest of them. She discussed the significance of the moment and the obstacles the Task Force was facing. On their side, the directors made it clear the city did not need another half-hearted investigation. The room was then cleared for a private discussion among the foundation presidents, and within minutes she secured a commitment of several hundred thousand dollars. The foundation directors also solved her staffing problem. Between them, they regularly supported a small nonprofit organization, the Chicago Consulting Alliance (CCA). CCA provides management and budgeting expertise to the small arts and theater groups, service providers, and community organizations they all funded. The foundations' police reform money went to CCA, which in turn could hire and manage the project coordinators, note-takers, IT and website experts, editors, logistics managers, and media relations staff the Task Force needed to get moving. Other organizations made contributions in kind. Subcommittee meetings were regularly held in office suites at some of the fanciest law firms in the city, and several donated the services of staff legal writers and paralegals to the project. The Task Force's large public hearings were held in community centers and high school gyms around the city. As their confidence grew, the Task Force appointed three needed new members to itself without asking anyone's permission. The morphing of the Task Force into an independent vehicle for reform was a remarkable example of the resilience of civil society and its ability to push back against government if sufficiently goaded. It also highlighted the complexity and scale of the effort it takes to have even a prayer of effectuating change in institutions like the police in large cities like Chicago.

The report met its goal of being data-driven. The data had principally been compiled by journalists, police reform activists, and local academics; the Task Force report pulled it together to quickly build a coherent story. As one media outlet described it, "The task force's claims rest on a mountain of data, cataloging major racial disparities in everything from police shootings to traffic stops to promotions within the CPD" (Fan, 2016). The fact that both

Chicago journalists and reform activists were importantly involved in generating, analyzing, and reporting based on data analysis was a relatively new phenomenon, but by the 2010s both groups had become visible players in the policy data arena. Police and 911 centers generate huge volumes of data on topics of broad interest. Illinois' Freedom of Information laws provide an effective backstop if requests for data access are denied. Powerful computers and software are remarkably inexpensive. Importantly, local watchdog groups were also successful in securing foundation support for their data-driven investigations, and their websites provided an independent channel for broadcasting their findings. The questions they asked were diverse, and often new. Who is losing their car because they cannot afford to pay fines and towing fees? In which neighborhoods are cars being towed when it is a snow clearance day, but it has not actually snowed? Where are residents being heavily ticketed for *bicycling* infractions? The answers to these and many other data questions seemed inevitably to circle back to the same conclusion: the poor pay more.

The Task Force report concluded "the CPD's own data gives validity to the widely held belief the police have no regard for the sanctity of life when it comes to people of color." It described "the callous and disrespectful way in which they had been treated by some officers," and how the McDonald incident was but "a tipping point for long-simmering community anger." The report cataloged racial disparities in everything from police shootings to traffic stops and promotions within the police department. In an interview the Task Force head noted, "The thing that was a tipping point for me was looking at the data on stops and shootings, showing a pretty significant disparity in the ways in which African Americans and everybody else experience policing in the city. It's pretty eye-opening" (Wogan, 2016). A version of Figure 4-1, documenting disparities in stops by race, appeared in the report. (Disclosure: I was active in the work of the Task Force.) The report also described "an utter lack of a culture of accountability" within CPD and a pervasive code of silence shielding individual officers and the organization itself from critical scrutiny. It noted, "Every stage of investigations and discipline is plagued by serious structural and procedural flaws that make real accountability nearly impossible."

Numerous recommendations flowed from the Task Force's findings. They called for new external accountability mechanisms. Two were the creation of a new Deputy Inspector General for Public Safety, who would audit the police department, and the establishment of a successor agency replacing the IPRA, which had been failing in its mission. Goaded by the panel, the city also formulated a new video release policy promising to put images from police body cameras (which they did not yet have in large numbers) into the public domain more quickly. The report also called for the formation of a new community oversight board empowered with a principal role in selecting new police chiefs and setting department policies. Other proposals included creating an office of diversity and inclusion within the department, new training in cultural sensitivity, accelerating the deployment of body cameras, and reinvigorating its flagging community policing initiative. Many of the concerns and recommendations in the 2014 report *Preventing and Disciplining Police Misconduct* were reiterated by the Task Force, which involved its author. Their recommendations included addressing the internal code of silence that hushed up police misconduct, the potential role for supervisors in preventing misconduct, and lengthening the disciplinary histories of officers the Police Board could consider when pondering cases.

The immediate significance of the Task Force's efforts was the positive reception of its report and the widespread endorsement of its conclusions and recommendations by many groups. The media stressed its data-driven character and the inescapable logic of many of its conclusions. Its focus on the experiences of ordinary Chicagoans rather than dryly reciting past calls for more training and supervision (although the Task Force favored those too) kept a focus on the human costs of police policies and practices. The Task Force understood the problems of the Chicago police were widespread and systemic, and not just attributable to individual rogue cops. This is a tough sell because it calls for hard thinking rather than finger-pointing. Most city and police leaders, and many leading politicians, prefer the latter because it promises easy and cheap solutions to entrenched problems. The Task Force's report avoided recounting individual instances of police misconduct, a journalistic staple encouraging finger pointing. Instead, they mobilized data documenting the widespread, long-standing, and systemic nature of racialized policing in Chicago. The findings of the Task Force loomed over discussions of police reform all through 2016 and beyond. A 2020 Google search for "police accountability task force" and "2016" still returned 10,600 website links. The Task Force concluded by calling for concrete action in the next 90 to 180 days.

Two of its organizational recommendations were implemented fairly quickly: the expansion of the auditing capacity of the city's Inspector General's office and the creation of a deputy position to oversee the police (by

2018) and replacing the existing IPRA with a new Civilian Office of Police Accountability (2017, with about 45 percent more staff). However, the mayor slow-walked responses to many other Task Force's recommendations; in a count by the *New York Times*, he ignored 70 percent of them in his initial policy proposals. Many of them would be picked up again during later investigations. The most radical recommendation, the creation of an elected civilian body providing oversight of the department and its policies, was approved by the city council in 2021.

The Justice Department Comes to Town

As the Task Force began its work, the U.S. Justice Department launched its own investigation of the CPD. Federal investigators and the local U.S. Attorney's Office sought to determine if the department was engaged in a "pattern and practice of unlawful conduct," and to discover what factors were leading to the situation. Their authority to step into the crisis in Chicago was created by an act of Congress, the Violent Crime Control and Law Enforcement Act of 1994. It was passed in the aftermath of the 1991 videotaped beating of Rodney King in Los Angeles and the riots that followed. The bill empowered the Justice Department to investigate local agencies, impose requirements on them (which are typically negotiated with city leaders), and sue if cities do not comply with the signed agreement. The U.S. Attorney General conducted frequent pattern and practice investigations during the Obama administration (2009–2017), and these had led to several negotiated settlements between cities and the federal government. At first, Chicago's mayor called the investigation of his town "misguided," but he backed down when it met with broad support. The federal investigation was launched on December 7, 2015, just two weeks after the release of the shooting video and the resulting clamor for change.

The federal investigation led to a formal report released in January 2017, far too late to directly account for the collapse of stop & frisk the previous year. The 161-page report concluded that the Chicago police had systematically engaged in the unconstitutional use of excessive force (United States Department of Justice, 2017). The report detailed incidents in which unarmed persons were shot by police, whose accounts justifying their actions were accepted by the city's civilian review agency without what seemed to be a critical investigation. Officers were described as ill-supervised, and the agency's disciplinary system was judged to be ineffectual. The training sessions federal investigators observed were poorly conducted and taught outdated legal principles. The report also described the collapse of public trust in the police, and a parallel collapse of morale within the department. Unlike earlier federal investigations, however, there was no resulting agreement between the Justice Department and the city to address these issues. The election of President Trump in late 2016 and the appointment of his new Attorney General put an end to federal pattern and practice enforcement. The mayor did try to negotiate a deal with the Trump administration calling for *suggested* recommendations but imposing no mandatory requirements, but this also collapsed in the face of popular pushback (Ruthhart, 2017).

The situation was rescued by the Illinois Attorney General Lisa Madigan. She strongly supported the investigation, and when it became apparent that the Trump administration was not going to follow through, her office sued the police department in federal court and managed to secure an agreement with the city that would be evaluated and enforced by a local federal judge. The final agreement of September 2018 called for 210 specific reforms and authorized the court to hire a monitor (and staff) to assess progress on those promises and report regularly to the judge. It came into effect in March 2019.

Because of its timing, any link between the Justice Department's efforts and the sudden collapse of stop & frisk could only have been due to the *investigation* rather than to the settlement or its implementation, which came later. However, the investigation and its aftermath lingered on for several years, during a period when stops did not creep back to their old levels. The investigation was certainly visible within the police department. Unlike the earlier reports described above, which were mostly carried out by well-meaning local attorneys, this time the investigation was conducted FBI agents and federal prosecutors, backstopped by experienced police consultants. They reviewed almost six years of use of force reports and investigations of officer-involved shootings, interviewed more than 340 officers and many staff members of the soon-to-disappear IPRA, and met with the unions representing officers, sergeants, lieutenants, and captains. FBI investigators rode along with patrol officers, and this got a lot of attention in police blogs. Unlike the Task Force, the Department of Justice had unfettered access to departmental records and police officers. Independent subject-matter experts were hired to review the department's policies, manuals, training materials, and internal and external reports. Informational meetings and "listening sessions" were held with more than 1,000 community members and representatives of more than 90 community organizations. They looked into internal matters like the department's hiring practices, officers' mental health issues, and morale. One of the consulting focus group leaders I know well told me the Chicago officers he met with were among the most dispirited he had ever encountered (see also Police Foundation, 2018). On their side, the city retained its own attorneys and consultants, including senior police leaders with experience in handling consent decrees. The events of 2016 thus opened a large window into the operations of the CPD that could have contributed to the continued subsidence of stop & frisk. The investigation and its threatened consequences were certainly on the minds of both city leaders and rank-and-file officers.

Mobilizing the Law

While the events surrounding the death of Laquan McDonald in Chicago triggered follow-up investigations, important moves to reform the city's stop & frisk policy had already been set in motion. Both the Illinois State Legislature and the local branch of the American Civil Liberties Union (ACLU) had been involved in amending the policies of the CPD, introducing significant changes in how stops were to be conducted and the documentation officers were required to submit justifying their actions. All these new requirements came into effect on January 1, 2016, coincident with the long-term collapse of stop & frisk.

An ACLU Effect?

The constitutionality of modern stop & frisk policies has been in question at least since the 2013 decision *Floyd v. City of New York* (2013). This decision voided New York City's stop & frisk practices because police failed to adhere to *Terry v. Ohio* (1958) standards and the 4th Amendment right to freedom from unreasonable searches and seizures. In Chicago, the local chapter of the ACLU began to dig into this issue seriously beginning in 2011. It was hard. Their FOIA request for data eventually yielded sketchy information on six months of stops but did not include useful detail on issues of interest to the ACLU, such as the circumstances and reasons leading to stops and searches. A follow-up request for information on stops yielded only 298 contact cards. The police insisted on reviewing and redacting information on each card they deemed sensitive. This was very labor intensive and took a great deal of time to complete, because much of the useful information on the card was handwritten in a narrative section. The narrative documented whether an encounter could even be classified as a stop & frisk. Officers also frequently noted personal information about suspects and other matters exempt from FOIA, and those notes also needed to be scratched out. After processing almost 300 cards the department was unwilling to put more into the task, and that was that. The ACLU was not alone in this situation. The same legal limitation on FOIA data requests—they could not be "burdensome" to the police—also kept the media from acquiring enough detailed information about stop & frisk to document what was going on.

Reviewing what remained unredacted on the processed cards, the ACLU concluded many did not document a basis for reasonable suspicion a crime had been committed or was about to occur, the legal standard for making a stop. The explanations they found for stops included "detained after being observed with a male who was smoking a cigarette," "subject standing on street corner loitering," "was in area known for high gang activity," "accused of rude behavior," and "observed walking through vacant alley." Based on what they could get from the CPD, the ACLU estimated one-half of the stops were unconstitutional. If they could extrapolate from what they had to all stops conducted during 2014, there could have been more than 300,000 unconstitutional stop & frisks (ACLU of Illinois, 2015).

Stop & frisk can also be legally suspect for its potential for unconstitutional racial bias, which is covered by 14th Amendment to the Constitution. Policies seemingly nondiscriminatory on the surface but applied in a discriminatory fashion can also be found unconstitutional. The judge in the New York City case concluded the NYPD's racially neutral policy was being applied in a discriminatory manner because of the high percentage of African American and Hispanic males being stopped. The ACLU's 2014 data for Chicago indicated 73 percent of stops had targeted African Americans while African Americans make up about 30 percent of Chicago's population. But few criminologists would think statements like this are always meaningful regarding discriminatory police decision-making; we know too much about who does what, and where they do it, to give simple percentages much standing (cf., Neil and Winship, 2019). In New York, Judge Shira Scheindlin accepted the validity of claims based on similar percentages and found the city in trouble on 14th Amendment grounds.

However, in Chicago all recorded stop & frisks at this time by definition involved only innocent parties. Prior to 2016, the stop data described a homogeneous group. If subjects of stops proved to be up to no good, they were not in the stop & frisk database. If all their stops had been based upon well-founded suspicions or discerning judgments when it came to weapon carrying and probable cause, the number of recorded stops could have been much lower. Instead, police were stopping innocent African Americans at six or seven times the rate at which they were making unwarranted stops of Whites, strengthening the basis for making a claim about discriminatory practice. At best, police were horrible at differentiating suspicious and unsuspicious African Americans. At worst, they were not trying.

Surprisingly, the outcome of the ACLU's investigation was a negotiated settlement rather than a lawsuit. Avoiding expensive and time-consuming litigation, in August 2015 the city, the police, and the ACLU entered into a negotiated yet legally enforceable agreement to reshape Chicago's stop & frisk regime. The city agreed to steps ensuring that police practices comply with the Constitution, which forbids unreasonable searches and seizures, and the Illinois Civil Rights Act, which requires government policies to not have a racially disparate impact. Both issues had been targets of the ACLU's examination of stop & frisk records. The negotiations also led to an agreement over new police training. Police were to undergo training to make sure they stop people only when there is probable cause to believe they were engaged in criminal behavior, and to pat them down only when there is reasonable suspicion the person stopped is armed and dangerous. There were to be regular audits by the department that could lead to retraining or the enhanced supervision or discipline of officers who repeatedly engaged in unlawful stops or pat-downs. The ACLU said the agreement incorporated many of the changes it sought while avoiding a protracted legal battle. From the other side, Superintendent McCarthy reported, "I've got to tell you, I'm pleased with the results . . . . Working with the ACLU is a very positive thing" (Sobol, 2015). He also promised policing in Chicago would be "based on crime data, patterns, statistics and community intelligence."

Importantly, especially considering the ACLU's experience with making sense of patterns of stop & frisk, their agreement with the city also required the police to begin keeping detailed records of every stop. No longer would stops leading to arrests or citations disappear into other paperwork. The new data could provide a more complete picture of the actual effectiveness of stops in uncovering guns and other contraband, among the justifications for making stops. The agreement also created a position for an outside monitor who would review all the data, including officers' written narratives and other information that in the past had not seen the light of day. The monitor, retired magistrate judge Arlander Keys, was to submit regular public reports regarding patterns revealed by the data, especially regarding race and gender bias, and assessing the lawfulness of police practices. He hired a well-known, out-of-town criminologist to conduct the data analysis. Judge Keys would also keep an eye on other elements of the agreement between the ACLU and the city, including the quality of the data, the appropriateness of the department's policies, and the department's compliance with agreed-upon changes in police training. It was agreed all of this would be effective beginning in January 2016.

The absence of systematic data on stop & frisks was an important feature of the debate in Chicago over its character and significance. The situation was quite different in New York City. There, officers submitted a standardized form (a UF250) for each stop. The data was entered into a database that early on became available to the public (I was a party to the lawsuit which accomplished this). Many elements describing the stop were recorded as checkboxes which were easily digitized. New York's stop records could be linked to parallel records on citations, arrests, and weapon seizures, so the outcome of each stop could be determined. Academics turned the data to the task of parsing out their contribution to reducing crime in the city. The New York Civil Liberties Union, media organizations, and interested community groups all could conduct their own analyses of the data and report their own conclusions. Both public debate and the lawsuits springing up around the city's stop & frisk policies were data driven, with everyone working from the same basic facts. Chicago's hard-to-access and sketchy data on stops during which not much happened, but without any information on why they took place at all, simply could not support the meaningful debates over stop & frisk happening elsewhere. As we will see later in this chapter, post-agreement debates had much more to work with because of the ACLU's efforts.

Some important issues were not addressed by the agreement. There was no commitment by the department to make *fewer* stops, only that they would respect reasonable suspicion and probable cause requirements for conducting them. In addition, the city did not agree that any of their previous stops were unconstitutional. These two points were related, as the ACLU could only demand unconstitutional stops cease. Importantly for the city, this construction of the agreement also gave them some legal cover from suits seeking damages for making illegal stops. At the same time that the agreement with the ACLU was being finalized, the city was being sued by six Chicagoans in a federal class action case alleging the police department had systematically violated the rights of hundreds of thousands of people with unconstitutional stops & frisks and unlawful searches and seizures (Crews, 2015).

But despite these wins by the city, there were skeptics of the settlement in policing circles. The head of the police union demanded the ACLU "remove the shackles that limit street stops to instances where officers either observe criminal behavior or spot someone who fits the description of someone reported to 911 as having committed a crime." He argued:

> It limits stop, question and frisk completely because it was designed by the ACLU and accepted as policy by the department, which is the main contributing factor to the drop in our street stops. . . . People think that police officers are standing down. Police officers aren't standing down. They're following policy. They're doing what the order requires. That's what everybody's missing. (Gorner, 2016)

The lament that the ACLU drove a spike through the heart of stop & frisk was common at the time the agreement was signed. Later, when the Great Crime Spike of 2016 cast a pall over the city, the term "ACLU effect" took on new meaning. As we will see in Chapter 7, in the eyes of some the spike was their fault.

Legislative Action

The ACLU was not the only player in the policy community surrounding the Chicago police. Even before the ACLU agreement and reports by the Police Accountability Task Force and the Department of Justice, the Illinois state legislature also turned out to be an important locus for stop & frisk policy-making. Many police researchers pay little attention to state statutes governing police activity, but legislatures are among the important arenas in which policing policy is fought out. We think of authority being decentralized in the American system of government, but it generally devolves to the states and not to cities. State laws often trump city ordinances, and there can be battles between state houses and city halls over how much autonomy the latter are going to have in making their own policies. Cities may want easy public access to body camera footage, for example, but across the nation states have been busily declaring body-worn camera recordings exempt from their open-records laws. "Blue lives matter" legislation imposing harsher penalties for attacking officers have been a common state response to big-city concern about police use of force, while few states have done anything to change the laws concerning when police are justified in using deadly force. In many places state "Police Officer Bill of Rights" legislation offers officers protection against investigations by their own agencies.

In Illinois, stop & frisk became the subject of debate in the legislature during its 2014–2015 session. One of the biggest pieces of legislation emerging from the session was the 2015 "Police and Community Relations Improvement Act" (SB 1304). Drafted with actual bipartisan support, it passed the House by a vote of 107–3–4 and was sent from the Senate to the Governor by a similar margin. The bill amended and tightened past legislation. Beginning in January 2016, SB 1304 required that officers complete a standardized form documenting their reasons for making a pedestrian stop; the race of the person stopped; whether a pat-down, frisk, or search was conducted; if contraband was found; and the disposition of the stop. Finally, officers were required to provide to everyone a card stating the reason why they had been stopped and listing the officer's name and badge number. This quickly became known as "the receipt." This act built on an earlier law adopted by the General Assembly in 2003, sponsored by then State Senator Barack Obama. A related "Traffic and Pedestrian Stop Statistical Study Act" handed authority to monitor all state data to the Racial Profiling Prevention and Data Oversight Board. This body had already been created by the legislature to watch for evidence of racial profiling in traffic stop data, which had been collected for some time.

When these rules were implemented in Chicago in 2016, the newly required data form was dubbed the Investigatory Stop Report (ISR). It included all the data elements required by the state. In an important move, Chicago went beyond state requirements by insisting the form be completed for *all* non-traffic-enforcement police encounters with the public. ISRs replaced the old contact cards. This policy was part of the deal the city had negotiated with the ACLU. In contrast, state legislation required data collection only for pedestrian stops featuring pat-downs, searches, summons, or arrests.

Thanks to the legislature's earlier requirements, Chicago's already-existing data collection requirements for traffic stops provide a case study of what

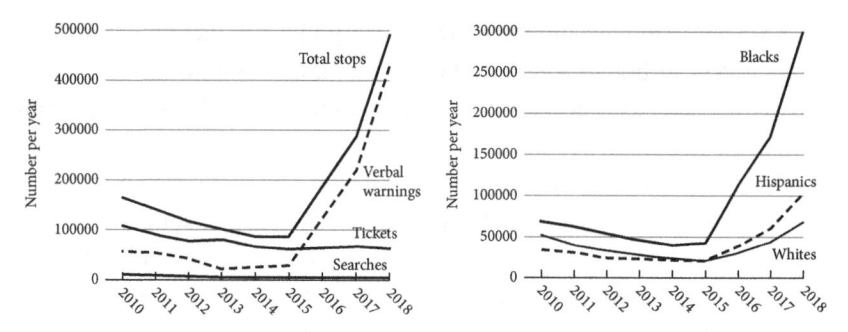

Figure 6-2 Trends in Traffic Stops

can happen when police are said to "stop doing stop & frisk." Officers were still on the street working, and a question in reply to this claim should be "well, what *are* they doing to fill their day?" Figure 6-2 provides one answer to the question. The required data collection documented that, prior to 2016, traffic stops had been declining in frequency. Tickets were routinely issued during stops, and a few searches were conducted. In 2015, tickets were issued in 70 percent of traffic stops. Following the collapse of stop & frisk, recorded traffic stops immediately surged, growing from less than 100,000 to almost 500,000 per year by 2018. This striking pattern is illustrated on the left side of Figure 6-2. But what surged were verbal warnings, not tickets or searches. During 2017, for example, of the about 285,000 recorded traffic stops, 220,000 resulted in verbal warnings, or 77 percent. As Figure 6-2 describes, traffic stops leading to tickets trended down as before, totaling 100,000 in 2010 but only 67,000 during 2017. Searches just continued to decline.

Clearly an enormous surge in significant traffic infractions was not what was driving the traffic stop rate, because of the (new) very high rate of verbal warnings. Rather, there was a sudden and large-scale switch between stop & frisk and a skyrocketing number of traffic stops—but not ones officers were inclined to press charges for. Importantly, in Chicago, "traffic stops" were officially not to be mistaken for "traffic enforcement." They are "vehicle enforcement missions." The department's General Order G10-01, issued January 1, 2016, noted, "A goal of targeted vehicle enforcement missions is to reduce gang violence, shootings, and drive-by shootings by enforcing the appropriate statutes and ordinances." Part of the order listed priorities for special attention using stops. These included suspicion of weapons or narcotics in a vehicle, a possibly revoked or suspended driver's license, playing music too loud, possible possession of spray paint by a minor in the vehicle, possession of an altered handicap permit, displaying a false temporary registration permit, soliciting a prostitute, fireworks in the vehicle, and fleeing a police vehicle." The rise in traffic stops is an example of a strategic change in police activity with big numbers behind it (for more analysis of this see Hausman and Kronick, 2021).

A second feature of traffic stops was who was caught up in them. The right-hand chart in Figure 6-2 tracks the distribution of suddenly numerous traffic stops by race. The race of the driver was assessed by the involved officers at the scene. As Figure 6-2 illustrates, most of the increasing number of stops targeted African American motorists. By 2018, more than 60 percent of traffic stops involved African Americans; Whites made up just 13 percent of the total. Stops also rose for other groups, but their totals remained relatively small. Interestingly, other features of stops changed very little. For example, the percentage of motorists who were searched after they were stopped was essentially the same for White, African American, and Latino subjects. This did not change, and the number of searches for all three groups actually declined. The big change was the explosion of warning stops, largely of African Americans, and fully 89 percent of all stops of African Americans resulted in verbal warnings. While the department's traffic stop strategy was a newly emphasized one, its targets remained virtually unchanged.

Other aspects of the state legislation bill imposed new requirements for body and dashboard cameras and established some (minimal) standards for investigating officer-involved shootings, including that a written report be filed with the State Attorney General. It created a statewide database recording confirmed instances of officer misconduct. This enables hiring agencies to check if applicants had been fired or had resigned while under investigation somewhere else in the state (for the issues involved, see Grunwald and Rappaport, 2019–2020). The act also set new standards for recruit training on procedural justice, human rights, cultural competence, implicit bias, and "constitutional and proper use of law enforcement authority." Agencies are now required to provide serving officers with more training on the same list of issues, and they must annually retrain all officers on use of force. Like the new stop & frisk requirements plus the agreements with the ACLU, all these reforms were inaugurated in January 2016.

During 2016, a major discussion point regarding the ensuing collapse of stop & frisk was the extent to which it was driven by the general aversion of police officers to paperwork. The new stop form was significantly longer than the contact card it replaced. In 2016, the head of the police union argued that "demands for increased paperwork contributed to why Chicago Police are down over 150,000 street stops this year." In April of the same year the department's press spokesman opined that most of the decline in stops was due to paperwork requirements. The new form was several pages long, and many officers reputedly found it excessively detailed and onerous. There were separate sections calling for detailed written narratives describing the source of their reasonable suspicion for making a stop, why they frisked a citizen, and why they conducted a search beyond a protective pat-down. The detailed information gathered in the stop report was put there to help Judge Keys evaluate whether officers were following the Constitution. The purpose for which the new information was being demanded did not seem endear the form to officers. Complaints about the form continued to be so vociferous the CPD and the ACLU agreed in January 2017 to simplify the stop form, and to remove the names and badge numbers of involved officers from any data available to the public. However, the head of the police union continued to insist the "monstrosity of a report" be scrapped entirely. The headline was "Too Much Police Paperwork to Blame for Spike In Murders, Union Boss Says" (Cox, 2016).

It is well known that one way to keep officers from doing things is to require them to "push paper" documenting what they have done. For example, a study of fatal force involving several cities discovered the major policy difference among departments notably affecting their use of force was the requirement by some that officers had to complete a written report every time they unholstered their gun. As the authors reported, almost every agency requires a report of firearm discharges; the new policy just further increased the hassle involved in making casual (weapon) threats (Jennings and Rubado, 2017; see also Epp and Erhardt, 2020). Along the same lines, some agencies require a separate justification form for each shot fired in discharge cases, wherever they landed. The goals of these policies are twofold: to remind officers to be mindful of the law and policy when drawing their weapon and to deter them from doing so by making them write something down.

In reference to stop & frisk, I found it curious that the media and the local policy community evidenced so little resistance to the argument that officers who had reasonable suspicion someone was armed or had detected a probable cause to stop them because of a criminal offense would not do so because they had to complete a report. The reason this argument remained unchallenged, I think, was because everyone involved just assumed a large fraction of stops actually *did not* involve probable cause or even reasonable suspicion.

Rather, most assumed they were being made without a legal basis or even real suspicion, so the prospect of recording them *would* serve as a deterrent to making so many unwarranted stops.

In a local police blog, an experienced officer passed along his advice for dealing with the new, post-2016 world of stops:

> If you don't have strong reasonable articulable suspicion do not make the stop. Period. If you are not sure what that is you'd better start discussing it with your fellow officers and sgts. until you do know what it is and more importantly is not. All these anonymous "suspicious man" calls should now be ignored unless you personally see something more. Just because somebody sees someone out their window that they don't want around doesn't mean we get to stop them automatically. Don't chase unless you have reasonable suspicion at that moment because running away is not enough on its own. And it's almost guaranteed that if you do catch that runner you're going to be using some level of force so don't even initiate the chase unless you're justified in making the stop. If there's any doubt about whether you have enough to make a legit stop you probably don't, so don't make the stop. (January 7, 2017)

New Media Scrutiny

A continuing consequence of the Laquan McDonald scandal and ensuing protests, firings, and investigations was a notable and sustained increase in media attention to the affairs of the Chicago police. Crime has always been a media staple, reliably producing easy-to-report material of interest to many readers and viewers. As we saw in Chapter 3, this does not mean crime coverage is *accurate*. Violent crime and the extent of stories about local violence in the newspapers rose and fell almost independently. Here, in contrast, we are interested in media coverage of police personnel, policies, and practices. In this arena, the media play an important role in *setting the agenda* for public discussion and political debate. Policy discussions and resolutions of political scandals routinely began in response to media accounts of community problems, programs gone awry, and public officials who have fallen down on the job. Various media prime their audiences to get interested in these debates, by letting them know what issues are important and by framing them in a way that makes sense to the public.

Research on the effects of the media is vast and addresses many topics. One has been the impact of media coverage of the police. Lisa Graziano has summarized research focusing on the impact of media coverage of episodes of police misconduct on the public. Taken as a whole, 42 studies of the issue confirmed links between perceptions of the police, exposure to coverage of high-profile incidents, and awareness of negative police stories. She concluded negative coverage was related to negative perceptions of police "at a rate which is not only comparable to negative personal contact with police and race-ethnicity of respondents, but is greater than that of neighborhood context, such as fear of and perceptions of crime problems" (Graziano, 2019, p. 221). She suggested that media depictions of such events should be a prime suspect in understanding turning points in mass opinion.

Events in Chicago at the end of 2015 defined a period of intense media scrutiny of police, their policies, and their use of deadly force. To examine this, I turned again to one of the principal newspapers in the Chicago area, the *Chicago Tribune*. The searches included the period from 2012 to mid-2018, which covered almost the entire administration of Superintendent Garry McCarthy and his mayor, plus the aftermath of the collapse of stop & frisk. The results document the ubiquitous nature of news about policing in Chicago. Over the entire period there was an average of about 104 stories each month involving the Chicago police. During 2015, the headlines ranged from good ("Chicago police are committed to treating citizens fairly, says Superintendent") to critical ("CPD stopped over 250,000 people—mostly Black—without arrests last summer"). Inevitably, there were mixed messages ("Police involved shootings down sharply in Chicago so far this year"). This being Chicago, even stories about promising moves by the city could not avoid negative scrutiny ("City body camera no-bid contracts raise questions").

Figure 6-3 depicts the steady drumbeat of policing news that provided a background for public discussion of policing over these seven years. For many months coverage hovered at around 90 stories, but there were spikes reflecting dramatic local events demanding media coverage. The first uptick in coverage reflected police responses to local marches and an encampment set up by Occupy Chicago, a local outcropping of the national Occupy Wall Street movement that captured public attention in late 2011. These stories coincided with discussions of the city's grave public employee's pension crisis. Together, these issues generated about 125 media accounts during January 2012. In May 2012, the city hosted a very large gathering of international

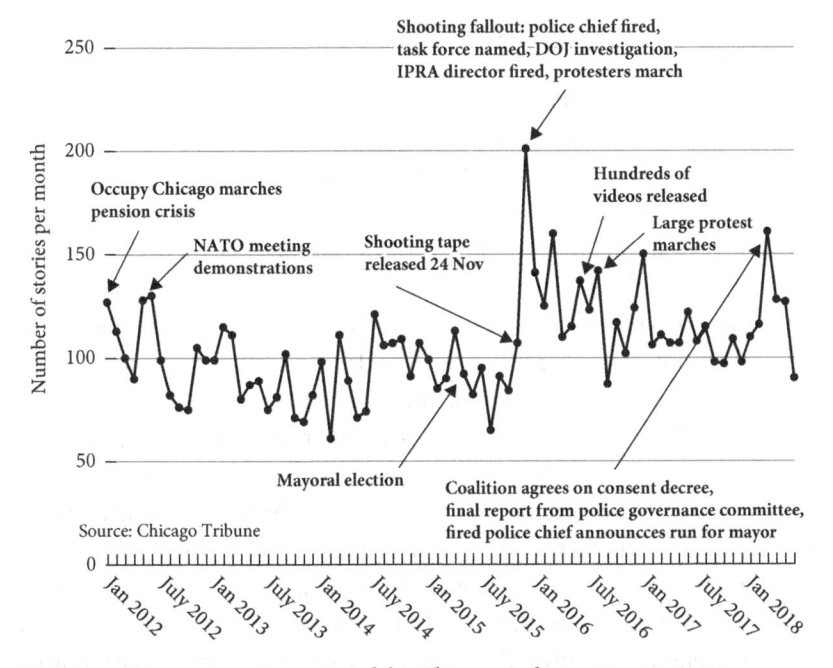

Figure 6-3 Newspaper Coverage of the Chicago Police 2012–2018

political luminaries at a meeting of NATO leaders. Local coverage of the event peaked at 130 stories in a month. Almost all the mainstream media coverage of demonstrations and the crowd control interventions that ensued was positive. This reflected careful (and widely touted) preparation by the police and city leaders for the continuous protests taking place in the city center during this event.

Then, following a long period of normal (three stories per day) coverage, came the Mt. Everest of media attention. It was generated by recountings of the McDonald shooting and breathless reportage of the ensuing political drama. The suppressed video was released on November 24, 2015, and the first protest march began at 4:30 pm the same day. Over the next seven days the *Tribune* printed 32 local policing stories. The next week it printed 31 stories. December 2015 was a particularly news-rich period, and more than 200 articles about the Chicago police appeared in the *Tribune*. During the week starting December 3, the American edition of the British newspaper *The Guardian* published 13 stories about events in Chicago. The firing of the police chief and the head of the city's civilian review agency, the mayor's *mea culpa* before the City Council, creation of the Policing Accountability Task

Force, reports Department of Justice investigators were coming to town, and prominent demonstrations during a prime holiday shopping period, sparked a compelling media firestorm.

Following months were also lively and commanded media coverage. In March, the findings of the Police Accountability Task Force began to leak out, and there were 160 stories that month. Hundreds of police dashboard videos were released in the June 2016 (137 stories). In July, marchers condemning police shootings clogged the city center and attempted to rush the city's Taste of Chicago downtown food festival. August 2016 brought repeated protest demonstrations around the city proclaiming Black Lives Matter, and marchers took over several lanes of one of the city's largest expressways (142 stories). Finally, as Figure 6-3 indicates, another spike in coverage followed a March 2018 announcement by the fired chief of police he was entering the race for mayor in the next election (the headline: "McCarthy pollster: Rahm unelectable, will 'embarrass' himself in reelecting bid"). The same month a coalition organized by the ACLU and including assorted community organizations, representatives of the local Black Lives Matter group, and the Illinois Attorney General, agreed on the terms for a federal consent decree requiring police reform. This was not the last required step in the process. The city had not yet signed on, but agreement on a legal strategy solidified a deal among the prominent political actors they could bring to a federal judge.

Overall, Figure 6-3 describes a political environment with increased media scrutiny of policing affairs in the months and years following the events of November 2015. Setting the obvious peaks aside, routine monthly coverage of policing affairs increased by about 20 percent. This set the stage for new public visibility of police policies and practices, and—as we will see in paragraphs to follow on public opinion—the public was primed to be critical of what they saw and read.

New Skepticism of the Police

Opinion polling in the immediate aftermath of the McDonald shooting confirmed Chicagoans were paying attention to the matter, and the mayor was in trouble. In April 2016, the *New York Times* conducted a poll in Chicago probing public responses to the events of 2015–2016. Some of their findings are summarized in Figure 6-4.[2] During this period in history Chicagoans were attending to events, and in turn their views about policing in general

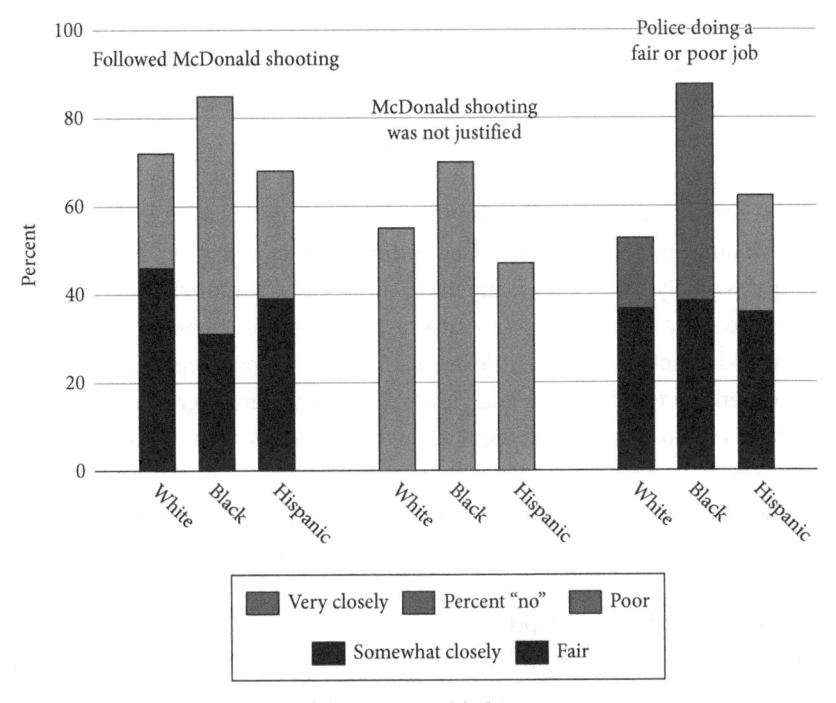

Figure 6-4 Negative Views of the McDonald Shooting

were linked to their responses to a specific incident, the McDonald shooting. About three-quarters of the respondents reported they had followed the case very or somewhat closely. African Americans were the most attentive: 85 percent of those interviewed reported they followed the matter somewhat or very closely. Whites and Latinos were not far behind, at around 70 percent. In another survey conducted during 2016, 92 percent of city residents recalled hearing about the incident. In follow-up questions, 77 percent of all respondents said they had seen the McDonald video themselves, and another 16 percent reported they had not seen it, but they had discussed the video with someone else.

As public affairs go, this is a lot of attention. Political scientists know the public does not have very coherent ideas about many policies, they pay little attention to the discussion of issues, and their vote often contradicts what they say they believe (Achen and Bartels, 2017). In this case their views seem more coherent than usual. Attention was high, and it was linked to other attitudes. In the *New York Times* survey, attention to the case was measured on a four-point scale, and the more attention respondents paid, the more likely they were to think the shooting was unjustified. Figure 6-4 depicts the number of respondents to the poll who reported negative views of the shooting. Again, African Americans were the most critical, but a slim majority of White respondents (55 percent) agreed it was a bad shooting. All this attention and the small number of "don't know" responses drawn by the survey was almost certainly motivated by the existence of the video. Its constant replaying on television and newspaper websites provided large numbers of city residents a compelling, almost live-action view of the event. Often political scientists ask about more abstract issues being decided far away, and which often have little dramatic or emotional content. In contrast, both attention to this matter and views of its justification were independently related to respondents' other opinions of the police. As one example, Figure 6-4 illustrates their responses when people were asked to "rate the job the police in Chicago are doing." Overall, two-thirds of all city residents thought the police were doing a poor or only fair job. White respondents were more positive than African Americans, but a majority also gave the police low ratings. In my experience this level of skepticism among White Chicagoans is not usual. In this case, a before-after study of opinion found that White Chicagoans were the ones who lost confidence in the police. Most African Americans already had (Kochel and Skogan, 2021). The link between attention to the McDonald shooting and popular judgments about its justification were also correlated with a longer list of questions about the police. For example, a majority of residents (including 52 percent of Whites) agreed Chicago police were more likely to use deadly force against African Americans. In addition, more than 40 percent of every group thought African Americans and Latinos were being treated unfairly by the city's criminal justice system either "always" or "most of the time." Like the "how good a job" question, people's views of these issues were closely linked to how they judged McDonald incident.

The mayor's strategy of withholding public access to the McDonald shooting video until after the election proved to be a success, in that he managed to win. In his initial run for office in 2011 Rahm Emanuel won votes in wards all over the city. He received 55 percent of the total in the primary election, winning handily and thus avoiding a second round of campaigning. However, by the end of his reelection campaign in the spring of 2015, even in the absence of a significant African American candidate he lost so much support among African American voters he was forced into a runoff against a Latino candidate. He won with a heavy turnout in better-off White wards, where being dubbed "Mayor One Percent" was not necessarily a bad thing.

By contrast, turnout was low—as usual—in Latino neighborhoods. Seven months later, after the election and the release of the video, his public support tanked.

Numerous opinion polls document the collapse of political support for the mayor following the release of the video. During the first week of December 2015 a survey of registered voters set his job approval rating at 18 percent, with two-thirds of respondents believing he had lied about the video and half thinking he should resign (ABC7Chicago, 2015). A January 2016 poll by the *Chicago Tribune* found that support for Mayor Emanuel had dropped by more than 50 percent in a year. The poll found "the vast majority of Chicagoans don't consider Emanuel honest and trustworthy, don't think he was justified in withholding the McDonald video, and don't believe his statements about the controversial police shooting" (Ruthhart and Bowen, 2016). The *New York Times* poll of April 2016 provided information about the views of all Chicagoans, and not just registered voters. It documented deep and widespread dissatisfaction with the mayor's performance. Residents were asked a general question about his performance: whether they approved

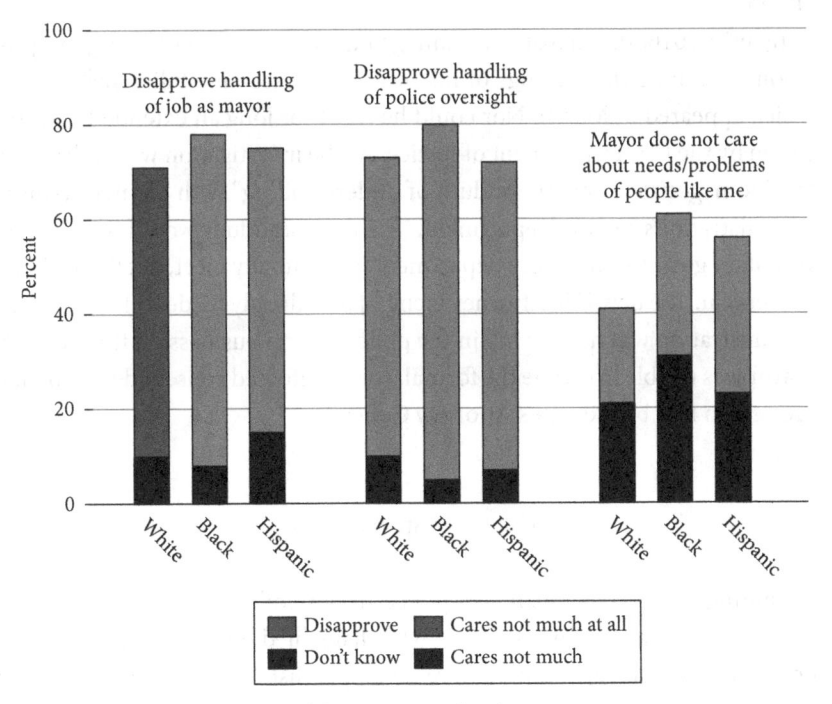

Figure 6-5 Negative Views of the Mayor and Policing

or disapproved of "the way he is handling his job as mayor." As Figure 6-5 illustrates, although Emanuel was just reelected, more than 60 percent indicated they disapproved, or they were not sure. (I am counting "don't know" replies as negative because respondents had proven themselves savvy about local events on many questions. They were saying they were on the fence.) Overall, almost 75 percent of those questioned viewed his job performance in a negative light. When asked specifically about how the mayor was handling oversight of the CPD, 74 percent gave him low marks. It was striking was how widespread dissatisfaction was; the differences between White, African American, and Latino respondents were quite small on both questions. A final political question brought their views of the mayor closer to home. Respondents were asked how much they thought the major "cares about the needs and problems of people like yourself?" Figure 6-5 reports their replies in a negative direction. Overall, more than 50 percent of Chicagoans reported he cared "not much" or (more often) "not much at all." He did best among Whites, but 40 percent still agreed he did not really care about them. Among African American and Hispanic voters, the most common response category was he cared "not much at all" about them.

By mid-2016, the mayor was damaged goods. He was not in a good position to dismiss the findings of his own Police Accountability Task Force, which appeared in March. Nor could he resist for long an extended investigation by the U.S. Department of Justice. As the investigation was ending, he tried to negotiate a "memorandum of understanding" with the new Trump administration's Justice Department. The memorandum would list a set of voluntary goals for the police department to eventually meet, but this did not get very far. The new U.S. Attorney General had already made it clear the new administration was not staying in the police reform business. In the end, the mayor was unable to escape the formal, court-enforced consent decree being pressed on him by the state's Attorney General.

The New Stop & Frisk

Beginning in 2016, the Chicago police began collecting a much broader range of systematic information on what happened during stops. Most importantly, recorded encounters were no longer just the innocent stops. ISRs were to be completed for every encounter. If subjects were patted down as a weapon safety measure, this was to be reported. If subjects or their vehicle was searched, and if any contraband was recovered, those actions and outcomes were to be recorded as well. Further, any ensuing enforcement action, such as making an arrest or giving a citation became part of the stop record. As before, the sex, age, and race of subjects was noted, now along with their home address and the street location of the stop. Officers were to record any gang affiliation they could divine during the encounter and if the incident was recorded on their body or dashboard camera. These were big changes. These data enable us to evaluate stops along more of the dimensions described in earlier chapters, including their effectiveness and efficiency.

There were still problems, to be sure. Most important, the CPD decided to delete all contacts with subjects who were classified as under age 18 from publicly available data. Even how many there were each month was not reported, much less any details—such as date or location—enabling outsiders to assess the impact of this exclusion on patterns in the data. There are two clues to the impact of this exclusion policy. In response to a request, the department's data group generated a count of under-18 stop subjects for 2016. Based on this, about 16 percent of all stops were excluded. Another clue is the number of subjects during earlier periods who were under age 18, because information about their stops was included in the data. During the period of 2013–2015, about 12 percent of subjects were either under age 18 or their age was missing or garbled in the data. By either measure, numerous stops were excluded from the post-2016 public record.

Based on the new data—on adults only—by March 2016, stop rates had begun to stabilize at a much lower level than in the past, even accounting for estimates of under-18 stops. Overall, there were about 12,000 to 19,000 stops per month, varying with the season. The innocent portion of these stops varied between about 10,000 and 13,500 per month. The difference between the two signals the inclusion of stops leading to arrests, citations, and/or seizure of contraband. Previously these stops had slid into other statistical categories. All these contingencies could now be identified in the data. During this period about 70–75 percent of monthly stops could be classified as innocent. That fraction was about the same for African Americans and White subjects; somewhat more stops of Hispanics—about 75 percent throughout—were classed as innocent.

Stop, Question, and Perhaps Frisk

Throughout his tenure, Police Superintendent Garry McCarthy insisted his stop & frisk initiative should fairly be described as one of "stop, question and perhaps frisk." Data now available on the new stop & frisk indicates a substantial minority of those stopped were frisked, but this was truer for some Chicagoans than for others. The CPD's "Guidelines for Field Interrogations" noted "protective pat-downs, or frisks, can only be used if the police officer has a 'reasonable and articulable' suspicion that a subject 'presents a danger of attack to the officer or another.'" In the *Terry* case, the Supreme Court noted "upon suspicion that the person may be armed, the police should have the power to 'frisk' him for weapons. If the 'stop' and the 'frisk' give rise to probable cause to believe the suspect has committed a crime, then the police should be empowered to make a formal 'arrest,' and a full incident 'search' of the person" (*Terry v Ohio*, 1967, p. 10; the Court's quotes). Here I frequently combine the two, defining as "frisk" as either being patted down for a weapon, searched, or both.

As noted earlier, one reason for gathering all this new information on stops was to enable the external monitor agreed to by the city and the ACLU to assess the conformity of stops with *Terry* and other legal criteria. Earlier, the concerns of many observers of the Chicago scene included the very large number of stops being made, plus a lack of confidence that this many appropriate circumstances for making a constitutional stop were presenting themselves. As one officer put it, on a local police blog:

> In the old contact card system, officers did not even write down what was the reasonable suspicion or probable cause to stop the person. They just wrote "subject stopped for field interview, a protective pat-down revealed suspect cannabis." What the fQ#k, man!!!! (July 1, 2017)

Only the monitor had access to officers' narrative statements regarding their reasonable suspicions and probable causes. However, the remaining data reveal a much richer profile of "the new stop & frisk." The new data details their frequency, contributes to our understanding of their efficiency, and raises equity questions regarding their distribution.

Overall, between 2016 and 2018 (during more than 500,000 stops), 42 percent of the subjects of stop & frisk experienced the frisk part of the city's stops regime. Pat-downs (33 percent of all stops) were more common than full searches (17 percent), for which the Supreme Court requires a claim that there was probable cause to believe a crime had been committed. As Table 6-1 documents, frisk rates varied by race. Less than 30 percent of Whites, but 44 percent of African Americans and 45 percent of Hispanics were recorded being frisked. These differences were driven by the more discretionary

Table 6-1 What Happened During Stop & Frisks?

	Total	Subject Race		
		Whites	Blacks	Hispanics
Who was frisked?				
No frisk, question only	58	71	56	55
Pat-down	33	20	34	35
Pat-down only	25	15	26	27
Searched	17	14	18	17
Frisked, pat-down or search	42	29	44	45
What did they find?				
Everyone stopped				
Nothing	94	95	94	96
Any contraband*	6	5	6	6
Found a gun (subset)	1	1	2	1
Everyone frisked				
Nothing	86	83	86	88
Any contraband*	14	17	14	12
Found a gun (subset)	3	2	4	3
Enforcement action taken?				
None	73	78	72	77
Any action	27	22	28	23
Arrest	14	12	15	13
Other non-arrest	13	10	14	10
Number of stops 2016–2018	500,197	43,400	358,099	93,966

Column percentages.

Column for total subjects includes persons of other races.

Contraband excludes marijuana and alcohol (see text).

Other non-arrest includes ANOVs, citations, and other actions.

suspicion pat-down for weapons. A key point is that a larger proportion of African Americans (26 percent) and Hispanics (27 percent) than of Whites (15 percent) were patted down but *not* searched. This signals that an initial inspection did not reveal a weapon *and* there was no apparent ground to proceed to a full search. These pat-down-only stops constituted 60 percent of all frisks. They could be described as unsuccessful hunts for weapons, and they were much more likely to involve racial minorities. Searches, presumably triggered by either probable cause, the discovery of a weapon during a pat-down, or the realization by officers they had a wanted person on their hands (see below), were much more evenly distributed, all in the 14-to-18 percent range.

Were They Quality Stops?

Did the new attention to stop & frisk, promises by the police to pay more attention to their legally required and agreed-upon standards for stops, and new monitoring of their performance promote good quality stops? One evaluative question regarding Chicago's program is how effective stops were at turning up guns and other forms of contraband. The ISR form enabled officers to account for the seizure of drugs (with some subtypes), drug paraphernalia, guns and other weapons, stolen property, alcohol, or "other" contraband. The table below excludes alcohol because the bulk of those stopped were over 21 years of age; in total, under one percent of stops involved contraband alcohol. It also excludes marijuana possession cases. Marijuana arrests in Chicago peaked back in 2007. By 2015, the last year of "old" stop & frisk, they had dropped by more than 50 percent, and by 2018 were down to only one-sixth of their former high. Marijuana consumption in Illinois was well on its way to being legal, and officers had long been encouraged to focus on serious possession-for-sale cases. In total, three percent of stops turned up marijuana. Other illegal drugs (at two percent) remain in the contraband category.

The figures presented in the middle of Table 6-1 (under "what did they find?") constitute the stop & frisk "hit rate"; in this case, the likelihood a stop resulted in the identification of contraband. This is a widely examined number. Low hit rates are frequently taken as evidence that stop & frisk is ineffective on its face. Over this three-year period, overall hit rates (seizures as a percentage of all stops) were low, six percent overall and for all groups.

However, since most Chicagoans were questioned but not frisked, this may not be the most important number. Another number to watch is what police find when they do pat-down or search someone; otherwise, they are unlikely to come across guns, knives, drugs or drug paraphernalia, or small stolen items of high value.

Variations in stop & frisk hit rates are often interpreted as evidence of possible discriminatory targeting by police. That is, when a bigger percentage of White subjects are frisked and discovered to be in possession of contraband, this is viewed as evidence Whites were more appropriately targeted for stops, thus accounting for their less frequent yet more productive stops. Lower hit rates for African Americans and others imply they were being swept up more indiscriminately. This is not exactly what we see in Chicago, during the new stop & frisk era. When White targets of stops were frisked, 17 percent of them were outside the law. For African Americans and Hispanics, the comparable figure was 14 percent and 12 percent, respectively. I judge the hit-rate difference between 17 percent (for Whites) and 14 percent (for African Americans) to be small.

Table 6-1 also presents a separate tabulation of gun seizures during stop & frisk. Shootings lie at the heart of Chicago's crime problem and keeping guns off the street should be one of the central missions of all of city government. This was the main rationale advanced for the tremendous increase in stops during the 2010s, and here the picture shifts somewhat. Although the percentages were small—between one and two percent of stops—guns *were* being seized. I did the math using exact figures, and over the period of 2016–2018 the gun recoveries reported from stop & frisks accounted for just over 7,000 firearms. According to their internal data, over this period the Chicago police seized 19,580 guns, so stop & frisk could have accounted for a large percentage—35 percent—of all the firearms taken off the street.[3] That's a lot, even if it is only approximately correct. Gun seizure totals need to factor into any assessment of stop & frisk.

A final evaluative dimension for stop & frisk is a broad "hit rate," the proportion of those stopped who were subject to arrest, ticketing, and other enforcement actions. The middle rows of Table 6-1 document that, in total, 14 percent of those who were stopped were shifted out of the innocent category because of contraband uncovered during frisks and full searches. However, there were other reasons why people fell from grace. Some were stopped because of what police call "on view" incidents, which means they saw them do it. Others turned up on wanted lists when officers checked their status online. Some stops involved pulling over suspects' cars, and traffic, licensing, or insurance coverage infractions could be identified (but there were not many of these). The bottom panel in Table 6-1 reports the percentage of persons stopped during 2016–2018 who faced enforcement action. Overall, 14 percent of those stopped were arrested, in roughly equal proportions for those of all races. An almost equal number, 13 percent, were ticketed, issued an ANOV, or had some other enforcement action taken against them. In general, enforcement actions during stop & frisks were more likely to involve African Americans by at most six percentage points.

So, by the broadest measure, which was whether they led to enforcement action of any type, about one-quarter of stops in Chicago during 2016–2018 were successful. It could be informative to compare this to the effectiveness of stop regimes in other cities, but that turns out to be difficult. Studies of hit rates vary greatly in what is counted as a stop and what is counted as a hit. The most comparable figures I could find were from New York City and Great Britain. The Chicago enforcement percentage was considerably higher than in New York City during the 2004–2012 period. There, 11 percent of stops resulted in an arrest or a citation of any sort, in contrast to 27 percent in Chicago. Lennon and Murray (2018) report the 2013–2014 one-year hit rate for searches in England and Wales was 12 percent, when measured by whether an arrest was made. In Chicago, 14 percent of those stopped were arrested. Scotland, on the other hand, measured success more broadly, by whether a "potentially actionable offense" was detected. By this measure their hit rate was 19 percent, but Lennon and Murray think this was significantly inflated by including very frequent but not separately recorded confiscations of openly carried alcohol. Public drinking is the bane of Scotland. In Chicago, the most comparable number was somewhat larger, 27 percent. Many other studies report numbers less suitable for making comparisons. For example, Epp and Erhardt (2020) looked at searches conducted during traffic stops in a middle-sized, mid-Atlantic city. They argued the rules surrounding these searches are like those for Terry stops. Their traffic stop hit rate, the percentage of searches yielding contraband, was 27 percent, which was about twice the comparable Chicago number, 14 percent. Focusing on the most comparable cases, Chicago's post-2016 stop & frisk regime looked at least as effective as elsewhere, but three-quarters of stops still turned out to have been unwarranted.

Finally, we would like to know if the new, post-2016 stop & frisk regime in Chicago was an improvement on the past. Many fewer people were being stopped, and it is possible this resulted from the more judicious use of officers' discretionary powers. Because of the changes in data collection mandated by the state legislature and agreed-to by the city and the ACLU, we know much more about the post-2015 period than the decade preceding it. One tantalizing comparison can be made: the percentage of *all* stops (thus bringing in enforcement stops) resulting in actual enforcement opportunities. This hit-rate measure stood at 27 percent for the new stop & frisk period, based on administrative data. For stops during 2015, the community survey described in the last chapter yielded its own hit-rate measure, based on reports by those who were involved. It was 25 percent. By this benchmark, while far fewer stops were being made in the new era, they were just as unselective.

The Fate of Stop & Frisk

After more than 50 months of rapid growth following the election of Rahm Emanuel and the arrival of his new chief of police, stop & frisks in Chicago dropped by almost 85 percent in a matter of weeks. This was a strategic, not tactical, withdrawal. Stops dropped virtually everywhere in the city, at about the same precipitous pace, and they remained many fewer in number for several more years. Other enforcement strategies picked up in volume, helping to eventually fill much of the quantitative gap.

The collapse of stop & frisk was driven by a confluence of events. Some were triggered by the dramatic release of a video documenting the killing of a young man late at night on an empty street, encircled by a squad of officers. But as many of the political and policy consequences of the event were in reaction to its elaborate (and expensive) coverup by civic leaders and the city's law enforcement executives. By the end of the first day, demonstrators were on the streets chanting "16 shots and a coverup." It was a very Chicago moment.

Cracks opened almost immediately in the establishment. Within days the mayor's political calculations led him to sacrifice his police chief, and the head of his civilian review body—who had been very effective at his job of finding little fault in the police department—also rolled down the steps of city hall. Others followed. His own party machinery and the voters who had just returned him to office turned against the next culpable public official who had to face them in this new political environment. Other forms of community pushback emerged quickly, as protesters confronted holiday shopping crowds.

Media attention to these events spiked even more quickly. When it comes to police policies and practices, local media can play an important role in setting the agenda for public discussion and the issues leaders need to respond to. In Chicago at the end of 2015, these were not abstract events in far-away Washington, D.C. Things had gone dramatically awry, and public officials known to voters had fallen down on the job. Media coverage of local policing went up, and over the long haul stayed up by 20 percentage points. Local opinion polling documented those assessments of the Chicago police were negative, and that support for the mayor had tanked.

We also saw ample evidence of the involvement of a wide-ranging policing "policy community" involved in both imposing new rules and fostering sustained attention and energy on police reform. Taking active roles in the Police Accountability Task Force were corporate lawyers and their firms, civil liberties activists, policy advocates (including, for example, for the mentally ill), foundation staffers, law professors, former prosecutors, heads of service providing organizations, serving public officials (the city's Inspector General and county Public Defender), retired police officers, and even a former Governor of Massachusetts. (Deval Patrick of Massachusetts was born in Chicago's perhaps most beleaguered public housing project, Robert Taylor Homes.) Surrounding them was a network of data-driven journalists and reform advocates, academics, and other researchers with data and evaluation experience to contribute. Local foundations paid their bills. During the federal investigation that came next, the state's Attorney General played a pivotal role in preventing the mayor from securing a sweetheart deal with the Trump administration, and then in securing agreement on a long and expensive reform agenda that rested in the hands of a federal judge and his court-appointed monitor.

Yet more constraints were piled on the Chicago police, and they came into effect precisely as stop & frisk collapsed. During the previous summer the ACLU secured an agreement with the police and the city requiring new and more extensive police training, audits of officer performance, and promises of changes in the department's disciplinary system. Their analyses and reports had for years played a significant role in keeping the constitutionality of stop & frisk alive on the policy agenda. An important item in their agreement was a commitment to recording stop & frisks in a manner facilitating external scrutiny of policing practices in Chicago. A monitor was agreed on who would submit regular public reports on stop & frisk. He would also keep an eye on other elements of the agreement between the ACLU and the city, including the appropriateness of the department's policies and its actual compliance with agreed-upon changes in police training. With some irksome redactions, stop & frisk data also became available to the public and various journalist and watchdog groups that have emerged in the world of Big Data. The state legislature weighed in with new requirements of its own. Passed earlier in the year, these would take effect on the same date as the policies extracted by the ACLU. In policing, state laws have real heft. In the sections relevant here, this legislation imposed significant data collection requirements, mandating that officers complete a detailed ISR recording what happened during many police–citizen encounters. For Chicago, the city's agreement with the ACLU extended this requirement to all stops.

Finally, in his newly crafted role as reformer, Mayor Rahm Emmanuel raised funds from private sources to support the creation of crime analyses centers within district police stations. Their mission was to put more cops at crime hotspots, and in more timely fashion. He found money for more tasers; recall Laquan McDonald was killed while officers were waiting for one to be delivered to them in the middle of the night. He also outfitted most of the department with body-worn cameras. These were widely touted as *the* technological fix for police encounters with the public. Their place among the policing reforms pursued by the Chicago police will be considered in Chapter 8, which considers alternative models for stop & frisk.

7

The Great Crime Spike of 2016

> No question about it, violent crime will go up if stop and frisk is
> abandoned by the NYPD . . . [and] this is not just a New York City
> issue, it's an issue throughout America.
>
> —Commissioner Raymond Kelly
> New York City Police Department[1]

Even as the city was still reeling from the impact of scandal, leadership collapse, new investigations into the inner workings of government, and rising challenges to the very legitimacy of the police, a new crisis arrived: The Great Crime Spike of 2016. Almost immediately, shootings and killings began to skyrocket. When the year was totaled up, almost 4,600 people had been shot. The number of shootings almost doubled from the year before and was up by 62 percent from the more placid 2014. Murders went from 478 (which was high-normal for the past dozen years) to 769.

Of course, the question on everyone's mind was "why?" Journalists, bloggers, and ordinary citizens looked for a culprit. Many suspects were identified, and bits of evidence were assembled against them. Among the prime suspects was stop & frisk. Described by its supporters as the city's first line of defense against guns and drugs, its collapse was quickly linked to the emerging spike in gun violence. This chapter looks in some detail at the post-2016 crime spike because upwellings of violence are often a feared possible consequence of cutbacks in traditional policing. Discussions in the 2020s of potentially de-funding, down-sizing, re-focusing, or otherwise significantly reforming the police inevitably brought that concern again to the front pages. In Chicago, the 2016 spike proved to be not a general upwelling of crime, but a very specific jump in unsolved, heavily concentrated, gun violence. Stop & frisk had been the response to that problem, so the question of its effectiveness stayed on the front pages.

Stop & Frisk and the Politics of Crime in Chicago. Wesley G. Skogan, Oxford University Press.
© Oxford University Press 2023. DOI: 10.1093/oso/9780197675052.003.0007

This leads to one of the questions central to this book: what was the impact of stop & frisk on gun violence? This is complicated to answer. Stop & frisk needs to be set within the context of a much larger set of national events, local police activities, and social and environmental trends. As noted elsewhere, cities and police departments have lots of moving parts, and stop & frisk is just one of them. The goal was to estimate the impact of this crime-deterrent strategy over the 180 months of Chicago history this book encompasses. This is an appropriate *policy* question, for the findings thus generalize across administrations, shifts in violent crime, and changing conditions (as they always change) in the city. The chapter comes to the uncomfortable-for-some conclusion that stops did have deterrent value but (uncomfortable for others) only a moderate one. It's effect, which is reported here, turns out to lie well within the range of other proactive policing interventions that have been carefully and positively evaluated. This is a range within which possible tradeoffs among proven policing strategies *and* with other values can be debated. Should it be stop & frisk, or something(s) else? The findings leave room on the debate stage for important social and political questions about the conduct and impact of stop & frisk.

The Spike

The year 2016 was a spike. To put it in perspective, Figure 7-1 traces the murder rate in Chicago from 1934. It describes crime *rates* because over this period the population of the city dropped considerably. Figure 7-1 reports population totals at key points along the timeline. In 1958 the city was home to 3.6 million people, but by 2016 it had slumped to 2.7 million residents. Visible is 1974, a horrific year recording the most killings in the city's history. The 1974 murder rate was four times that of 1958. This was a period dominated by a drug epidemic and huge, highly organized gangs claiming control of many city streets. However, the peak year for the murder rate was 1992, when the homicide count hit 940 but the city had shrunk by another 400,000 residents. That year, the murder rate was *five times* the rate in 1958, when the city was at its largest. Next came 2016. During the 2016 spike, the murder rate in Chicago stood at about 29 per 100,000 residents. This was off a bit from its historic highs but stood close to some unattractive benchmarks. During 2016, the city's murder rate approached that of Brazil (also 29 per 100,000) and Guatemala (27 per 100,000). By contrast, during the height of the Al Capone era in the 1920s, Chicago's murder rate was around 12 per

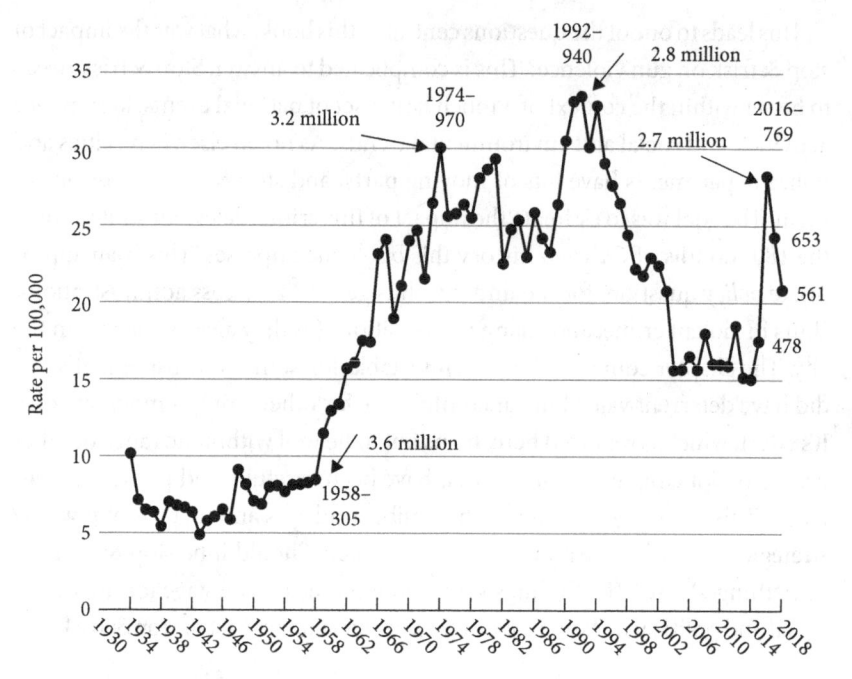

Figure 7-1 Chicago Murders Since 1934

100,000. The murder count during 2016 was 769, up from what seemed to be the new normal a year earlier, 478.[2] That was a 61 percent increase, in one year. Every month during 2016 the body count was higher than in the same month in 2015. It was a spike.

The Spike Was in Gun Crime

One of the notable features of the spike was that it was largely confined to gun violence. Figure 7-2 contrasts trends in gun and non-gun murder. It is apparent that during the spike non-gun murders followed their own trajectory, plugging along at a low rate. It was the gun murder count that soared in 2016. In 2014 (prior to the summer 2015 homicide "pre-spike" depicted in Figure 7-2), 408 homicides involved a firearm; during 2016 it was 690, a 69 percent increase. Figure 7-2 also presents the post-spike trend in the larger measure of gun violence—shootings. In parallel with homicides, shootings spiked during 2016. The number of shooting victims grew from just under

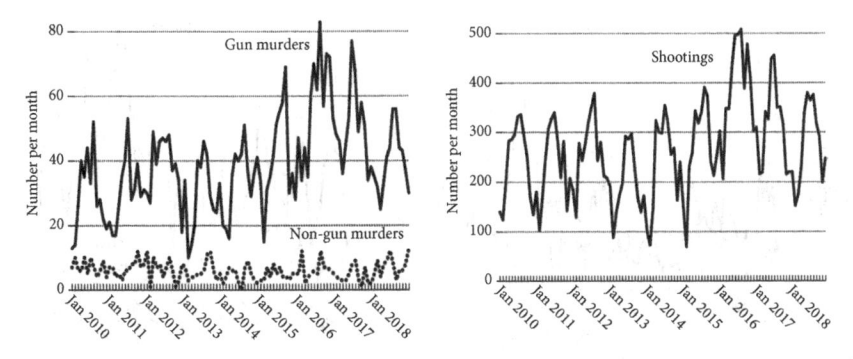

Figure 7-2 Trends in Gun and Non-gun Violence 2010–2018

3,000 to more than 4,600 in just one year. The crime spike was not across the board, however. The general rule was, like homicide, if a gun was involved, crime spiked. Otherwise, not so much. Aggravated assaults involving a gun went up by 61 percent, while those limited to physical attacks or weapons such as knives went up by only seven percent.

The fact that gun robberies increased alongside other forms of gun violence suggests the increase in 2016 and beyond was not driven exclusively by gang feuds or altercations, as robberies generally have a financial motive. Carrying a gun opens opportunities for crimes such as robbery and rape. On the other hand, one of Chicago's murder mysteries is that many other acquisitive crimes did not spike, and in fact continued to decline. Burglary in 2016 was lower than in 2014, and then dropped again in 2017 and 2018. Car theft reached decade lows in 2017 and 2018. In this sense, the public was right to focus on scary gun crimes because they were the ones spiking.

The Spike was in Unsolved Crime

Beginning in 2016 there was a further collapse in Chicago's inability to solve shootings and killings. Unsolved offenses drove the spike in crime. Figure 7-3 charts trends in solved and unsolved murders (on the left) and solved versus unsolved shootings (on the right) over this period. It depicts the magnitude of the spike in unsolved crime. During the 2010–2014 period the city solved about 33 percent of its murders. The August 2015 pre-spike drove this down only slightly; however, during 2016 the solution rate for murder in the city was only 23 percent: 180 solved murders and 586 unsolved ones. The

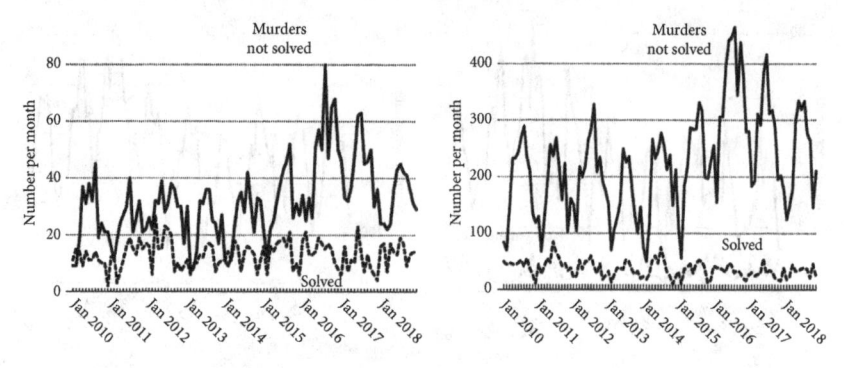

Figure 7-3 Solved and Unsolved Murders and Shootings 2010–2018

following year the murder clearance rate dropped further, to only 19 percent. As noted in Chapter 2, Chicago police have never done very well when it comes to solving shootings, but the spike beginning in 2016 hugely exacerbated this problem. The number of solved shootings grew not at all as their numbers skyrocketed, dropping the shooting clearance rate to only 8.8 percent during 2016 and nine percent the following year. Between 2015 and 2016, unsolved aggravated assaults jumped by 35 percent, while the solved ones went *down* slightly. In Chicago, people were getting away with murder, and even more were getting away with trying.

A corollary of this decline in crime clearance is that it leaves us with more of a murder mystery than before. With clearance as low as nine percent (for shootings during 2017), it is hard to say much about offenders. Who did it? Why did they do it? Is one incident linked to others? Who else knows they did it? Where did they get their gun? When the public and policy makers pressed for *reasons* for the crime spike, the best they could get was a reading of tea leaves. But the sheer fact that no one (relative to the past) was being caught could provide an important clue regarding the spike itself. As the spike rose, deterrence should scarcely have been a part of anyone's crime calculations. The standard model of policing, which we have seen was already under stress, was not holding offenders to account.

Violence Remained Concentrated

The bulk of the crime spike was concentrated in just a few Chicago neighborhoods. Ranking Chicago's community areas from highest to the lowest, the top six of 77 contributed 50 percent of the 2014–2016 crime spike. North Lawndale's murder count rose by 162 percent. The top 13 community areas (adding just seven more) accounted for more than 75 percent of the spike. In contrast to the highest crime areas, the 13 communities at the bottom of the list actually subtracted 29 murders. The crime hotspot we encountered in Chapter 2—the five-by-five block area constituting census block group 2315/6—remained hot. It was still among the top five percent of shooting locations citywide, and by 2018 it had claimed this distinction for 27 straight years. Between 1991 and 2018 380 people were shot there, and the area topped the city over the entire period with a total of 83 murders.

Concentrated meant the increase in shootings and killings was largely confined to predominately African American neighborhoods. There were other correlates of the crime spike, most of them very similar to the factors related to higher levels of neighborhood crime generally. Comparing crime rates for 2016 with 2014, violence rose more in lower-income census tracts with a larger youth population, in places where people rented rather than owned their homes, where education levels were low, and in the midst of a lot of abandoned buildings. But race was highly correlated with all these factors.

Figure 7-4 traces trends in violence during the 2010s. As in Chapter 2, census tracts were clustered by the predominate race of the area, and victimization rates were calculated per 10,000 residents of each grouping. The needle moved slightly in the city's most racially diverse areas (predominately including Hispanic, White, and Asian residents) in 2016. The impact of the spike on predominately White census tracts was imperceptible; the number of murders there grew from 17 in 2014 to 19 in 2016. The spike in violence was more pronounced in concentrated Hispanic neighborhoods,

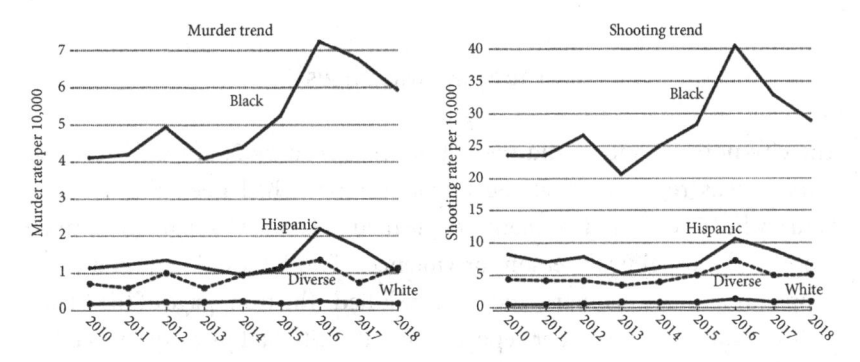

Figure 7-4 Murder and Shooting Rates by Race 2010–2018

where homicides more than doubled. But as is apparent in Figure 7-4, the vast bulk of shootings and killings in Chicago remained concentrated in the African American community. In the first year of the spike, 72 percent of all homicides took place in African American neighborhoods. Looking just at the increase in shootings and killings, fully 75 percent of it was concentrated in the African American community. Any analysis of increasing and decreasing crime in Chicago must take into account conditions there.

The Spike Receded Slowly

Another feature of the spike is it did not fade away in a few months. That is the fate of many apparent crime spikes, usually within a few weeks or months. But after three years, homicides and shootings still stood above their early-2010s high. While the monthly shootings count reached its peak (at just over 500 incidents) in August 2016, the weekend beginning the evening of August 3, 2018 saw 75 people shot, 13 of them fatally. On that Sunday (which began after midnight on Saturday night), 47 were shot. This was the worst weekend for shootings in almost a decade. Between 2016 and 2018 Chicago lost the benefit of winter. Shootings no longer fell to a comparably low level during the coldest months. In 2015, May was the first month counting more than 300 shootings; in 2016, there were 302 shootings in January. During 2014 the highest homicide month was August, while in 2016 there was an identical number of murders in January. Tracking where the spike receded reveals the decline was greater in better-off census tracts. Compared to 2014, by 2018 the shooting rate was down the most in predominately White, lower-poverty, home-owning areas well-stocked with senior citizens.

The Spike was News

The city noticed, and so did the nation. By February 2, 2016, the *Chicago Tribune* was reporting that the previous month had been the deadliest January in 16 years, and "as many people died in January as in many summer months, the usual peak season for violence." Two hundred and ninety-two people were shot in January, and 51 were killed. The front page of the March 1, 2016 edition of the paper reported that the city had just experienced its "most deadly start to the year" (now 95 homicides) in two decades. They labeled it "a spike." On April 1, the *Tribune* forecast the city might hit 500 murders for the year, and noted it was outpacing New York and Los Angeles. During the three-day Memorial Day weekend in May, 69 people were shot, six fatally. July 3 brought new reporting arithmetic; the front page of the *Tribune* reported the city was averaging "10 shootings a day," and added Chicago now had more homicides than New York and Los Angeles combined. By August the city's other news outlets had already written the year off. "Chicago writes another violent chapter in a year full of anguish," reported the *Chicago Sun Times* on August 8: "The city's bloody 2016 crossed another tragic line this weekend," when nine people were killed on the same day. A local online news source declared "Bloody July Sees Spike in Chicago Gun Violence as Shootings Up 45 Percent" (*DNA Chicago*, August 2, 2016). In September, Presidential candidate Donald Trump described Chicago as a "war-torn country" during his first debate with challenger Hillary Clinton.

Local opinion polls also dug into the issues involved. What they found was a mix of concern about policing and crime. A poll conducted by the *Chicago Tribune* found a record-low approval rating for Mayor Rahm Emanuel's handling of crime. Approval of his leadership had dropped from 45 percent in polls conducted during 2012 and 2013, to 19 percent in January 2016 (*Chicago Tribune*, February 23, 2016). A *New York Times* poll conducted in April 2016 asked residents, "What is the single biggest problem facing Chicago today?" Almost everyone's responses fell into the "crime/violence/gangs" category. Education (11 percent) and the economy (13 percent) were serious contenders only among White Chicagoans, 35 percent of whom stuck to crime. Among African Americans crime was given top billing (at 63 percent), and among Hispanics it was 60 percent. Concern about crime did not divert city residents from the issue of police reform, however. Asked if the new police superintendent should focus more on reducing crime or on reforming the way the police department operates, African Americans, Whites, and Hispanics all put police reform at the top of their list. A January 2016 poll discovered "a strong majority of Chicagoans don't think the city's cops treat all citizens fairly and believe a cover-up "code of silence" is widespread in the Police Department (*Chicago Tribune*, February 23, 2016).

It should be no surprise that in this agitated environment many explanations were advanced to account for the spike. Several reflected the interests of the claimants. They included the police union with a political agenda, social service providers in search of contracts, victim advocates with experiences to relate, out-of-office politicians seeking a place, and leaders of critical social movements. Having a concrete stake in their explanations does not mean they were wrong. Rather, they often reflected what claimants hoped to *do* about the situation, by securing funding and applying their organizations' solutions to the problem. Explanations by local criminologists reflected generations of research on the causes and correlates of crime. These proved remarkably un-useful, because their research usually focuses on conditions (such as neighborhood poverty, or racism) which change only in the long term (Rosenfeld, 2018). A crime spike is rapid, falls outside the normal range of events, and is usually unanticipated. Spikes can be difficult to explain.

Was it Stop & Frisk?

Despite the confident analysis of the New York City Police Commissioner quoted at the top of this chapter, research presents a mixed and frequently modest portrait of the impact of stops on crime. Unfortunately, a great deal of everyday discussion of this question draws its evidence from looking at yearly trends in crime and stops. New York is a favorite specimen for examination because a large decline in crime there followed the launch of an aggressive stop & frisk program. But this is not much evidence. Stops are only one slice of police activity, in Chicago and elsewhere. In Chicago, other efforts frequently associated with crime reduction did not falter, and an aggressive program of traffic stops quickly ramped up as stop & frisk hit bottom. We have just seen violence itself also changed in character, evolving in directions leading it to be more lethal and more difficult to police. The neighborhoods were not standing still, either; in Chicago, this is easily evident in its declining African American population. And back in New York City, crime continued to drop even after the city abandoned its stop & frisk initiative following 2013.

However, arguments that the causal link between stops and crime is obvious because one set of numbers went up as the other went down plagued discussions of crime in Chicago, as well as New York City. The tie between the two appeared clear to many looking at trends in stops and violence. Figure 7-5 provides a detailed closeup of trends in stop & frisks (on the left axis) and shootings (on the right axis—they are many fewer in number). As in Chapter 6, these numbers are comparable across time. We have already described the decline in stops; they totaled about 529,300 unwarranted adult

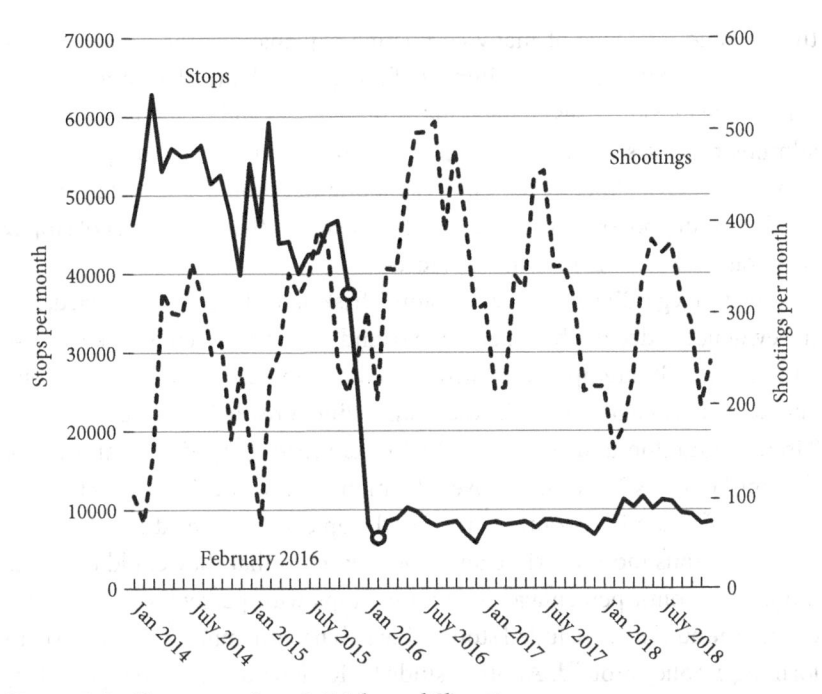

Figure 7-5 Closeup on Stop & Frisks and Shootings

stops in 2015, but only 66,000 in 2016, a drop of 82 percent. At the same time, shootings went from 3,180 to 4,600—a 45 percent increase. Murders jumped by 42 percent in just a year. Stops went down, violent crime went up—case closed! As a police blogger put it at the time, in reference to the negotiated agreement between police and the American Civil Liberties Union, "ACLU got exactly what they asked for—less stops. Now deal with it. Less stops equals more crime—it's as simple as that. The blood is on ACLU" (June 16, 2016). A somewhat measured academic analysis agreeing with this conclusion dubbed the 2016 spike in homicides as "the ACLU effect" (Cassell and Fowles, 2018). A representative of the ACLU called their study "junk science." In Chicago, as elsewhere, views of stop & frisk were polarized.

The Impact of Stop & Frisk on Crime

Here we will examine in detail the impact of Chicago's stop & frisk strategy on crime. The findings are based on statistical analyses which controlled for the possible influence of many competing explanations for trends in violence to isolate the distinctive impact of a stop & frisk over 180 months. This time frame encompasses changes in the preferences and strategies of various administrations, shifts in the character of violent crime (including declining clearance rates), shifts in the city's demographic profile, and deteriorating conditions in poorer parts of the city. The answer is that the impact of stop & frisk was between eight and nine percent.

Research regarding the impact of stop & frisk on violent crime is varied, and the evidence is decidedly mixed. One strand of this research is—like here— correlational. It attempts to control for competing explanations of the ebb and flow of crime over time. These studies differ greatly in their approaches. Tiratelli, Quinton and Bradford (2018) examined merged stop and crime data for London's 31 boroughs over 108 months (it was a "fixed-effects panel regression" analysis). Monthly crime and stop counts were adjusted relative to the previous month's crime and stop counts so that they could correlate month-to-month percentage changes in stops with percentage changes in crime. The authors concluded stop and search had no impact on crime worth forming a policy around. Another study by Rosenfeld and Fornango (2014) examined yearly rates of robbery and burglary for New York City's 75 police precincts. They controlled for precinct measures of immigration and population turnover. They concluded there were no statistically significant effects of stops on various measures of crime.

Closer to home, Cassell and Fowles (2018) reported a regression analysis of 60 months of citywide data on stops and crime in Chicago. They concluded the 2016 decline in stop & frisk, compared to the four years before, led to an additional 245 murders and 851 non-fatal shootings that year. These were headline numbers. There are significant differences between their project and mine, including in the length of the time series (60, versus 180 months), the scope of the control factors included (10, compared to 21), and the statistical approach employed (see below). Perhaps most significantly, their analysis involved only one stop & frisk collapse year, 2016. As we have seen, shootings and killings in Chicago trended back downward during 2017 and 2018. At the same time, stops remained down by about 80 percent, the character of violent crime continued to evolve, and police pursued other crime prevention tactics—notably traffic stops. Another study of Chicago using an entirely different methodology attributed a spike of 18 murders per month during the first six months of 2016 to "de-policing and civilian behavior simultaneously changing" (Ba and Rivera, 2019, p. 1). However, Ba and Rivera examined no actual measures of the extent of policing, and the "citizen behavior" they linked to the crime spike was measured by complaints against the police (which went up). It is hard to know how the latter caused a lot of crime in a few months. Importantly, robbery and assault rates during the same period were not significantly affected by this presumed de-policing. It is hard to know why policing would affect some crimes and not others in the same personal crime category.

A second strand of research on crime and stops examines the impact of policing strategies on crime in geographical units, such as police districts, and compares what happened there over time with trends in similar areas which experienced only police business as usual. In recent decades the best of these studies were fielded in multiple program and comparison areas, and random selection was used to decide which areas receive which kind of policing. To increase the analytic power of these experiments, typically all the study areas are, to some degree, crime hotspots. A problem for comparing the findings of these experiments to the Chicago case is that what police do in selected special study enforcement areas is typically highly varied and the actual dosage they deliver is badly documented and often went unmeasured. In reports of these projects, police are described as having engaged in "saturation policing," "directed patrol," "increased patrol," "dedicated patrols," "car checks," and "problem solving." Often the intervention is described as "more of all [of] the above." Usually, they do not reveal *how much* was done, an important policy and cost detail. In a systematic review of the findings of 62 experimental and quasi-experimental evaluations of policing interventions, Braga, et al. (2019, p. 289) concluded that there was "a *small* [my emphasis] statistically significant mean effect size favoring the effects of hot spots policing in reducing crime outcomes at treatment places relative to control places." They also report problem solving strategies were a bit more effective than the remaining mixture of traditional proactive policing. However, except for problem-solving policing, there were not enough evaluations of individual strategies to say anything about their specific effectiveness.

Other stop & frisk studies are cross-sectional and correlational, looking at geographical variations in stops and their correlation with area levels of crime during one slice in time. Some are quite sophisticated. For example, Weisburd, et al. (2016) concluded that during New York City's peak year, stop & frisks accounted for a two percent decrease in crime citywide. There are also "difference in difference" studies of the issue relying on sharp breaks or policy changes to examine before–after changes in patterns of police activity and crime across areas such as police precincts (for an example see Sullivan and O'Keefe, 2017). A study in this tradition by MacDonald, Fagan and Geller (2016) concluded New York City stops based on probable cause were associated with more arrests and lower rates of crime in hot spot zones. However, stops without any enforcement potential were not linked to more arrests—not surprisingly—or less crime. They report that New York City was emphasizing non-productive stops, dragging down the overall effectiveness of their strategy. Geographic studies are quite distinct from the time series approach used here, relying mainly on variations in crime and stops across places during narrower timeframes.

A good summary of all this research on police interventions in hot spot neighborhoods appeared in the National Research Council's 2018 report, *Proactive Policing: Effects on Crime and Communities* (Weisburd and Majmundar, 2018). A takeaway from both the report and the Braga et al. (2019) systematic review is that there is plenty of evidence police can deter crime when they focus their efforts intelligently, but in the absence of more specific guidance from research, decisions about exactly what those enforcement efforts should be, how much effort should be invested in them, and if they could be paid for, remain almost entirely political choices.

This Project

This Chicago analysis is decidedly non-experimental. Instead, it relies on "naturally occurring"—in other words, initiated by the police—variation in stops and many other police activities and community trends. The major problem with this is that, under many circumstances, police activity is positively correlated with stops. This does not mean cops cause crime. Rather, at any moment crime is, to a significant degree, causing the distribution of stops. Cops gravitate toward the dots on their crime maps. Officers are sent to locations where crime has spiked, perhaps only the night before. More generally, all reactive policing is driven by crime. Squad cars speed to the scene in response to victims' calls. Planners in headquarters pour over crime patterns when drawing beat boundaries and deciding how many officers to assign to districts long-term. In research terms, stops can be "endogenous" to crime, determining how, when, and where stops are distributed. The experimental studies described above are one solution to this problem. For further discussion of these issues, plus other approaches to the problem, see Wu, Koper and Lum (2021).

One strength of strategy employed here for estimating the impact of stop & frisk on crime is both crime and stops varied a great deal over time. We are not looking for the effect of a policy that changed only incrementally, or at slowly shifting trends in crime. Another aspect of this approach is that it encompasses the *entire* 180-month span of organized stop & frisk to the end of this project, rather than selecting a subset of years that might have implications for what is found. The goal is to make a general statement about stop & frisk, and data clustered just around a historical crime spike are unlikely to reveal one. Also, more data facilitates the inclusion of more theoretically and empirically important control factors—in this case 21 of them. However, perhaps the most important rationale for accepting a causal interpretation of the findings is that Chicago's stop & frisks were significantly policy- and event-driven. They did not go up and down just in response to crime. As documented in Chapters 3 and 6, some police chiefs were more devoted to them than others and were variously hounded by the media and their mayors to "do something," and elections kept coming up. Chapter 3 noted the simple correlation between de-seasoned stops and shootings was an almost non-existent +.03 between 2004 and 2015. Further, the collapse of stop & frisk at the end of 2015 was politically, legally, legislatively, and media driven. If anything, the 2016 spike in shootings called for more, rather than fewer, stops. Instead, stops dropped by more than 80 percent. Importantly, they *stayed down* in the face of shifting but still-high levels of violence persisting for the next three years. In Chicago, the push-and-pull relationship between violence and stops witnessed in other places was additionally shocked by many and complex external events.

The Measures

This analysis of stop & frisk is based on 180 months of data, from January 2004 to December 2018. This includes three full years of data following the collapse of stop & frisk. This section describes the measures employed and presents some detail about them. The discussion also touches on some of the numerous factors determining levels of crime not involving police actions. It highlights the many and diverse things police do to influence crime. There certainly was a great deal of continuing police activity over this entire period.

Even after the collapse of stop & frisk, officers were still coming to work and driving around their beats, and their supervisors were keeping them busy. Headquarters still demanded documentation of their activity. "Ending stop & frisk" meant officers were doing *something else* to fill their day. Discussing his new agreement with the ACLU, Superintendent McCarthy noted, "We expect police officers to do their job. They're collecting their salary, and we expect them to give an honest day's work for an honest day's salary" (Gorner, 2015) Any accounting of the effects of stop & frisk in Chicago has to incorporate the adoption of new policing tactics and the effects of officers shifting to other tried-and-true activities also targeting shootings and killings. To investigate these alternatives and find out how officers were filling their day required digging through many police activity databases.

A great deal of information on trends in police activity in Chicago can be found in data maintained by the city's communications center. Excluding a multitude of administrative matters, the Emergency Communications Center handled about 2.2 million incidents per year over the period from 2010 to 2018. Some were initiated by 911 calls from the public, but the database also tracks many events officers themselves observe and respond to (these are called "on view" incidents). They also radio in reports on actions resulting from the many missions their commanders send them on, and the problems they are assigned to deal with by dispatchers. Some decisions by officers, including issuing an order to a street gathering to disperse, require they radio in to obtain a special event number to include in their documentation. Beginning in 2020 (which was outside the scope of this study), they were required to call in whenever they pointed their gun at a citizen. In all, the Communications Center tracks 1,778 different kinds of officer activity, as well as citizen's reports of crime.

Early on, the 2016 spike in violence was widely attributed to Chicago police "going fetal." They were described as keeping their heads down and doing as little as possible. Their fetal status was attributed to a long list of factors. It was claimed officers did not want to become a news story and they were fearful of appearing in the next misconduct video. By early 2016, dashboard cameras were widespread and body cameras were on their way. However, "citizen cameras" were already a problem for them, and officers expressed concern about being captured by bystanders on smartphone video (Sweeney and Gorner, 2016). It was said officers were policing less aggressively because they feared being punished for making mistakes—which implies this was not a problem before!—and the about-to-be-reformed civilian review agency charged with looking into their use of force would be aggressive (same implication). They also did not like the many new rules imposed by the legislature's racial profiling and no-choking laws. As a police blogger posted in early 2016, "don't chase anyone and don't shoot at anyone unless they are shooting at you. Let them go. Everything will be turned against you for headlines or for lawsuits." Plenty of observers commented that new paperwork was plaguing the lives of officers, who did not enlist to be "paper-pushers" (Konkol, 2016). The new stop form required that they complete two pages documenting their reasonable suspicions and probable causes for making stops and conducting searches, and this was seen to be a great burden. Finally, inattention to duty was ascribed to bad morale among the rank-and-file. Disgust was frequently expressed with their own organization's leaders, who apparently gave in to pandering politicians and the media. We saw in Chapter 5 that in 2013 officers already thought they were not appreciated, and the public could not be trusted.

In this dispiriting environment, "de-policing"—a phenomenon already widely known as "The Ferguson Effect"—was claimed to be the order of the day. It was alleged that police withdrawing from the street during 2014 in Ferguson, Missouri because of complaints about them had led to widespread disorder and looting. This has led to a host of studies of media coverage, public opinion, crime, and de-policing (Capellan, Lautenschlager and Silvac, 2019; Shjarback and Maguire, 2021; Kochel, 2019). In Chicago, the now-former police chief alleged, "Why would you stop anyone if you're a police officer in Chicago today. Criminals are being empowered, and we're investigating police" (Hinz, 2017, p. 2). However, this review of 165 million indicators of policing activity from the 911 center did not find much evidence of a *general* collapse in enforcement efforts, nor in the many other important things police do on a daily basis. The tempo of policing picked up by many measures. Despite the collapse of stop & frisk, officers were otherwise mostly going on with their routine business, and some old routines—including traffic stops—were being pursued with much greater vigor.

Actions: Arrests and Dispersals. Arrests for crime and dispersals of loitering "toughs" provide perhaps the most direct link between police activity and crime deterrence. Durlauf and Nagin (2011) describe the threat of punishment as central to deterrence theory, noting that research documents that the deterrent effect of certainty of punishment is far stronger than the effects of its severity. Certainty includes the risk of apprehension, which can be communicated by personal encounters with police and by the visible presence of policing (Lum and Nagin, 2017). Because we are examining the impact of innocent stops on crime, arrests provide an important complimentary explanation for variations in crime needing to be considered. There are certainly many of them. Over the 2004–2018 period, Chicago police made millions of arrests of all kinds. These varied a great deal in number over time and had a shifting relationship with levels of stop & frisk, leaving their potential link to stops and crime an empirical question.

During 2004–2018, Chicago police made arrests on more than 2,418,000 occasions. Some of these doubtless stemmed from stop & frisk encounters, but the post-2016 data described in Chapter 6 suggests many more arrests were made by officers in response to 911 calls and during their investigations. By the end of 2015, arrests in almost every category had been dropping for a long time. Drug arrests peaked in 2005 at 5,000 per month, and eventually dropped to 1,000 per month. Earlier, most involved marijuana possession. In 2016, arrests began to drop at a faster rate. During the two years prior to the collapse of stop & frisk, Chicago police arrested an average of about 8,300 people per month; in 2016, the arrest total dropped by 28 percent, down by more than 2,300 arrests per month. Arrests lingered at this new low through the end of 2018. The statistical analyses reported here controlled separately for personal and property crime arrests, drug arrests, and arrests for disorderly conduct. The latter is a misdemeanor category which is used to clear the streets.

The final arrest type potentially playing a role in violent crime falls in the weapons violation category. Unlawful use of a weapon (UUW) typically is the most serious charge when a search reveals an unlicensed weapon but no other offense (such as a robbery or an assault) is associated with the incident. Over time, the correlation between violent crime and weapons offense arrests was positive (+.36 with shootings, between 2004 and 2018). This is consistent with the view that uncovering firearms is a measure of gun *carrying* in high crime areas, which in turn should generally be associated with the frequency of gun use. These arrests also reflect taking guns off the street, reducing opportunities for casual gun violence. Data on monthly gun *seizures* are available for the 2010–2018 period, and they are correlated +.89 with UUW arrests. Of course, gun enforcement efforts could also discourage people from carrying guns in the first place, a general deterrent effect. A study by McGarrell, Chermak and Weiss (2002) is just one of several documenting targeted gun enforcement can significantly reduce gun-related violence. In a systematic review of evaluations of deterrence strategies focusing on guns,

Braga and Weisburd (2015, p. 64) concluded that, as a group, they had a "strongly significant effect," that they judged "medium" in size and described as "relatively large compared with assessments of interventions in crime and justice work more generally." In Chicago, there was no noticeable letup in weapons arrests around the emergence of the crime spike. They averaged 3,310 per year during 2014–2015, and 3,660 during 2016–2017.

Chicago police also have the power to order people to move on. "Dispersals" have a long and politically charged history in Chicago. Following the violent summer of 1991 the City Council enacted a "Gang Congregation Ordinance." It made it an offense for "apparent gang members" (and anyone associated with them) to "remain in one place with no apparent purpose." If when ordered to move along they did not do so, they could be arrested (City of Chicago, 1992). There is only scattered evidence remaining of the number of times officers ordered people from the street, but in the early 1990s about 20,000 dispersal orders were issued each year, and about 10,000 persons were arrested annually. Finally, in 1999, the U.S. Supreme Court (in the case of *Chicago v. Morales*) found the statute "void for vagueness." Earlier, so had the Illinois Supreme Court. For a detailed political history of Chicago's loitering ordinance see Levi (2009).

But as the Gang Congregation Ordinance went away, the city created a new, more constitutionally defensible strategy for dealing with suspected gang loitering or narcotics-related loitering. It was not hard to convince many members the City Council to go along with it because they were hearing complaints from their constituents regarding threatening street activity by young toughs. However, most African American aldermen opposed the new measure, noting that their communities were bearing the brunt of this highly discretionary crackdown tactic (Roberts, 1999). Under the new ordinance, areas could be officially designated by the police as district crime hot-spots or high-level gang conflict locations. As instructed by a departmental order, officers are to "verbally inform all of the persons engaged in the gang loitering that they are doing so in an area where loitering by criminal street gangs is prohibited," and "order all such persons to disperse and remove themselves from sight and hearing of the place where the order was issued." Further, officers are to "inform those persons that they will be subject to arrest if they fail to obey the order promptly or return within sight or hearing of the location where the order was issued," and "arrest any persons who do not remove themselves in a prompt manner." Note loitering groups are defined as "two or more persons."[3]

Dispersals were most frequent before 2010, a period when shootings and killings were fewer in number. Between 2010 and 2015 about 180–280 dispersals were initiated every month, fluctuating with the weather. The number of arrests for noncompliance never approached those in the 1990s, but during 2013–2015, about 820 gang or drug loitering arrests were recorded each year. Then dispersals collapsed, in concert with the reduction in stop & frisk and in parallel with the spike in gun violence. Post-2016, the CPD issued only 50 or so dispersals monthly, and an average of only 170 individuals were arrested each year for drug or gang loitering during 2016–2016. Over the entire 2004–2018 period, the monthly frequency of dispersal orders was correlated –.22 with homicides and –.26 with shootings.

Actions: Crime Solvability. As we saw earlier, crime solvability collapsed in concert with the crime spike. The large drop in homicide and shooting clearance could well have signaled a falloff in the deterrent capacity of the criminal justice system, and research documents the likelihood of getting caught is a primary factor in choosing whether or not to commit crimes (Nagin, 2013). The possibility that police were not deterring anyone could also have contributed to more widespread carrying of guns for self-defense. In an interview study involving 195 young African American males from high-violence neighborhoods in Chicago, 50 percent reported having carried a gun, and 93 percent of them explained they did so for self-protection (Fontaine, et al., 2018). In their world, being prepared to shoot back—or better, shoot first—could be their best line of defense.

Although they later improved, during the first three months of 2016 the clearance rate for shootings dropped below *two percent*, and clearances for homicide below 17 percent (see Arthur and Asher, 2016). Monthly clearance rates were calculated from the clearance status of individual crime incidents. A crime was counted as solved if anyone was arrested for it, or if it was (as few were) administratively cleared. Care must be taken with clearances. This analysis avoids clogging the analysis with related numbers on both sides of the statistical analysis; for example, by regressing the number of shootings on the shooting clearance rate, which has the same shooting number in its denominator (for the problems this creates statistically see Bartlett and Partnoy, 2020). Instead, the model incorporates the *general* deterrent effect of solving crimes by examining the effect of broad measures of police effectiveness. For example, during 2014, prior to the crime spike, shootings made up only 20 percent of the violent crime count in the city; during the 2016 spike in shootings this fraction rose to 26 percent. This is a modest-enough overlap to justify including the solvability rate for violent crimes in general as an independent explanatory variable.

The final analysis model included the solvability rate for all personal crimes and major property crimes. Over time, personal crime clearance was correlated –.50 with homicides and –.53 with shootings. Between 2004 and 2015, the monthly personal crime solvability rate ranged from 28 to 38 percent but traced a stable line. During this period the shooting count remained stable as well. Then crime solvability dropped, and shootings skyrocketed. Between 2014 and 2016, the solution rate for shootings dropped from 16 percent to nine percent, and murders from 33 percent to 24 percent. The more general solvability measure used in the statistical analysis, one representing all personal crimes, dropped less sharply, from 32 to 24 percent. The sharp 2014–2016 decline was followed by a two-year period of steady recovery in clearances, and by a parallel decline in shootings. In short, the sharp drop in violent crime solvability and the erosion of deterrence this threatens remains a prime suspect in the story of the great Chicago crime spike. Higher property crime clearance rates were also negatively correlated with shootings and killings, but unlike personal crime clearances they did not drop following 2015. They were never high, averaging about 14 percent during the 2004–2015 period, but they stayed right at the mark during the crime-spike era.

Actions: Traffic Enforcement. Traffic enforcement is a key role for the police. It is important to recall that law enforcement is a "public safety" function. Many lives are at risk daily on the traffic front. During 2017, 17,284 Americans were murdered, but more than 40,000 were killed in traffic accidents. The principal factors involved in traffic fatalities are speed and alcohol, which are very much policing concerns. The role of traffic enforcement in crime deterrence more generally is widely recognized as well. Some of the best-known early studies of the impact of proactive policing on crime used traffic ticketing and arrest rates as general measures of the aggressiveness of city policing (cf., Sampson and Cohen, 1988; Wilson and Boland, 1978). Traffic enforcement increases the visibility of active policing, perhaps serving as a general deterrent to crime, and signals that it is risky for offenders to transport stolen goods, weapons, and other contraband because they might be stopped.

Chicago police make many traffic stops each year. During the decade prior to 2016 they generated between 20,000 and 35,000 routine traffic stops monthly. Just between 2010 and 2018 these totaled more than 3.6 million traffic stops. They were "generated" because the resources police departments devote to traffic enforcement are driven largely by internal and organizational factors (Gardner, 1969). In truth, there are enough people speeding on just a few of the city's prominent highways to occupy however many traffic enforcement units the city could afford to assign there. Traffic-related encounters are initiated by officers who decide whom to stop and sanction from what Schafer and Mastrofski (2005, p. 225) described as the "never-ending flow of traffic law violators."

One lesson of the 2015–2016 period is that policing is fungible. As stop & frisk collapsed, the districts turned instead to traffic stops, and their numbers skyrocketed. Assembling the data on traffic enforcement made it apparent how much Chicago police ratcheted up the number of traffic stops following the collapse of stop & frisk. After a brief downturn, traffic enforcement picked up tremendously. This is apparent in Figure 7-6, which is based on counts of units radioing into the city's communication center as they were initiating a traffic stop. By 2018, traffic stops approached the stop & frisk numbers recorded during 2015, peaking above 60,000 per month. As we saw in the last chapter, most stops recorded following State of Illinois statutes led only to verbal warnings, and not to citations or arrests. The volume of traffic stops

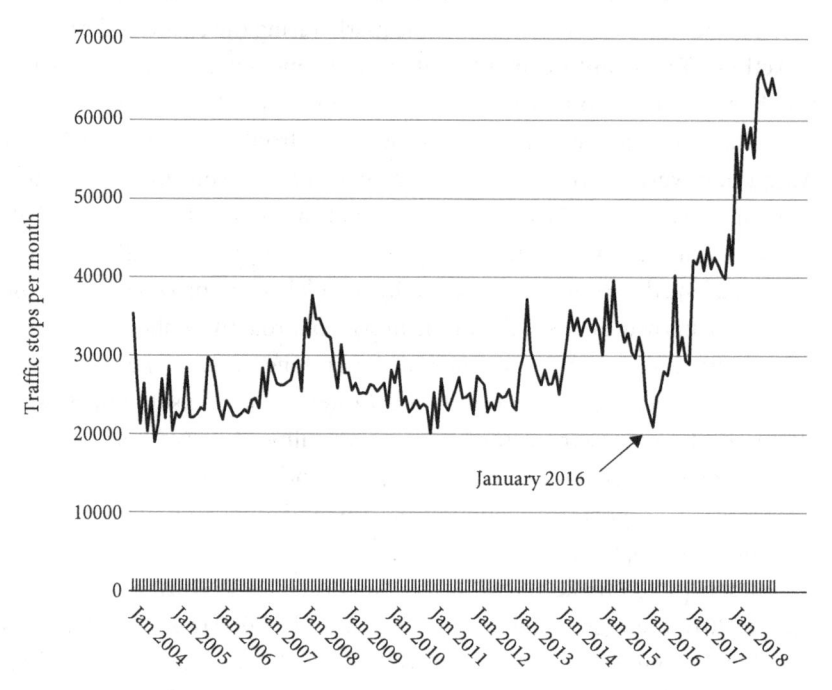

Figure 7-6 Traffic Stops 2004–2018

depicted here (which come from a different database) is not consistent with the claim that officers were going fetal beginning in 2016, but rather points to the agency's shift to another tried-and-true, high-volume enforcement strategy. Statistically, it turns out that the frequency of routine traffic stops, those which sometimes led to a citation but did not lead to an arrest, was a consistent correlate of lower levels of violence. These stops remain on the list of prime suspects because this correlation became apparent after controlling for other factors on the list. In particular, traffic stops continued rise during 2017–2018, when violence in Chicago began to subside from its 2016 highs.

Actions: Routine Dispatches. There was little evidence of any significant police slackening during the crime spike in any of the high-volume activities filling their day. The highest-volume dispatches provide a measure of the extent of visible police activity and contacts with the public, factors considered a crime deterrent. Dispatches in response to reports of "disturbances" were the largest component of reactive police activity in Chicago. During the 2013–2015 period, the CPD averaged just under 37,000 disturbance dispatches per month, rising to about 45,000 each summer month. The disturbance category included events involving drunks, noisemakers, "teen disturbances," vague reports of "threats," pleas for help in handling people with mental problems, and complaints about disorderly or potentially dangerous activities taking place in parks (there were 850,000 dispatches to parks alone during this period). There was no sign of slackening police activity during the crime spike. During 2016, disturbance calls dropped by only two percent compared to recent years, and that number remained nearly constant in the years following.

Two other high-volume activities are "assisting citizens" and responding to disruptions dispatchers identify as "domestic situations." Chicago police spend a lot of time helping people. Events in the assist category involved calls for help, lost and found property, lost and found people, delivering medical services, attending to fire scenes, responding to vague reports of "man down," transporting individuals needing help, and animal bites. (My favorite dispatch category is "Animal Bite; Perp. Gone"). Public assistance dispatches peaked after 2015. Officers were responding to these calls on about 16,000 occasions each summer month. Some of the largest activity codes in the domestic situation category were "domestic related," "restored peace," "advised legal help," and "perpetrator gone," or "perp not found." Dispatches to domestic situations declined a bit during 2018 but showed no decline earlier in the supposed "fetal" period. Responding to complaints about "suspicious persons" is another frequent police activity. One officer described this as, "they look out the window and see someone they don't want around." Police enforcement actions were recorded only in about five percent of suspicious person incidents. More often, officers reported giving advice and "restoring peace." Suspicious person dispatches actually rose during from 2016 to 2018. Finally, responding to ringing alarms was the second most common policing activity, and is one of the banes of police work because little ever comes of them. These dispatches were equally frequent both before and after the onset of the spike.

In short, Chicago police were keeping busy, remaining a visible presence on the street, and in frequent personal contact with a broad spectrum of the public about a wide range of public concerns. This how they spend much of their time, and these are among the most important things police who are not on television do. In the statistical analyses described below, routine visible policing will be represented by its highest-volume component—disturbance dispatches.

Reactions: Police Legitimacy. As we saw in Chapter 4, one of the claims of procedural justice research is that fair treatment by the police builds their legitimacy and encourages compliance with them and with the law. It is also often argued that, by extension, crime can be expected to be lower as a result, and a procedurally just society can be a safe society. This proposition is widely discussed in research on procedural justice policing, which focuses directly on legitimacy building. The theoretical link between legitimacy and crime is described in a review of research on community policing by Charlotte Gill, et al. (2014). They concluded that the legitimacy of the police needs to be reinforced before any longer-term effects of innovative policing strategies can occur. By extension, declining police legitimacy could be tied to increasing levels of crime. In the period encompassing the release of the Laquan McDonald video and the emergence of the crime spike in 2016, observers quickly drew a link between the two. Cassell and Fowles (2018, p. 221) describe the scene in Chicago following the Laquan McDonald incident. They report stories of police officers being "taunted and harassed" by bystanders, and worried "[t]he bad element knows that policemen aren't willing to do the job the way they did it [before]." In June 2016, the head of the police union complained that "the level of boldness has increased in some of the higher-crime areas," and officers were facing "a level of disrespect we have not seen" (Cox, 2016). In November, the chief of police noted "I've never seen the level of disrespect out there on the streets" and "I've never seen that before. So, it is a tough time right now. But we'll get through it" (Gorner, 2016).

However, assessing the state of police legitimacy on a monthly basis for 16 years is a thorny problem. Data on complaints against the Chicago police are available only after 2007, and we saw in the previous chapter that how complaints were investigated changed radically beginning after 2016. An alternative could have been monthly counts of the number of persons shot by the police. Securing this is difficult, however. Chicago media outlets fight continuous battles with the city over its unwillingness to release useful information regarding shootings by police, and before 2010 monthly reports of persons shot and killed (which is a minority of those shot) are scattered. Further, police shootings of civilians in Chicago have also been on a downward trajectory. During the 1990s, Chicago police shot an average of 55 people per year; during 2004, it was 33, and in 2018, 21 people were shot, most non-fatally. For months where there are data, the correlation between the number of persons shot and the overall number of complaints filed was about +.50, so the two measures point in the same downward direction.

Another rough and ready measure of legitimacy available on a monthly basis is the number of individuals arrested for obstructing officers in the line of duty. This includes actions such as refusing to cooperate with officers, concealing fugitives, and aiding persons in escaping. This measure conceptually reflects a weakening of moral bonds and the loss of police legitimacy, concepts often measured by people's perceptions of their obligation to obey the law and instructions by the police. During 2016, obstruction cases numbered between 80 and 100 per month. More interference with officers was booked during the highest-crime months and, over the entire period, obstruction charges were correlated +.30 with murder and +.38 with shootings. This is in general accord with the view that deteriorating legitimacy may undermine law and order. However, although the rise and fall of murders and shootings coincides with Chicagoans giving police a hard time, resistance peaked most noticeably during 2011–2015, in advance of the spike in crime. Still, during 2016–2018 resistance to the police remained well above the 2004–2010 levels and deteriorating legitimacy potentially could have played a role in the crime spike.

Controls: Population and Poverty. Over this time period the city's population dropped. Residents left for reasons ranging from seeking more sunshine to finding better economic opportunities elsewhere. In the statistical analysis it proved important to account for this change in the size of the population at risk of being a victim or an offender. The city's African American population has been particularly impacted by gun violence, and a drop in their numbers was the most notable feature of Chicago's population decline. Between 2000 and 2018 alone the African American population declined by about 275,000, a drop of 25 percent. The analyses control for both city total population and the size of the African American population. Monthly population estimates were interpolated between yearly population estimates made by the Census Bureau for big cities. In the analyses, the size of the African American population was a notable predictor of homicide trends: more people, more murders.

Another factor to be accounted for is Chicago's increasing economic and social inequality, which has been horrific. This was measured using an index combining census data on the percentage of female-headed households with children, unemployment as a percentage of the working age population, the percentage of residents who lived below the poverty line, and the percentage of persons ages 25 and older who did not have a college degree. These measures were available for the decennial census years 2000 and 2010, and yearly beginning with the American Community Survey in 2011. For each data year, tract-level measures of these four factors were converted to standardized scores (z-scores) and combined into a single poverty measure. Then population-weighted average poverty scores were calculated for the sets of tracts classified as predominately White, Black, Hispanic, and diverse in composition. Monthly poverty-score estimates were interpolated between yearly scores for each group of tracts. The statistical analyses controlled for this estimate of the monthly trend in poverty in predominately African American neighborhoods, and it remained a strong predictor of both murder and shootings. Over the 180-month span, variations in the extent of African American poverty correlated +.39 with the level of homicide and +.43 with the number of shootings.

Controls: The Weather. Chicago has a lot of weather. The city's average temperature is reasonable, but often it is not average. Over this period, one month included 19 days with highs above 90 degrees, and another month saw 26 days with lows below freezing. One month it snowed (not always a lot) for 21 days. Other events are certainly affected by the city's weather, including attendance at its monthly police–citizen beat meetings (Skogan, 2006b). Weather is the most important factor in understanding month-by-month levels of violence, so we will be taking it into account. However, the 2016 spike was not likely to have been caused by the weather; monthly temperatures during 2016 were close to their historical averages. As we have seen, violence remained seasonal, but the traditional effect of normally cold weather on shootings and killings dissipated. That year, January looked more like May.

A preliminary examination of the crime-control effects of rain and snowfall, average monthly minimum and maximum temperatures, and the duration of bouts of extreme heat and cold, found crime went up and down with everything involving weather. The bottom line was that most of the effects of weather could be captured by one number, the average monthly temperature. The 180-month correlation between the average monthly temperature and shootings was +.78, and for murders it was +.67. In addition, a visual inspection of the predictive power of the model recommended adding the number of days each month above 90 degrees. This helped account for bump-ups in homicides and shootings occurring during July and August each year. Overall, shootings were correlated +.51 with the number of extra-hot days. There is a possibility that long-term changes in the earth's climate portend higher levels of violence; it looks like this would be driven by the adverse influence of mild winters (Harp and Karnauskas, 2018). However, no real winter warming trend was visible during the 2004–2018 period in Chicago. The weakening of the effect of winter on crime post-2016 was due to changes in the character of crime, not the temperature. However, the very close correspondence between violent crime and the weather—and in the frequency of stop & frisks, which are also seasonal—requires it be accounted for as well.

Controls: 911 Calls. In many instances, crimes recorded by the police come to their attention because they were reported by victims and other members of the public. The extent to which they do so is highly varied, depending on the nature and seriousness of the incident, any relationship between the parties, and if there is hope of gaining restitution or an insurance check (for a review see Tarling and Morris, 2010). There is also evidence of revelations of nasty police misconduct independently affecting crime reporting in effected communities. Desmond, Papachristos and Kirk (2016) examined the impact of a widely publicized police beating of an unarmed African American man on the subsequent volume of 911 calls in Milwaukee. They found a legacy of this event was a reduction in calls to report crimes, especially in the city's Black neighborhoods. They concluded "police misconduct can powerfully suppress one of the most basic forms of civic engagement: calling 911 for matters of personal and public safety" (p. 858).

The general risk is clear. Did the extensive media coverage and continuing political fallout from events in Chicago at the end of 2015 spill over into crime reporting? Because we are focusing here on shootings and killings—incidents producing hospital admissions and dead bodies—this is probably less of a risk than otherwise could be the case. Nonetheless, it was prudent to include measures of the frequency of 911 calls as a control factor in the analysis. Three measures were involved: total 911 calls, calls to complain about gang activity or drug sales, and calls to report incidents coded as either "person with a gun" or "shots fired." Over time, the latter was correlated +.66 with the murder count, and +.72 with monthly shooting totals, and it was among the most consistently strong correlates of monthly violence. Unlike the Milwaukee trend, 911 shooting reports *increased* in Chicago following the Laquan McDonald episode, from about 240 per summer month to over 300 in 2016. In fact, 911 calls tracked the increase in recorded shootings imperfectly because they rose *more sharply* than recorded crime during the period.

Controls: The Crime Climate. As indicated in Chapter 2, crime goes up and down in the United States for reasons eluding our clear understanding (see Rosenfeld, 2018). Statistical analyses of long-term trends in crime across large samples of cities find there is a "non-local" component to the city-by-city oscillations that in the aggregate make up national cycles. Hiding behind individual ups and downs in city crime is a common, shared trend. McDowall & Loftin (2009) calculated that this deep trend accounted for about 20 percent of the variation in crime over time and across cities, a considerable fraction. This was not true for all the cities they studied, but they found that in an average year about two-thirds of cities and their residents were affected by the deep trend.

The source of this co-variation across cities over time remains obscure. It could be the result of shared economic trends, the (very) rapid diffusion of new criminal or policing strategies, common cultural shifts, or the shared impact of national media events. Even before the events engulfing Chicago at the end of 2015 it was commonplace to hear that a police legitimacy crisis was sweeping the country. Prior to the Chicago shooting, the nation was reminded of the depths to which police–community relations had sunk by Eric Garner's police chokehold death in New York City (July 2014); Michael Brown's police shooting death in Ferguson, Missouri (August 2014); 12-year-old Tamir Rice's police shooting death in Cleveland, Ohio (November 2014); Walter Scott's shooting death in North Charleston, South Carolina (April 2015); and Freddie Gray's death in police custody in Baltimore, Maryland (April 2015). As noted earlier, research suggests any resulting legitimacy crisis could undermine the authority of the police and weaken the moral bonds helping to informally control crime. But however significant common events and conditions sparking general urban trends might be, the goal here is to isolate the effects of Chicago's local stop & frisk regime on local crime. In this light, any common crime trend due to other factors is a distraction needing to be accounted for.

The analysis therefore includes a measure of the violent crime trend in other regional cities during the 2004–2018 period. Because of the focus here on a rise in shootings and killings, this measure combines monthly assault, robbery, and murder rates per thousand (because the cities varied in size) for Milwaukee, St. Louis, Kansas City (Missouri), Indianapolis, Detroit, Cincinnati, and Cleveland.[4] We can think of this as a "control" time series, one reflecting common, non-local city trends. It is a "synthetic" control because it is constructed from a group of racially diverse Midwestern rust-belt cities that, prior to the late-2015 collapse of stop & frisk, tracked the ups and downs in shootings and killings in Chicago (Abadie, et al., 2010).

Figure 7-7 illustrates the close relationship between violent crime trends in Chicago and these seven cities over much of the post-2004 period. Before 2016, Chicago tracked regional trends, which predicted the local number of shootings quite effectively for 12 years. During this period, the correlation between violent crime across these seven cities and shootings in Chicago was +.61. But, beginning in 2016, the synthetic trend in the crime climate for the previous 12 years predicted continued *stability* in shootings and killings in Chicago, not the spike in violence coming on the heels of the collapse of stop & frisk. As the shaded area illustrates, during 2016 there were 1,800 more shootings in Chicago than the common trend in other regional cities would predict; during 2017 there were 880 unanticipated shootings, and an unexpectedly high shooting count during the summer of 2018 is also visible. Controlling for the general crime climate should help sharpen the picture of Chicago's local crime scene.

Dependent Variables: Shootings and Killings. The key measures of interest are monthly counts of the number of murders and the number of shootings. The latter includes most murders, but (for example) during 2015 almost 80 percent of shooting victims survived, so the monthly shooting count is a much larger number. About 10 percent or less of the murder count each year involved stabbings and other non-gun incidents. The overlap between these two measures means the separate analyses discussed here are not fully independent. However, there would be little interest in separately examining the number of *non-fatal* shootings, which would have been independent

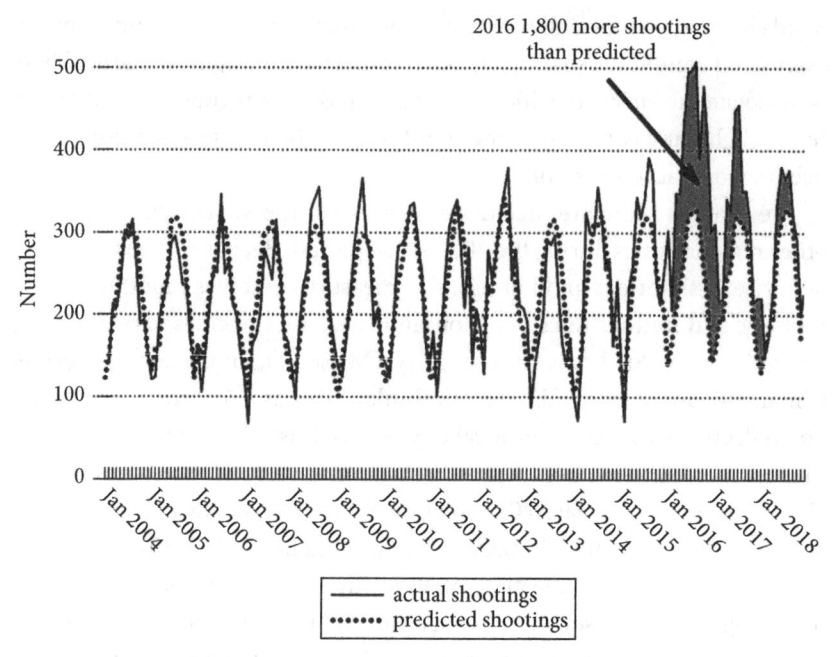

Figure 7-7 Chicago's Regional Crime Climate 2004–2018

of homicide. In the media and in politics it is shootings and killings that capture the headlines and drive policy. As noted in earlier chapters, there is not much distinctive about non-fatal shootings—except detectives pay much less sustained attention to them and give up on investigations of non-fatal shootings more easily, perhaps because non-fatals are not featured in the media. Otherwise, researchers report there is not much difference between fatal and non-fatal shootings except the distribution of good and bad luck, good and bad marksmanship, and perhaps a more effective weapon (Cook, et al., 2019).

Measuring Stop & Frisk. There was a lot of variability in the extent of stop & frisk, which (statistically, at least) is a good thing. Early on, stops ranged between 200 to 300 per month. With the arrival of police chief McCarthy at the end of 2011 the count ratcheted up, hitting 33,000 per month by the spring of 2012. Then, as we have seen, stops soared. They hit 50,000 per month in January 2013 (and this was in the dead of winter!). Stops peaked in early 2014, at almost 63,000 in a month. Later, following the collapse of stop & frisk at the end of 2015, police commonly reported only about 8,000 stops per month.

As they are throughout this volume, stops are better described as monthly counts of innocent stops. Prior to 2016, only unwarranted stops were recorded, while those resulting in an enforcement outcome were diverted into other administrative categories, such as arrests. From 2016 onward I filtered the data to remove stops involving arrests, citations, or seized contraband to extend the comparable innocent time series through 2018. The original and adjusted time series were very highly correlated. During 2016–2018, raw stop counts were correlated +.92 with the innocent version created by subtracting out non-innocent stops. Many of the non-innocent stop & frisks, both pre-2016 (not known) and post-2016 (filtered out), should be captured by the other measures included in this analysis. This includes stops leading to arrests or citations. We saw in the previous chapter that post-2016, arrests were made during 14 percent of stops, while tickets or ANOVs were issued in another nine percent. Those were all filtered out here but were represented by other variables in the analyses.

Summary

Table 7-1 summarizes the measures discussed here. Because of the very close association between murders and shootings (many of which could be called "attempted murders"), all the statistical controls are included in the analyses of both crime categories. This involved fitting a regression model correcting for first order serially correlated errors to 180 months of time-series data. Again, the goal is not to estimate the effects of the individual measures or clusters of explanatory factors on trends in violence. Rather, it is to account for them and then assess the apparently distinct impact of stop & frisk on crime in Chicago.

An important limitation of this approach to assessing the impact of stop & frisk is not so much the variables included, but those which are not. The concern is any apparent correlation between stops and crime may be "spurious" due to other causal factors correlated with stops but were not included in the analysis. There are, of course, many unlisted causes of violence. One hundred years of criminological research has produced a huge compendium of general and category-specific causes of crime. Many are not represented here. However, there are some statistical protections built into time-series analysis that flag whether omitted variables are having a systematic effect on

Table 7-1 Statistical Control Variable Summary

Actions Potentially Influencing Crime	Control Factors Influencing Crime
Legitimacy	Weather
Complaints	Average temperature
Public resistance	Days over 90 degrees
Crime Solvability	Regional Crime Climate
Personal crimes	7-city violent crime trend
Property crimes	Population and Poverty
Arrests and Dispersals	Total population
Personal arrests	African American population
Property arrests	African American poverty index
Drug arrests	Citizen Incident Reporting
Weapon arrests	Total 911 calls
Disorder arrests	Drug and gang 911 calls
Loitering dispersals	Shots fired 911 calls
Other Enforcement	
Traffic stops	
Disturbance dispatches	

the data. These protections are summarized below, as part of the discussion of the statistical findings.

What Was the Impact of Stop & Frisk?

The top rows of Table 7-2 summarize the statistical estimate of the impact of stops on murders and shootings. The bottom line is that stop & frisk apparently reduced the victim count by eight and nine percentage points. This figure was derived from the estimated impact of 1,000 stops each month, which (rounded) was –.14 murders and –.87 shootings. While this may seem like a small number being deterred, recall that there were almost five million stops during the 2004–2018 period, including more than 50,000 every month during most of 2014. Another row of findings in Table 7-2 reports that, over 180 months, there were an estimated 739 fewer murders and over 4,300 fewer shootings due to stop & frisk.

However, these large totals depend on this being a long time series. A more useful figure is the estimated average *monthly* crime reduction attributable

Table 7-2 Statistical Summary

	Murders	Shootings	Comments
Crimes Averted			
Per thousand stops	–0.141	–0.868	For every 1,000 stops (net of other factors) subtract this many victims
Total averted 2004–2018	703	4327	Estimated total not victimized (estimated effect multiplied by number of stops) in 180 months
Percent averted 2004–2018	–8.4%	–8.8%	Estimated averted victimizations divided by total of actual victims plus averted victims
Average averted per month	–3.9	–24.0	The overall total divided by 180; in any month this depends on the number of stops
Statistical significance of estimate	0.051	0.002	Likelihood that the estimated effect could include zero; should be small
Variance explained R^2	0.76	0.91	Overlap between actual and predicted crime; maximum is 100%
Durbin-Watson Test of correlated errors	1.999	1.989	Errors in monthly predictions not correlated in adjacent years (very important); should be 2.0
Dickey-Fuller Test for stationarity	–6.47	–4.92	Relations between variables should be the same throughout (important); should be negative
Rho (stationarity measure)	0.006	0.007	The mean and variance of the series should remain the same throughout; should be small
Standardized residual outliers	2 of 180	2 of 180	Monthly error in crime predictions; values over 3.0 need investigating
Likely upper and lower estimates define by plus/minus one semi-robust standard errors around estimated coefficients			
Maximum likely percent averted	–0.121	–0.114	Averted six murders and 32 shootings per month
Most likely percent averted (above)	–0.084	–0.088	Averted four murders and 14 shootings per month
Minimum likely percent averted	–0.043	–0.061	Averted two murders and 16 shootings per month

to stop & frisk, which was (rounded) four homicides and 24 shootings. Be sure to note the estimated number of victimizations averted in any month depends on the number of stops, which varied. For example, in 2010 Chicago had a police chief who was not very interested in stop & frisk, and there were only about 280,000 of them. The findings reported here predicted 41 homicides were averted in 2010, which otherwise would have been added on top of the 436 which did occur. That was an average reduction of 3.4 killings per month. By contrast, during 2014 there were 629,000 stops, which may have averted 91 murders, or 7.6 per month.

Because these are statistical estimates of the impact of stop & frisk, there are other plausible values they might have taken. A section at the bottom of Table 7-2 indicates the top and bottom of those ranges. In this case they form the interval within which about two-thirds of all likely estimates of the impact of stops would have fallen if the measures in the analyses fluctuated reasonably when they were measured again. For example, for homicide, this range ran from −4.3 percent to −12.1 percent; for shootings the range was −6.1 percent to −11.4 percent. However, it remains more likely that the "true" population figure was much closer to the middle figures of −8.4 percent for murders and −8.8 percent for shootings.

Is an eight to nine percent reduction in shootings and killings a credible estimate, based on other research? As indicated, time-series analyses of this type have diverged widely in their methods and findings. The London study found no substantively significant reduction in crime due to stop and search. On the other hand, applying some arithmetic to the crime reduction estimates reported by Cassel and Fowles (2018) for Chicago suggests the effect of stop & frisk on homicide was almost 4 times as large as my estimate. Their study involved a much shorter time series, so the ranges of likely estimates like those at the bottom of Table 7-2 would be notably wider. They also focused on just five years of data, concluding with the 2016 spike and the collapse of stop & frisk. Here, the data extend both further back in time and two years further into the future, over a period in which violence continued to evolve and stops remained low. Framed by the rest of this book, the goal here is to examine the impact of this crime-deterrent strategy over the long haul, generalizing across administrations and changes in policing policies, shifts in the character of violent crime, and changing conditions (as they always change) in the city. The Braga, et al. (2019) review of research on the impact of proactive policing did not report overall average reductions at all; instead, it featured "effect sizes," which are good for comparing results across studies but are not interpretable in the real world. Their report concluded the combined results of 62 studies pointed to a statistically significant but "small" impact of proactive policing. The eight to nine percent reduction described here might fall in their small category.

Some Details

The middle panel of Table 7-2 summarizes some technical features of the analyses. One is the statistical significance of the estimated coefficients relating stops to shootings and killings. Neither was likely to vary enough to include zero on more than one out of 20 occasions, which meets a standard statistical threshold. Table 7-2 also reports the variation in the two dependent variables explained by the statistical model. This is a measure of how well the modeled data fit the real data. The fit measure for shootings was very high at 91 percent. For homicide it was 76 percent. This is still high, but low enough that visual inspection of the data might reveal improvements in the model. Figure 7-8 plots the monthly murder count in conjunction with murder as predicted by the statistical model. They track each other quite strongly. Figure 7-8 shades the most prominent differences between the two. They are scattered across the entire series, which is a good thing statistically. Sometimes the variables

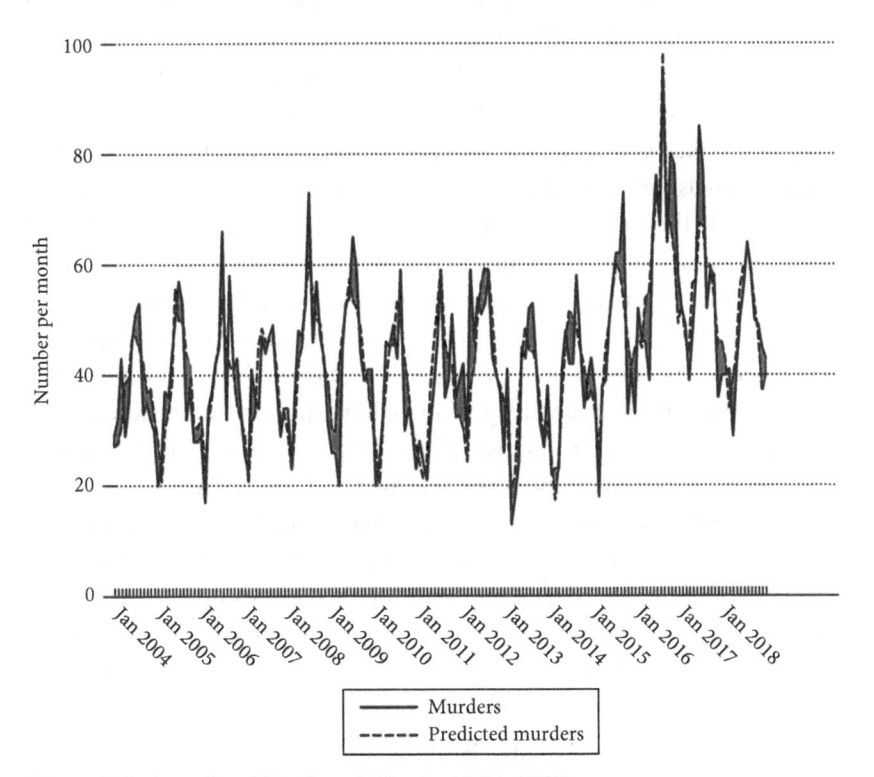

Figure 7-8 Actual and Predicted Murder 2004–2018

included in the analysis fail to catch extreme summer highs. This was true of the spike years 2016 and 2017, but there were misses at the high (and low) ends earlier as well. After examining such plots, adding weather measures beyond average temperature and the number of hot days each month did not improve the prediction of extreme highs and lows in violence, and no other modifications had much of an effect on the observed model discrepancies.

Statistically, the most important issue addressed by Table 7-2 is serial correlation. Time-series models are biased if errors in their predictions are correlated with errors in other months. The bias is generally in estimates of the statistical significance of the independent variables, but not in the coefficients themselves. The Stata 14 PRIAS software used to do these analyses is designed to correct for precisely this problem. Social and economic data are often characterized by first order serial correlation, which means mispredictions of data points are correlated with mispredictions of the next month's data points. A major remaining source of correlated error is the omission of important independent variables from the analysis. The absence of serial correlation is, therefore, good news. The Durbin-Watson statistic is a formal test of the independence of the mispredictions across the entire time series. In an ideal world, the value of this statistic should be 2.0. This is almost exactly the value for the models of both shootings and killings.

Another issue is whether the data are stationary. Stationarity is good because it signals that the effects of the explanatory variables do not fluctuate over time. If they do, many key assumptions of statistical theory do not apply; the computer will continue to run, but the output will be misleading. Two tests for stationarity are reported in Table 7-2. Both point strongly to stationarity not being a problem. The stationarity measure "Rho," which is zero when a time series is well-behaved and 1.0 when there is no observable pattern in the data, is exceedingly small for both shootings and killings.

Finally, a way to assess a statistical model is to visually inspect the errors (the "residuals," or monthly differences between the actual and predicted values). Standardizing first (by dividing each residual by its standard deviation) helps interpret them. A convention is that the resulting values are a problem if they exceed an absolute value of 3.0. In this case, for each crime measure only two of 180 residuals exceeded this threshold. Three of the four residuals fell *prior* to the 2016 spike, in 2009, 2012, and 2014. Figure 7-8 illustrates this for Chicago murders. It compares the number each month predicted by the statistical model with the raw figures. The biggest miss was for March 2009, when the model predicted 41 murders but there were only

20. For October 2016 the model predicted 399 shootings, while there actually were 478 shootings. No sensible adjustments to the data made this go away—October 2016 was truly a spike.

In addition to stops, what other factors seemed consistently related to higher or lower levels of violence? Recall the goal was to isolate the effect of stops by controlling for as many as possible potential determinants of trends in crime. As a result, the list of control factors was a long one. To test the robustness of the statistical models, one experiment involved removing any measures not having any notable independent effect on crime trends but were included for theoretical completeness. In summary, this changed the estimated size of the stop & frisk coefficients only at the third decimal place. Among the most impressive remaining variables were personal crime arrests (more arrests less homicide, in particular), poverty in African American neighborhoods (more violence generally), the common rust-belt crime climate (correlated positively with both Chicago trends), the city's African American population (more people, more homicide), traffic stops (fewer shootings and killings), and—of course—the weather.

For the same reason tables do not display individual regression coefficients and significance tests for the many included variables. The control variables were overlapping, intercorrelated, and sometimes redundant, selected for theoretical completeness and to make up for empirical uncertainty over which was "best." For example, there were five different measures of arrests and two of crime solvability. This strategy was facilitated by the long, 180-month time series. In light of this, the coefficients attached to the control variables were not informative individually. Rather, the question was, once they were accounted for, were stop & frisks still associated with violent crime?

Stop & Frisk and Crime

Over the 180 months examined here, this statistical model indicates stop & frisk was about an 8.5 percent solution for murders and shootings. This estimate was smaller than a few, but larger than the findings reported for several other time series and cross-sectional studies. It is in line with the conclusions of the National Research Council's review of proactive policing (Weisburd and Majmundar, 2018), and with tabulations of the findings of a substantial number of rigorous experimental and quasi-experimental studies (Braga, et al., 2019). They report generally modest effects.

Although this discussion of the impact of stop & frisk was motivated by the intense political debate that broke out following the collapse of stops and the Chicago crime spike of 2016, this analysis extended both backward and forward in time. The focus here was the impact of stop & frisk as an organizational strategy, including across its entire high-to-low range and through its significant variability due to leadership changes, shifts in the political environment, and the crisis of late 2015. This extended time frame also facilitated including presumably important features of crime itself, such as the collapse of crime solvability and its deterrent consequences, and significant changes in local policing strategies, most prominently Chicago's massive shift toward traffic stops as a crime prevention tool. It also accommodated measures of community conditions, and Chicago's neighborhoods were evolving markedly during this period. Working with a more complete theoretically, empirically grounded model encompassing the findings of past research on crime trends required the many months of data that could be assembled.

This approach still did a good job modeling the Great Crime Spike of 2016 and its subsequent downward trend. During the 2014–2018 period surrounding the spike, the correlation between the number of shootings and a statistical prediction of the monthly shooting count was +.95. However, there are many caveats and perhaps heroic assumptions lying behind this (and the conclusions of all the studies cited above). Many of these were discussed already. Being an "observational" study, measures of relevant factors possibly influencing levels of crime in the city remained unaccounted for. Some bother me more than others. An example of the latter: research has pointed to the importance of community factors, such as neighborhood cohesion, in controlling crime, but these tend to change only slowly, and whether they have much to do with monthly ups and downs in crime is doubtful. On the other hand, sociologist Patrick Sharkey reports that, over a 20-year period, adding a notable number of community organizations focusing on crime and community life to the social mix in moderate- and large-sized cities could have had about the same effect on violent crime as stop & frisk in Chicago. Across his large sample of cities, 10 more organizations led to a nine percent reduction in homicide and a six percent decline in all violent crimes (Sharkey, Torrats-Espinose and Takyar, 2017). I also wish there were more appropriate measures of police legitimacy, which is widely discussed as contributing to social stability through its positive effects on law-abidingness and cooperation with authorities. However, research on these topics has just examined attitudes about the police and offending or (in a few instances) self-reports of behavior. At this writing, the closest legitimacy measures have come to the messy world of crime data is in studies of national crime rates, matching them to survey and other indicators of national police or governmental legitimacy at one point of time (as an example, see Nivette and Eisner, 2013).

There remain important questions raised by the 8.5 percent solution provided by stop & frisk. The criterion of "effectiveness" is one metric for assessing public policies. Was 8.5 percent effective enough? Were there other, more effective policies on the table that were not chosen? A 2009 evaluation of a Chicago intervention program dubbed "Cure Violence" found that among the six troubled study neighborhoods where the program was active, shootings declined in the range of 20–28 percent in four of them, and gang homicides (a special target of the program) went down there as well. At a cost (then) of $250,000 per neighborhood, per year, Cure Violence was also *much* cheaper than stop & frisk (Skogan, et al., 2009). Police-led interventions are expensive. At this writing, the average Chicago police officer (the lowest rank) costs $150,000 per year, each. Or, as reported above, seeding communities with more neighborhood organizations promised about the same effectiveness as stop & frisk, and could have many other ancillary benefits for neighborhoods as well. In addition to effectiveness, stop & frisk raises the related issues of efficiency and equity, and these too will be addressed in the final chapter.

8

Assessing Stop & Frisk

While police have always made stops, this chapter documents how stop & frisk, as an organizational strategy, was something new by contrasting it with some of the city's earlier intensive enforcement efforts. It then turns to three evaluative dimensions on which to judge this practice: efficiency, effectiveness, and equity. Equity issues evidence themselves as both over-policing and under-policing. Next, the chapter briefly examines some potential options for "fixing" stop & frisk. These include optimizing them to minimize over-policing, improving officer adherence to procedural justice standards, and relying on body cameras to reshape police and citizen behavior. None of these appear especially promising. The chapter concludes by suggesting instead to consider *alternatives* to stop & frisk that could speak to the on-the-ground realities of gun violence in Chicago while avoiding some (but not all) of the liabilities associated with the city's stop & frisk regime.

Was This Anything New?

Police have always used their discretionary powers to make stops. When it comes to making arrests, they point to statutes, shifting among them over time as the laws themselves and our understanding of their appropriate use changes. By the 2000s, some arrest categories police had historically relied on for authority to stop, question, and frisk people had disappeared. For example, arrests for vagrancy, spitting in public places, "suspicion," and loitering were once common in Chicago, but by 1970 they had dropped essentially to zero. Part of Chicago's stop & frisk story is that policing moved beyond the statute books. Rather than reacting to evidence of a specific offense, the goal of stops was to identify potential offenses. Stop & frisk was governed by rules of procedure rather than criminal statutes, because they were just stops and frisks that were not searches, unless something actionable turned up.

How distinctive was Chicago's stop & frisk era, compared to earlier times when other grounds were used to make stops aimed at deterring potential

Stop & Frisk and the Politics of Crime in Chicago. Wesley G. Skogan, Oxford University Press.
© Oxford University Press 2023. DOI: 10.1093/oso/9780197675052.003.0008

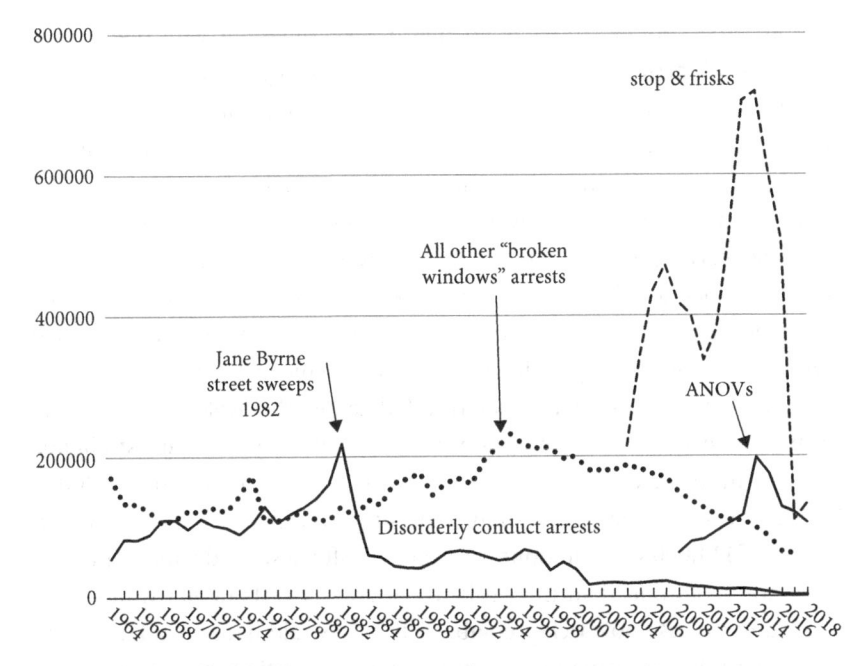

Figure 8-1 Trends in Arrests, ANOVs, and Stops 1964–2018

troublemakers? Were stop & frisks just a substitute for them, with little net change in the breadth of the city's social control efforts? To examine this, Figure 8-1 charts the 2004–2018 trend in stops and compares them to the deployment of policing tools of earlier eras and different legal categories. These data points extend back until 1964; a huge scandal prior to 1964 led the police department to stop releasing useful public reports for several years.

One comparison with stop & frisk is with the trend in misdemeanor arrests. These are arrests for relatively minor offenses, frequently crimes without a complaining victim, which depend on officers taking the initiative to identify and act upon them. The misdemeanor arrest list illustrated in Figure 8-1 is generous. It includes all non-traffic, "non-index" (generally less serious) arrests. The trend line subtracts out only assaults and arrests for unlawfully carrying a gun, plus the disorderly conduct arrests that are presented separately. During the 1970s the biggest remaining arrests were for marijuana possession, drunkenness, minor assault, vandalism, gambling, and undifferentiated "other minor" offenses that are only summarized in the department's reports. In the mid-1980s, efforts to crack down on such offenses became known as "Broken Windows" policing. Defending this strategy, Kelling and

Bratton (2015) noted, "some assert that it is synonymous with the controversial patrol tactic known as 'stop, question, and frisk." They rejected this and argued instead, "it is a more broadly based policy mandating that police will address disorderly illegal behavior, such as public drinking and drug use, public urination, and other acts considered to be minor offenses, with responses ranging from warning and referral to summons and arrest." Their reasons for pursuing this strategy included that it was popular with the public and that "ample evidence makes clear that Broken Windows policing leads to less crime." They cited declining crime in New York City and claimed "Broken Windows-style policing was pivotal in achieving these results."

Figure 8-1 also presents brief trend data on the ANOV tickets that began to substitute for some offenses that previously were arrest-eligible misdemeanors. ANOV counts are only available for the period of 2008–2018, but it is clear they play a significant role. Over this period, there was an average of 114,000 such citations per year and, after a surge during 2014, they were more common than the Broken Windows arrests depicted in Figure 8-1. Many of these now ticket-eligible offenses would have been familiar in earlier periods, including public drinking and urination, minor drug possession, selling untaxed cigarettes, and violating park closing hours. The addition of high-volume cell-phone-and-driving infractions helped drive up the ANOV total around 2014. Later, those infractions were moved to a more serious category and the ANOV total went down.

The final comparison to stop & frisk is with the volume of disorderly conduct arrests. In the 1980s, the city's Municipal Code defined disorderly conduct as an offense committed any time a person "knowingly does any act in such unreasonable manner as to provoke, make or aid in making a breach of peace." For a period, disorderly conduct arrests were the workhorse for social control in Chicago. Vagrancy, suspicion, and loitering had effectively been erased from the statute books by the courts, and disorderly conduct filled the void. In 1982 (admittedly the high point; see Figure 8-1), disorderly conduct accounted for more than one-half of *all* the arrests made in the city, not just those illustrated in Figure 8-1.

The year 1982 was special because it was the high point for "Jane Byrne street sweeps," which were famous in their time. In October 1981, Mayor Byrne pushed Police Superintendent Richard Brzeczek to reorganize her police department by creating a Bureau of Gang Crime Suppression. Headed by Joseph McCarthy, who was chosen directly by the mayor, this unit made many of the city's disorderly conduct arrests. Significantly, disorderly

conduct arrests during this era almost never resulted in convictions because officers did not appear in court to defend them. Their job was to clear
the streets. As Officer Bob Suess explained to a reporter: "Because of the
bad economy, people have more time on their hands. We break up groups
of people to prevent serious crimes from happening" (Cruz, 1982). An
ACLU lawsuit successfully challenged this pseudo-arrest practice, arguing
that many were made without probable cause. Of course, without officers
showing up in court, there was no one to claim they were. Disorderly conduct arrests promptly plummeted. The net impact of this reduction in stops
included about 100,000 Chicagoans each year not spending a night in a police lockup or days in the county jail, awaiting a hearing that would almost
automatically free them.

Figure 8-1 contrasts these earlier policing strategies with the city's post-
2004 stop & frisk campaign. During its first year, there were 214,000 recorded stop & frisks, compared to just 18,600 disorderly conduct arrests. As
Figure 8-1 illustrates, during their first year stop & frisks also exceeded the
city's total misdemeanor arrests, 186,500. In fact, during 2004, stop & frisks
almost exactly matched the total number of arrests made for all offenses by
Chicago officers, 216,600 (this is not shown). Stop & frisks then took off,
rising by more than 340 percent. Only following the collapse of stop & frisk
in 2016 did these encounters revert to "normal" levels, in the same range
as other enforcement efforts. Some of the large number of ANOVs during
the most recent period could fairly be added to the Broken Windows total.
However, the 2014–2015 surge was fueled by a widely-publicized enforcement effort targeting driving while using a mobile phone, which generated
59,000 ANOVs in 2014 alone. This offense has rarely surfaced earlier. Even
adding other ANOVs to Broken Window arrests would not rival stop & frisk
as the city's preferred crime control strategy. Most striking is the comparative magnitude of the locally famous wave of disorderly conduct arrests
conducted during the early 1980s. They were a response to four consecutive
years witnessing more than 850 murders. This was considerably more than in
the 2016 crime spike, and the city was then seen to be collapsing into lawless-
ness. But at their peak, stop & frisks were almost 3.5 times as frequent as Jane
Byrne's greatest yearly haul.

In short, almost from the outset, Chicago's stop & frisk regime represented
a massive increase in the scope of policing. By these comparative measures,
stop & frisk was, by a large margin, the city's greatest enforcement effort in
modern times.

Efficiency, Effectiveness, and Equity

Efficiency, effectiveness, and equity are important evaluative dimensions on which stop & frisk should be considered. The *efficiency* of stops has long been measured by their "hit rate," or the proportion of encounters interdicting criminal activity, turning up contraband, or identifying individuals already wanted by police. Stops are inefficient when they come to naught; they have contributed no individual deterrent value. The *effectiveness* question focuses on the broader crime prevention effects of stop & frisk. Has there been a decline in crime attributable to the general deterrent effect of this enforcement strategy? As previous chapters have reported, various approaches to examining both the hit rate and the question of the general deterrent effectiveness of stop & frisk have accumulated in a mixed bag of findings. The *equity* issues raised by stop & frisk form a third important evaluative dimension, and they will be examined separately.

These are not new ideas. The standards of efficiency, effectiveness, and equity were introduced (at least to police research) by John Eck and Dennis Rosenbaum (1994). They described them as things citizens want and expect from their police. More recently, Robin Engel and John Eck (2015) applied these criteria to evaluate different policing philosophies. Here, definitions of these terms are adapted to evaluating stop & frisk.

Efficiency

While it can be described by a narrow number, an efficiency criterion for evaluating stop & frisk addresses a *very* big question. It is the extent to which innocent stops are being conducted. One potential consequence of stop & frisk is that from the point of view of many of the citizens involved they will be unwarranted. Even in crime hot spots most people, most of the time, are just going about their daily lives. The ability of officers to accurately select suitably hot people from among them can be very limited. This is especially true when the local policing style isolates them from the neighborhoods they drop into. Officers may have no idea who is who, or whom the troublemakers are in the eyes of other residents. By the end of his tenure this is what Superintendent Garry McCarthy had wrought, after stripping the districts of officers to staff mobile units to make stops. These units had few policing options other than rounding people up and taking their names. At best, stop & frisk may provide what Kennedy, Kleiman and Braga (2017, p. 158) dubbed "clumsy and unfocused deterrence." They lamented the "strategic bankruptcy" of pursuing a policy that was not delivering on the deterrent effects being touted to justify police intrusion in the lives of many ordinary people. Chapter 3 documents that this was of concern to McCarthy, but for political reasons he ended up going down this path anyway.

The efficiency of stop & frisk has been examined elsewhere, most notably in data-rich New York City. Between 2004 and 2012, NYC police documented more than 4.4 million stops. Of these, 11 percent resulted in an arrest or a citation of any sort. Many of these stops were apparently pretextual, made to support conducting a frisk or full search. Overall, 1.1 percent of stops in New York City yielded a firearm, and an overlapping 1.5 percent turned up other illegal items. Because prior to 2016 Chicago's stop & frisk forms were completed only when nothing turned up at all, it was only later that the hit rate question could be addressed. Beginning in 2016, when reporting procedures changed, firearms turned up during one percent of all stops, and in three percent of the stops during which subjects were searched. These figures were comparable to those in New York and in a few other studies. On the other hand, about one-quarter of Chicago stops turned up an opportunity for making an arrest or issuing a ticket, about twice the rate for New York City and in England and Wales. Not to be forgotten is that stop & frisk also seems to have accounted for around 35 percent of all the guns seized in Chicago during 2016–2018. New York's similarly low hit rate for firearm seizures still yielded about 7,700 guns during 2011 alone, and getting guns off the street should be among any city's most important public health measures.

In other words, by narrow but important measures, Chicago's stop & frisk regime looked at least as efficient as elsewhere, and more so than some. However, in many months, upwards of 80 percent of stops routinely turned out to have been unwarranted. Based on the community survey, which was designed to produce a people-based estimate of the stop & frisk rate, almost 30 percent of adults aged 16 and older recalled being stopped by police in the past year. This was a staggering figure, but doing the math indicated it was broadly comparable with estimates from administrative records after accounting for survey reports of repeated stops. Some among the 30 percent admitted they were stopped because they were speeding, driving badly, or were involved in other infractions. They made up 25 percent of those who recalled being stopped, a fraction that closely resembles post-2016 stop records. The remaining 75 percent described involvement in encounters looking just like unwarranted stop & frisks. This group added up to 22 percent of Chicagoans aged 16 and older being swept up but then released in just a year. This was still a very large number, meaning in human terms stop & frisk was imposing an unwarranted ("inefficient") burden on a very large fraction of the residents of this great city.

The low rate at which Chicago officers turn up firearms and contraband can also be questioned in the more conventional language of efficiency. Stops are not cheap. As noted earlier, in 2019 the average Chicago patrol officer cost the taxpayers $152,000 per year in wages, benefits, health care and retirement contributions, and various special allowances. This figure alone highlights that how they spend their time is important. As I have observed them, officers approach parked cars and convince all the passengers to step out. Or they approach and then question pedestrians, after calming them down. They check whatever identification those involved may offer. They record fairly detailed descriptions of them plus any identifying information they can glean using a data terminal in their patrol car and wait for the results. They run the license plates of any associated vehicles through a national database, as well as through a local one. If there is any detailed questioning, but they do not find anything to act on, this takes at least 10 minutes, but searches take longer, and more data fields must be filled in. By my estimate, the 718,000 stops made in this way by Chicago police during 2014 cost at least 180,000 hours of expensive officer time.

Effectiveness

The collection of research findings on the effectiveness of stop & frisk in deterring crime is particularly jumbled. For New York City alone, some analysts report modest crime reduction effects (MacDonald, Fagan and Geller, 2016), some have concluded aggressive New York stops created *more* crime (Sullivan and O'Keefe, 2017), and others suggest they have little or no effect (Rosenfeld and Fornango, 2014). Perhaps the most influential project focused on 2011, the peak year for stop & frisk in New York City. Statistically, the almost 700,000 stops conducted during 2011 were estimated to have reduced reported crime in impacted areas of the city by two percent (Weisburd, et al., 2016). Weisburd and colleagues describe this decrease in overall crime as a "small" crime prevention gain.

Most of Chapter 7 focused on estimating the effectiveness of stop & frisk in Chicago. Stops went up and down over time, reflecting changes in department priorities, pressure from the political environment, and the independent voice of the media (which frequently included being independent of the actual crime trend). Stop & frisk then collapsed in the face of an extended political crisis, another external force which helped separate out the independent effects of stops on crime because stops were moving in response to exogenous events.

That chapter reported that, over the period of 2004–2018, for every 1,000 monthly stop & frisks of innocent residents there were –0.14 murders and –0.87 shootings. These values may seem small, but there were often a very large number of stops. Across the entire period, the estimated average monthly crime reduction attributable to stop & frisk was four homicides and 24 shootings, or about 50 murders and 290 shootings each year. However, the estimated number of victimizations averted in any particular time frame depended on the number of stops, which varied. There were 73,000 stops during March 2013 alone, which may have averted more than 60 shootings. During 2014, there were more than 50,000 stops every month, and by the end of 2015—when stop & frisk collapsed—Chicago police had recorded more than 5.5 million unwarranted stops. Overall, stop & frisk averted about 8.5 percent of shootings and killings over this period.

To be sure, Chicago's 8.5 percent was bigger than New York's two percent crime reduction, but these were also very different studies. Both figures are larger than those reported for the monthly impact of stop & frisk on non-domestic violent crimes in London (Tiratelli, Quinton and Bradford, 2018). However, what is clear from these studies and others is that stop & frisk as an effective strategy depends on *volume*. Based on the Chicago results, the benefit of stopping and then releasing 1,000 residents per month would be one homicide every seven months. That could be hard to spot. To be a notable deterrent, stop & frisk demands a huge volume of activity, involving significant percentages of the population. In 2014, there were 765,000 African Americans aged 14 and older living in Chicago, and African Americans were stopped on 453,000 occasions before being allowed to go on their way. Unwarranted stops of very large numbers of innocent people are a necessary component of stop & frisk to drive general deterrence.

Equity

The equity criterion involves the *distribution* of fairness. How well was stop & frisk aligned with the norms that constitute fairness in society? There are several relevant norms. An important one is adherence to *constitutional* standards. This involves making stops only when there is reasonable suspicion that an individual was involved in a crime. Pat downs are justified only when there is reasonable suspicion that a person is armed, and a full search is justified only if there is probable cause (a higher standard still) for making an arrest. Another norm is that police need to treat all members of the community in a *fair and impartial manner*. This does not mean there are equal outcomes of stops. Some people are carrying contraband, and some are not. Rather, the standard is that they are seen as fair by the citizenry and the courts. Unfair treatment, like legally shaky stops, imposes unwarranted costs on innocent people who live or work in proximity to crime, and more broadly on people who might *appear* to be criminals. The risk is their apparent race, age, social class, and gender may provide the principal flags by which officers misidentify hot people and fail to treat them with respect. In the United States, race is easily the most consequential of those risk factors. In Chicago, race proved to be intimately connected to the conduct and consequences of stop & frisk.

Equity and Over-policing

When it comes to the judicious evocation of the legal authority of police to challenge and implicitly threaten to use force against passers-by, Chicago's stop & frisk program was unfair to almost everyone. As we saw in Chapter 1, the vision of stop & frisk underlying the decisions of courts in the United States was that they are preceded by careful surveillance and a nuanced analysis of the situation by experienced officers who are wise to criminal opportunities in the area and the ways of those who are up to no good there. Reasonable suspicion and probable cause were to be their guiding standards. This was the understanding of policing evidenced by the U.S. Supreme Court in one of its leading endorsements of stop & frisk, *Terry v Ohio*. But when stop & frisk scales to hundreds of thousands of encounters per year and pressure from management is for volume and not quality, stops can easily impose a heavy and unwarranted burden on generally law-abiding people.

Figure 8-2 details the burden of over-policing in Chicago. On the left, it charts the percentage of the population that was swept up in unwarranted stops, by month, once new stop & frisk data became available. These encounters did not lead to the seizure of contraband, the seizure of guns or drugs, arrests, routine citations, or ANOVs. In the end, the citizens who were involved walked away. As it indicates, this happened most of the time. At or close to *80 percent* of stops were unwarranted through the entire period. The mistargeting rate was a general one. African American, White, and Hispanic residents all were over-policed, measured by the fraction of stops in which they were involved that were unwarranted. Differences among them were not large, and they fluctuated. When stop & frisks collapsed by 85 percent following the political crisis of late 2015 it seemed that there could be scope for the much smaller remainder to be more surgically targeted. The numbers pressure was clearly removed. However, there is no evidence that this happened. Stops continued to be largely unwarranted.

There was a time when this many stops would have raised an alarm. The Jane Byrne street sweeps of the early 1980s captured headlines and sparked concerted action by civil libertarians. Those arrests featured harassment rather than prosecution via the policy of having arresting officers not appear in court. But in the era of stop & frisk, freed of any routine court oversight, seemingly every one of note has come to believe that stopping very large numbers of people for no demonstrated good reason is just a byproduct of effective policing. A key legal point—that stops cannot be conducted

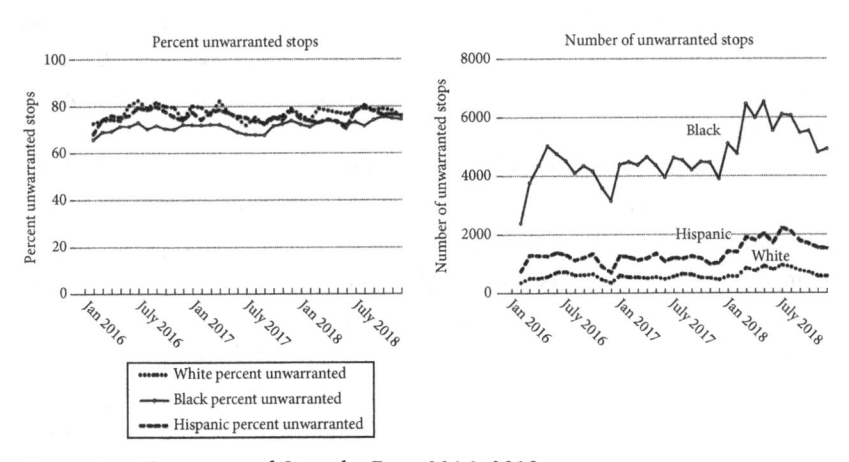

Figure 8-2 Unwarranted Stops by Race 2016–2019

lawfully without reference to the actual behavior of the individual being stopped—has gotten lost in the enthusiasm for spreading a general deterrent message.

The right-hand panel of Figure 8-2 is a reminder that while the unwarranted stop fraction was high for all groups, the number of people that were affected was not. During this period, even following the collapse of stop & frisk, almost 70 percent of the 359,000 unwarranted stops charted there were of African Americans.

Equity and Under-policing

Over-policed does not mean over-protected. While some claim that places plagued by violent crime want to see less of the police, there was limited evidence of this in Chicago. Addressing this question, policing scholar Cynthia Lum concluded:

> How important a problem do you think under-policing is in poor black communities, both historically and today, and does under-policing reflect structural racism? My response is that under-everything is a problem in poor black communities. (Lum, 2021, p. 5)

In a review of national polling results, Richard Rosenfeld, et al. (2017, p. 21) concluded "Black Americans want greater police presence on their streets than do whites." They cited further evidence that African Americans were *twice* as likely as White survey respondents to want a larger police presence that currently existed in their neighborhood. Likewise, in Chicago, African Americans in particular wanted more effective and responsive policing.

Two measures of under-policing are presented in Figure 8-3. Both are based on the community survey conducted for this project. They examine the extent of satisfaction with three measures of perceived police performance and levels of worry about different crimes. The chart benchmarks the police ratings and fears of African American and Hispanic respondents against those of Whites, addressing the distributional nature of equity issues. The further the bars drop, the greater the perceived under-policing. For example, respondents were asked, "how good or poor of a job do you

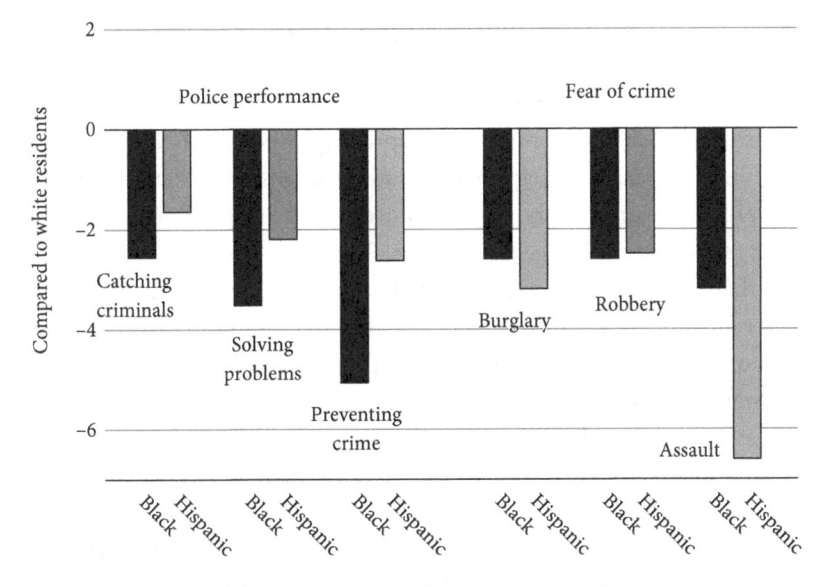

Police performance and fear ratings compared to whites

Figure 8-3 Distribution of Fear and Police Performance Ratings

think the Chicago police are doing" at "preventing crime in this neighborhood," "solving people's problems when they call the police for help," and "catching the people who commit crime in this neighborhood?" They could choose ratings ranging from "extremely good" to "extremely poor." When it came to catching criminals, 15 percent of Whites were dissatisfied, contrasted to 38 percent of African Americans, for an under-policing ratio of 2.6. We saw the role fear of crime played in encouraging support for expanding stop & frisk in Chapter 4. Here, by all three measures both African Americans and Latinos felt relatively under-protected. For example, when it came to worry about burglary, African Americans and Hispanics were two-and-a-half to three times as worried as White respondents. When it came to their personal safety, less than four percent of Whites were very or extremely worried about being assaulted, while the comparable figure for Hispanics was 25 percent. Using the exact figures, this yielded a 6.5-to-1 ratio. As Figure 8-3 illustrates, both African Americans and Hispanics were most concerned about the ability of the police to prevent crime, followed by the capacity of police in their neighborhood to solve the problems that concern residents.

A Better Stop & Frisk?

Could Chicago-style stop & frisk be fixed? Police will inevitably keep making stops, so, are there ready options for improving police practice? Stop & frisk is not just a Chicago strategy, but one adopted to some extent by virtually every policing agency in the nation. Those heavily invested in a stop & frisk strategy should consider the alternatives. Part of the problem is how agencies focus their efforts, which seem inevitably to concentrate huge numbers of unwarranted, innocent stops in a few heavily impacted minority communities. A question is, are there more efficient (in the sense I am using that term here) ways to identify dots for the cops? Another issue is what police *do* when they gather at their prime locations. Can they at least meet the standards for stops that they have been trained in? Also, are there technological fixes on the horizon that might improve the efficiency and effectiveness of stop & frisk? In their New York stop & frisk study, White and Fradella (2016) concluded there was a continuing role for stops "under very specific conditions." Their agenda for fixing stop & frisk includes careful recruit selection, better training and supervision, better management, and more external accountability. In short, they want to fix all of policing. Here we will walk through some specific elements of the "fixing stop & frisk" agenda to see how promising it looks in practice.

By Optimizing Stops?

One policy option would be to (a) stop fewer people, but (b) target those stops more accurately. This would align with what we know about the concentration of offending among a relatively small proportion of the population. In the late 2010s, Chicago officers were failing to turn up anything actionable during 80 percent of stop & frisks, despite focusing their stops in just one-seventh of the city's small census tracts. Could they do even better at finding the balance point between the two competing risks this strategy raises—over-policing and under-protection?

This proves to be a very difficult balance point to locate. Chapter 2 looked into the heart of the problem: the distribution of violence in Chicago neighborhoods. Crime is concentrated geographically, violent crime is more concentrated than most offenses, and gun crimes are particularly concentrated in poor and minority communities. In 2014, the year of peak stop &

frisk in the city, 68 percent of its 788 small census tracts had no murders at all. Another 18 percent reported only one murder in a year, so 86 percent of the city was a low/no homicide zone. If the goal is to deter potential gun violence, these are not the places to go. By focusing instead on just the top 10 percent of places in the city, the 78 tracts with the most shootings, Chicago police would have piled onto 45 percent of all the shootings in the city that year. But in 2014, 85 percent of the residents in those high-risk places were predominately African American, 14 percent were Hispanic, and one percent were White. The unwarranted stops this optimizing rule could generate would clobber those communities.

In a study of resource optimization, criminologist Andrew Wheeler (2020) tackled the tradeoff between allocating police resources to the highest crime areas while simultaneously minimizing the unwarranted racial disparity generated by focused stop & frisk. In the language of linear programming (Wheeler's mathematical tool), he was minimizing "false positives." Here, I have dubbed it maximizing efficiency. This effort focused on crime and stop data from New York City that were aggregated to 500- by 500-meter boxes on the map. The boxes covered the entire city, so there was an ample supply of both high and low crime and people of all backgrounds to be mathematically manipulated. But he could not do it. It proved impossible to identify a focusing model that would allocate officers reasonably in response to where crime happens *and* meaningfully reduce racial disparities in their stops.

This situation was simply another legacy of the high level of segregation in American cities, overlaid with the closely matching spatial concentration of a very long list of crime-generating and community-destroying social, economic, and infrastructure factors. There is no such thing as "race blind" resource allocation in this situation. Ignoring race in allocation algorithms does not make it so (Brayne, 2014). Noting that Black–nonBlack segregation is significantly higher in Chicago than it is in New York City, it does not appear that linear programming will come to the city's rescue.

By Being Nicer?

One of Andrew Wheeler's fallback suggestions (as he could not make optimizing stops work) was to focus instead on optimizing fairness in how people are *treated* when they are stopped, especially when they are stopped without reason. In other words, it may be more realistic to focus on what police *do* when they stop people, and not *where* they do it. We saw in Chapter 4 that stops were both ubiquitous (for some) and often failed to meet the standards being taught in the training academy (also for some).

Beginning in 2012, Chicago's police department had fielded a department-wide program of procedural justice training. It took a few years to get to all the agency's 13,000 members, but they were done before the resident survey described here. Two evaluations of this program reported positive results. A study of administrative records concluded this training reduced both complaints generally and payments for legal settlements with victims of misconduct (Wood, Tyler and Papachristos, 2020; Wood et al., 2021). My own evaluation found the training increased officer support for four components of procedural justice theory: voice, respect, neutrality, and trust. A six-month follow-up concluded trained officers were still more supportive of three of these dimensions, but they were no longer more likely to endorse ideas reflecting trust in the public (Skogan, Van Craen and Hennessy, 2015). Trust was officers' least favorite dimension of procedural justice in every survey I conducted in Chicago during the 2010s.

The department-wide training program was well-organized and labor intensive (classes were capped at 25 participants), and, therefore, expensive. After it concluded, a new "refresher" round of training began, albeit at a slower pace. However, the 2015 city survey findings were not particularly heartwarming. Almost one-half of the many stop & frisk contacts reported by African Americans were rated poorly on measures of their fit with procedural justice, as were those described by Hispanics. The gap between White residents and others remained large on all of its sub-measures. Discouragingly, the lowest rated aspect of their experience should have been the easiest for officers to deliver on: paying attention to what the citizen had to say.

By Fixing the Organization?

Training is only one step toward redirecting police behavior. Even staff members at the Chicago police academy were not sanguine about relying on a day of training to change the culture. In their view, the next steps had to involve performance monitoring, supervision, and the exercise of discipline directed toward reinforcing behavior change. A difficulty is that everything about policing makes officers' actions on the street hard to penetrate, and police organizations have always struggled to maintain control of their field force. To fill this lacuna, supervisors need to do their jobs: allocating the workload correctly, showing up to observe their officers in action, staying alert for behavior problems, and managing the needs of both employees and the organization. Studies suggest it is in combination with effective management and clear policies that align with training that learning at the academy works best.

Supervisors also need procedural justice training as much as anyone in the organization. However, their training also needs to focus on exercising the principles of procedural justice *internally*, as well as with the public. In research, this is known as *organizational justice*. Studies have shown that perceived fair supervision increases officers' compliance with supervisors and the policies of their organization (Van Craen and Skogan, 2016; Bradford and Quinton, 2014). It also fosters compliance by enhancing officers' moral alignment with their own organization—a belief that they and their department share values and a sense of what is right and wrong (Tyler, Callahan and Frost, 2007). This further encourages officers to hew to the policies and recommended practices of the organization. But beyond the skills of sergeants and lieutenants in the districts lies the hard stuff: fairness in hiring, promotions, internal investigations, and the imposition of serious discipline. Discussing improving street policing practices, Superintendent McCarthy told me that change had to proceed from the inside out, and reforms had to bring the officers along. In his typically forthright style, he concluded "We can't kick their asses until they are nice to people."

However, fixing the organization was beyond him. Observers usually do not take long to learn that one of the biggest sources of dissatisfaction and stress in police work is often the organization itself. Achieving fairness in hiring, promotions, internal investigations, and discipline is a tall order. Chicago's department is rigidly rule-bound yet rife with rule-breaking. Disciplinary paperwork gets lost. The informal structure of the organization is dominated by dense networks of interpersonal relations. These include intergenerational family ties, links based on ethnic, religious, and fraternal associations, and bonds among friends, neighbors, and members of the same rookie class. (A later reform mayor described these networks as the department's "friends and family program.") There are powerful patron–client relations between many younger department members and senior officials who promote their careers. Documents leak selectively supporting this or that policy. Senior managers with other assignments sometimes meddle in the staffing and management of their old units. Politicians often play a key role influencing personnel assignments, and City Hall vets all important appointments politically. The search for racial balance is an important component of many personnel decisions. The density of these informal avenues for influence facilitates favoritism, mutual assistance, string-pulling, and subversion of formal decision processes. They mitigate against making hard personnel decisions and promotions that are truly based on merit. These informal networks are an important feature of the "good old boy" character of the organization, which covers up for its members and lets everyone slide gracefully into retirement at age 51. An unfortunate few are allowed to retire before they are fired. I have seen three mayors driven to a fury by their inability to grasp hold of the mushy governance structure of "their" police department. Reforms to stop & frisk predicated on serious internal procedural justice reforms are heading down a long, hard road in Chicago.

Technology to the Rescue?

Could technology harness stop & frisk? Technologies are now frequently suggested as solutions to many police problems, and first among them is body-worn cameras. It is thought that requiring officers to wear and activate them will change police behavior, and perhaps the behavior of those they encounter. On the police side, supervisors could watch and judge how their officers approach people, perhaps heightening their officers' inclination to comply with department policies. It also might narrow the range of people officers decide to stop, putting more of a focus on citizens' now-visible public behavior. Being on camera, actual punishment for being out of bounds regarding department policy might also be more certain.

However, the general pattern that is that body-worn cameras have had a difficult-to-summarize effect on police–citizen encounters. A review of 30 high-quality studies that examined 116 different hypothesized effects of body cameras found few clear or consistent findings (Lum, et al., 2020). The outcomes included various measures of police use of force, complaints against officers, arrests, the frequency of a variety of proactive police activities, assaults on or resistance to officers, and citizen's calls for police assistance. Of particular interest here, cameras did not affect the rate of pedestrian stops. While the authors of this review rightly call for more research on this important topic—body-worn camera use has surged across the country—what we know about the matter through the early 2020s is not as promising as promised.

Further, investigations of actual practice in the use of body cameras in Chicago indicate there has been little organizational will to make them work. Although distribution of the cameras began in 2017, in 2021 it was still questionable whether the department's budget would cover their routine use by all operational units. An investigation by the city's Inspector General found that they threatened to become a "high-tech vest ornament." There was no workable program for systematically reviewing videos (which had been promised), and when incidents came up requiring investigation there was often no video to be found. A review of 300,000 stop & frisk encounters failed to find any video about 20 percent of the time (Chicago Inspector General, 2021). The (reform) mayor's office also tried to block required public and media access to videos that were widely suspected to document police misconduct. For his efforts, the Inspector General was not renominated for a new term, and left office at the end of 2021 with many of his most important reports blocked from release.

Finally, as body cameras began to spread through the organization, there was no visible evidence that stop & frisks were improving. Based on the promises of body camera advocates, one hope was that ubiquitous camera coverage might increase the quality of stops, encouraging officers to be more selective. But we saw in Figure 8-2 that, despite growing camera coverage, there was no evidence of any clear, parallel changes in the selectivity or efficiency of stops. As camera coverage of stop & frisks went from 10 percent in 2016 to about 80 percent in 2018 the "hit rate" actually went down. Most stop & frisks were still ending up in the unwarranted category. There was no sharpening of the agency's focus on gun carrying, measured by finding them. Measured by making stops that justified conducting searches, suspects were not more likely to be stopped based on probable cause. It was hard to find any evidence in the data of any improvements in the efficiency, effectiveness, or equity of stop & frisks in Chicago.

Alternatives to Stop & Frisk

In larger scope, we need to evaluate public policies comparatively by asking the question, "is there *another*, perhaps more efficient, effective, equitable, and even cheaper way of increasing community safety?" In addition to (or instead of) trying to fix their stop policies, could cities and their police do something *else* to prevent violent gun crime, something perhaps better than widespread stop & frisk? Choosing to devote an agency's most important resource—their officers' time and skill—to a strategy is to say, "this is the best we can do." In light of what we have seen of stop & frisk in Chicago, the answer to this question might start with "maybe stop & frisk is not the best we can do."

There is no shortage of ideas regarding improving policing. Since the 1980s the field has seen the emergence of community policing, problem-oriented policing, zero-tolerance policing, hot-spots policing, procedural-justice policing, and intelligence-led or predictive policing (the two differ). They all promise to contribute something unique to maximizing public safety. Researchers have been working for years to identify what are variously described as "best practices," "what works," "promising projects," "crime solutions," and "evidence-based strategies." The findings of individual research and evaluation projects have been collected, classified, and analyzed to draw general conclusions highlighting the potentially most effective policing initiatives.

But the first step to choosing among promising alternatives is to carefully specify the problem that needs solving. Rather than selecting the most fine-sounding solutions, Chicago needs policies and practices reflecting realities on its ground. We saw most of them in Chapters 2 and 7, on crime in the twenty-first century. (1) It was specifically Chicago's *gun-related* violence that was spiking, as well as drawing most of the attention of the media and the attentive public. There were a lot of guns out there, moving hand-to-hand in market-like fashion. (2) Few gun crimes were being solved. (3) Gun violence was concentrated in a few places, and it was seemingly resistant to traditional policing strategies. (4) Most (and usually almost all) of the people inhabiting those places and times are going about their own business, concerned with their own safety, and not making trouble. The low efficiency of Chicago's stop & frisk regime, with its hundreds of thousands of stops each year that turn up nothing, illustrated how much twenty-first-century gun crime springs from a small cadre of hard-to-find chronic offenders. Yet the reality is that there are times and places where serious gun crime requires carefully targeted action to deter violence and save lives. While I have tremendous sympathy for "long term solutions," these places need help now—if not sooner. People will be dying there by the weekend.

A group of carefully evaluated interventions addressing on-the-ground conditions in Chicago are collectively known as "focused deterrence" strategies (Braga and Kennedy, 2020; Braga, Weisburd and Turchan, 2018; Kennedy, Kleiman and Braga, 2017). Most important, focused deterrence casts a narrow net. These initiatives zero in on a relatively small number of prolific offenders and the gang networks fostering them. They try to engage with other parts of the criminal justice system (although this can be surprisingly hard). Some have also found creative ways to link community resources to their gun agenda. These agencies try to mobilize social services on behalf of wavering young (usually) men (mostly), linking them to drug counseling, job training, and high school completion programs. They use violence interrupters and other street workers to communicate with gangs and budding troublemakers about the risks they face.

In 2018, Anthony Braga, et al. offered a summary review describing place-based and gang-oriented gun interventions conducted in Oakland, Boston, Los Angeles, and Chicago (Braga, et al., 2019). These focused efforts recorded 20 to 30 percent reductions in gun violence by identified gangs, and similar drops in violence in the areas they operated in. Chicago's focused deterrence effort targeted individual gangs. Their leaders and prominent members were placed on notice that they had to stop killing people. By two measures, shootings involving members of the targeted Chicago gangs declined by 23 and 32 percent (Papachristos and Kirk, 2015).

More generally, a systematic research review by Braga and Weisburd (2015, p. 64) concluded the effects of carefully targeted gun-focused interventions were "large compared with assessments of interventions in crime and justice work more generally." In the main, their effects were larger than those recorded by conventional hot spot policing strategies, which Braga, Bureau and Turchan (2019) judged to be "small." In their updated review comparing many styles of proactive policing, Braga, Weisburd and Turchan (2018) concluded that focused deterrence projects generated the largest crime reductions. Certainly, steps must be taken to ensure these projects are implemented properly. In my experience, the hardest parts are creating networks of partner service providers and finding ways to sustain these projects over time.

Focused deterrence speaks to some key issues raised by stop & frisk as practiced in Chicago. First, it emphasizes the core problem: gun-carrying for illegal purposes. These programs relentlessly focus on guns, rather than every problem that comes along. Second, they do not involve every young man who happens by. Focused deterrence helps limits the scope of policing. The emphasis is on identified individuals and gangs or area cliques, networks rather than neighborhoods. Crime policy expert Thomas Abt stresses the importance of limited scope:

> Given that crime is so hyper-concentrated, stigmatizing entire groups of people or neighborhoods as uniformly violent is not only morally wrong, it's factually inaccurate. Even in the most dangerous neighborhoods, most of the people there are not dangerous, and there are many parts of that neighborhood that are not dangerous. Police should be more proactive in crime hot spots, but they need to still know the community and be looking out for specific people and behaviors. If hot spot policing is practiced with zero-tolerance, it's not just unfocused, it's unfair. (Gressier, 2019)

It is important to note that paring down the focus of enforcement efforts is unlikely to make much of a difference in the class and race distribution of the individuals involved. Violent criminal networks find their home in down-trodden areas, and then make them worse. Rather, immediate relief promises to come via stepping back from the vast numbers of people who are swept up because they live or work in targeted areas and whose involvement appears to be required to describe stop & frisk as a solution to violence. It also provides relief from a trend lamented by sociologist Alex Vitale (2017), that of viewing all social problems as policing problems. Focused deterrence is built instead on the tremendous concentration of chronic and dangerous offending which we know characterizes a relatively small number of locally networked individuals who move guns and are responsible for a disproportionate fraction of the serious twenty-first-century violence marking poor neighborhoods.

Where does this information come from? Some grows out of routine police "detecting," an intelligence source which is underused when every police district is required to produce increasing "numbers" each month and has little capacity for planning and executing surgical interventions. More is likely to come from community members. They can know a lot and may be willing to share it, especially when it involves chronic troublemakers and local gang factions who are threatening *them*. People understand the high overlap between violent offending and victimization, which can easily be seen among the young men participating in those networks. Unlike stop & frisk, police are no longer focusing on sweeping up people known by the neighbors as *not* up to no good. The legitimacy of police operations could be further enhanced by the provision of a serious menu of support and services which could help meet the immediate needs of impacted youths. Braga and Kennedy (2020) provide a wish list of services including relocation to shelter them from further harm; helping them in getting drivers' licenses and other documents; providing food, clothing, and shelter; and lending assistance in navigating such obstacles as outstanding warrants, fines, child support judgments, and criminal records. However, they also note making the support side of focused deterrence projects work has not often been successful.

Finally, focused deterrence strategies evaluate their effectiveness by reductions in various crime-related measures, not by the number of stops they have conducted. In a sense, they call for getting back to the basics of local crime analysis and locally derived responses which (as Chapter 3 argues) originally characterized CompStat in Chicago before it became a venue for imposing stop & frisk from police headquarters.

Is focused deterrence a "silver bullet," or the project that will solve the violence problem in American cities? No, but perhaps it can buy some time for longer-term investments. Like any policy focused on a complicated problem, there are informed critics of focused deterrence. Their concerns mostly involve practice, and less so program theory. There are complex implementation issues involved in coordinating the work of police, independent street workers, service providers, and community representatives. These programs too easily slide into arresting people rather than extracting them from their gang context and protecting them from victimization. Evaluations of focused deterrence could have been better. They usually focus on recorded crimes and targeted arrests but avoid examining the many other planned moving parts of the program that are featured in their reports (cf., Roman, 2021).

Assessing Stop & Frisk

Noting that police have always made stops, this discussion began with the question "is this anything new?" It concluded that Chicago's stop & frisk regime was indeed something new, off the scale in comparison with the sometimes-feverish responses of earlier administrations to the threat of crime. The practice of stop & frisk in Chicago can be attributed to several intersecting factors. First were the legal, political, and cultural shifts that facilitated wide acceptance of the notion that the job of police is to prevent crime from happening in the first place. Then came the role played by police and political leaders in New York City in valorizing stop & frisk as *the* tactic producing the apparent New York Miracle, a dramatic drop in violent crime. This legitimated the adoption of stop & frisk as a core organizational strategy of the Chicago police, not just something cops did. The neighborhood focus and aggressive activities of street cops were in turn driven by the other widely touted component of this miracle, data-driven CompStat-style management. The concentration of violent crime directed the department's efforts toward events taking place in about one-seventh of the city's real estate, so their officers would be on the dots. Good detective work would not do the job because detectives no longer could catch anyone. The dogged focus of proactive policing of all kinds on these areas was politically acceptable in the corridors of power because the people who lived there were generally poor and marginalized, and mostly African Americans. Further, an important fact about stop & frisk is that in practice it is not particularly efficient (in the way that term is used here) at identifying and stopping people carrying guns and drugs. Most who were stopped were not, as crime experts would predict. Stopping a lot of people, accumulating some guns, and perhaps generating a bit of general deterrence through intimidation of the neighbors seemed to be required to make stop & frisk seem a success.

The seemingly inexorable logic of stop & frisk dominated Chicago policing for some years. It worked politically, the media was happy with reports of vigorous efforts, and the result was an ever-mounting number of unwarranted stops. By the end of this telling, they totaled over five million. The targets of these stops were mostly not happy, as most were African Americans and Hispanics who were not being treated well. The numbers involved were huge; based on the survey, 30 percent of Chicagoans were stopped by police in a year. While courts assumed that most of these stops would be quick and painless, this was not the case. We also saw that during 2013–2015 there were more proactive policing encounters in the city's predominately African American neighborhoods than there were people. Chapter 5 documented that the cops who were making the stops viewed them as if they were from another planet.

But while forces in civil society primed to challenge the claims of stop & frisk seemingly had gone underground, there was life there yet. The inefficiency, ineffectiveness, and inequity of stop & frisk produced a toxic mix of both over-policing and under-policing that could not remain unnoticed. Even before the trigger incident sparking a cascade of political events that roiled the city beginning in 2016, activists in the civil liberties community and enough state legislators to pass significant legislation had already organized a push-back. Others joined them, and the media awoke. In just a few years, a mayor, police chief, prosecutor, and investigative agency head were out of a job, and reformers claimed their seats. During 2016, opinion polling in Chicago produced results that would not be recorded nationally until events of 2020–2021 began to show cracks in the national consensus that "the policeman is our friend." White Chicagoans, in particular, became more skeptical; others already were (Kochel and Skogan, 2021). But the future of reform lay, as always, in the future.

Epilogue

Mayor Rahm Emanuel surveyed the political landscape in mid-2018 and declined to run for re-election. In March 2016 he had forced the appointment of a new police chief, Eddie Johnson, effectively by-passing the required selection process. But continuing a Chicago tradition (see Chapter 3), his appointee was forced to retire in a December 2019 scandal. This gave new Mayor Lorie Lightfoot, inaugurated in May 2019, a chance to choose a new police leader. Lightfoot's role in reform was documented in Chapter 6. She appointed as temporary interim chief Charlie Beck, a retired head of the Los Angeles Police Department and himself noted reformer. During his four months on the job, he made a number of important structural and personnel changes in the department, in close consultation with city hall.

Neither Johnson nor Beck was particularly interested in stop & frisk. Stops crept into the 10,000 per month range by 2010 but were still 80 percent below their 2014–2015 high. How they were spread around did not change. During 2019 the median stop & frisk rate for predominately African American neighborhoods was ten times that for largely White areas. For Hispanics it was three times the White rate. At the median, 50 percent of stops in African American areas involved a frisk, compared to 29 percent in predominately Whites census tracts. And everywhere fully 80 percent of all stops were unwarranted.

Mayor Lightfoot had been elected in a campaign featuring police reform, and this turned the spotlight on the city's progress in fulfilling the terms of the federal consent agreement. Although Lori Lightfoot won all 50 city wards, and even with her own appointee (David Brown, in April 2020) at the helm of the police department, keeping reform on track proved difficult. In their first report, the independent federal monitor concluded that the city had not met a single one of its promised deadlines. In the next report, this figure rose to 13 of the 50 specific reforms that were at or past their due date. By March 2020 the city had hit 22 of 74 agreed-upon deadlines (Independent Monitoring Team, 2020).

The monitor's March 2021 report complained that the 100,000-or-so ANOV citations the department handed out each year—many during stop & frisks—were proving unreviewable by them, were not included in any department reports, and were impossible for the public to find out about. They were concerned about the "equity and fairness" with which ANOVs were distributed (Independent Monitoring Team, 2021, p. 164). In the same report the monitor felt the need to remind the city:

> The CPD should give more attention to (1) the process of applying the law—i.e., conduct guidelines for police interactions with community members when officers stop, question, search, and/or arrest subjects—and (2) the risk of bias in decision making. Public trust of the police is directly impacted by the level of procedural justice exhibited during these interactions, both verbal and nonverbal. The successful execution of these encounters with minimal conflict rests heavily on how people feel they are being treated. Whether someone believes that a search is consensual, for example, is likely to depend on what the officer says to that person and how the officer says it (Independent Monitoring Team, 2021, p. 145).

But the city was already confronting the Tempestuous Twenties. In the face of the March 2020 onset of the pandemic, stop & frisks immediately dropped by 60 percent from their recent low-normal level. Many other measures of discretionary police activity slumped as well. In March 2020 there were just over 10,000 stop & frisks; in April the total was 4,100. In parallel, there were 45,000 registered traffic stops in February 2020 and just 6,800 in April. Many officers were in quarantine or were ill, and everyone was being more cautious on the often-empty streets. By the time spring arrived the police union elected a particularly incendiary new president dedicated to thwarting the new mayor at virtually every turn—including any monitoring (even without requirements) of officers' vaccination status. On the last day of May 2020, the city center was disrupted by large-scale protests over the death of George Floyd in Minneapolis. These protests became violent, and eventually more than 1,200 arrests were associated with the event. Three nights of large-scale looting began immediately, first in the downtown and then spreading to city neighborhoods and nearby suburbs. Most bridges over the Chicago River were eventually raised to impede the mobility of looters. This outbreak was followed by widespread and organized late-night downtown looting on August 10, 2020, surprising again a still-unprepared city.

A cloud hanging over these events was an enormous run-up in violent crime. In May 2019 the city saw 240 shootings; in May 2020 the count went above 400. Homicides and shootings for all of 2020 matched the Great Crime Spike of 2016, and in 2021 the homicide count exceeded the 2016 total, going over 800. In 2021 more than 4,420 people were shot. During 2020 my numbers—which began to diverge from the department's press releases—showed police solved less than 20 percent of homicides and only *nine percent* of shootings. Despite this continuing spike in violence, stop & frisks did not climb back. The April 2021 total was less than 6,000, about the same as the summer 2020 monthly average. Continuing COVID-19 restrictions on police activity doubtless played a role. In addition, during 2021 police numbers were notably impacted by a wave of unexpected retirements and resignations, plus there had been only a few graduates from the training academy. A lot of resources were going into forestalling more looting, everyone was working overtime, and officers had not had a regular life for many months. They were tired and grumpy. In the face of all of this, most of the organizational and personnel changes made by interim Superintendent Charlie Beck and city hall were jettisoned.

Police reform in Chicago continued its bumpy course. In the face of the crime wave of the Twenties, the mayor fell into a continuing spat with the local prosecutor, whom she claimed was too cavalier when it came to letting the accused out on low or no bail or monitored with an ankle bracelet (a restriction with a notable failure rate). Other critics pointed to patterns of non-prosecution and alleged that common offenses were "decriminalized." A few noted that there was no good data on any of these claims. This divergence between mayors and prosecutors had not been typical in Chicago, where the party organization kept many officials on the same page, but it infected several prominent American cities during the Twenties. On the other hand, at the end of 2021, the mayor and city council agreed on one of the more dramatic recent reforms in big-city policing—electing 66 community counselors at the police district level. Besides speaking for their neighbors, they nominate candidates for a civilian oversight commission with considerable authority and backed by a professional staff. Commissioners will be selected by the mayor and city council from the district representatives' list. The commission in turn will play a role in selecting police superintendents. They will also nominate candidates to the mayor for membership on the public body that reviews appeals of disciplinary decisions by the police department, and select candidates to head of the civilian agency that investigates complaints against Chicago officers. Finally, they will have a voice in writing department policies. The Commissioner's views of stop & frisk at this writing remain unknown.

Data Appendix

The Community Survey

The community survey was conducted during 2015, a period when stop & frisk was near its peak. The project was financially supported by the John D. and Catherine T. Macarthur Foundation, and the field work was carried out by a professional, university-based survey research organization, the University of Illinois Chicago Survey Research Laboratory.

Responding households were selected to represent residents of the seven types of neighborhood clusters that make up most of Chicago. The clusters were home to concentrations of (a) poor and better-off African Americans, (b) better-off and blue-collar Whites, (c) long-settled and recently arrived Hispanics, and (d) other recent immigrants, many of whom are Asian. They were identified by analyzing recent demographic and economic data for the city's 788 census tracts. Representative samples of residential blocks located within each of these seven clusters were selected proportionate to their population size. Survey staff members next walked the sample areas, adding any residential addresses that did not appear on the United States Post Office's list for the block and removing incorrect or non-residential addresses. Then, sample addresses were randomly selected from the list for each block. Interviewers knocked on those doors and conducted personal interviews with a randomly selected resident age 16 and older.

Respondents were offered a cash incentive of $40, and interviews were conducted in either English or Spanish. More than 30 percent of the Hispanics interviewed for this study were questioned in Spanish. Up to 10 contact attempts were made at each sample address. Follow-up validations were conducted for 10 percent of each interviewer's completed cases. The response rate for the survey was 28 percent, due in part to our inability to establish if anyone was even living at sampled addresses in areas with high rates of building abandonment. Chicago's declining population and the high level of eviction and abandonment characterizing many poor neighborhoods doubtless contributed to this. Another group that proved very difficult to approach was affluent Chicagoans living in high-rise residential buildings. At addresses where someone could be contacted, the overall cooperation rate for the survey was much higher at 52 percent.

A total of 1,451 residents were interviewed: 457 Whites, 436 African Americans, 437 Hispanics, and 121 persons of other races. As in the daily life of the city, Hispanic respondents will frequently be described as "Latinos." Chicago's Hispanic community primarily has its origins in Mexico, and 44 percent of the Hispanics interviewed for this study were foreign-born. Of all Hispanics, 26 percent reported they were not citizens. Among respondents classified as "others" on race, 44 percent were Asian in origin, primarily from the Philippines and Southeast Asia. Other blocs of respondents in this category came from the Middle East and North Africa. Almost 40 percent of all "others" were foreign-born, and in total 10 percent were not citizens. Because of their relatively small numbers and diverse backgrounds, persons of other races are frequently excluded from the detailed charts that are presented here, but they are included in analyses describing the entire adult city population.

Sampling weights were developed for the survey. They were used to adjust the data for several factors. One component corrects for differences in the probability of selection for residents of multiple-adult households. Otherwise, individuals living in larger families would be less likely to be selected than adults living alone, who would always be chosen. In addition, respondents were weighted to bring them into their correct demographic proportions across the city. In general, the descriptive statistics presented here are based on weighted data, but the multivariate analyses that are reported are based on unweighted data. Weighting had little effect in the findings, in any event.

One purpose of the survey was to examine the frequency with which Chicagoans contact and are stopped by the police. When they were interviewed, respondents were first presented with questions about crime and disorder in their neighborhood, fear of crime, their participation in community organizations, and their responses to local problems. Next, they were asked about their neighbors and things they may have done to prevent crime. Further questions gathered their general impressions of the police on several dimensions, including how much they trusted them. Only then did the survey turn to their personal experiences with the police. Respondents were presented with multiple and redundant verbal cues to aid them in thinking about their involvement in police-initiated encounters.

The Officer Survey

Chapter 5 is based on a survey of Chicago police officers conducted during 2013, while stop & frisk was in its prime. The project was financially supported by the John D. and Catherine T. Macarthur Foundation, and the field work was carried out by the University of Illinois Chicago Survey Research Laboratory. The project was conducted independently of the CPD, but with their general endorsement. The department made no recommendations concerning the survey's content, which they did not see until I delivered a briefing summary of the findings to the Superintendent. Later, I made a presentation on the findings to the 125 exempt staff members who make up the department's command staff.

The survey was carried out in each of the city's 22 police district stations. This ensured that most respondents were officers working in uniform and on neighborhood assignments. At each station police officers (the bottom rank) and sergeants were randomly selected in fixed proportions from the current duty roster. Differences in the sizes of the districts were accommodated by drawing somewhat larger samples in the largest districts and smaller ones in the smallest districts. Everywhere we selected officers proportionally to the number who worked on each duty shift, to ensure that people who worked midnights and those who came in during the day were accurately represented. Finally, after the data were collected, we used sample weights to put officers and sergeants into their correct proportions before analyzing the data.

Advance roll call presentations, flyers, wall posters, and an offer of coffee and donuts were used to promote participation. The interviews were conducted via laptop computers the research team set up in a station conference room. The team made repeat visits to each district, around the 24-hour clock, to make sure officers with a day off or on special assignment had a chance to participate. Based on the names randomly selected from district rosters the response rate for the survey was about 28 percent. A total of 621 police officers and 95 sergeants were interviewed.

As a descriptive tool, the survey was designed to quantify the depth and breadth of some of the concerns of both police leaders and rank-and-file members. As a research tool, the survey was designed to examine aspects of "organizational justice," which is an extension of procedural justice to conditions in the workplace. There is a very large literature on organizational justice in the workplace, including solid studies of police officers and members of related occupations, such as FBI agents and army officers.

Importantly, the survey also assessed the extent of officer support for delivering aspects of procedural justice when they come into contact with the public. There were measures of the extent to which officers supported offering "voice," "neutrality," "respect," and "trust" to the public. There have been few studies using the conceptual framework provided by procedural justice theory to frame a survey asking officers about their relations with the public, rather than their own supervisors.

Finally, there were questions gauging support for the city's homegrown community policing program and for discerning what officers think about their union. A few items probed aspects of aspects of police culture.

For more details on the survey, see Skogan (2015).

Recorded Crime and Arrests

Virtually every section of this book makes use of detailed data on Chicago crime. When sociologist Richard Block and I began to assemble the data in 1994, driving regularly to police headquarters to pick up large reels of fragile magnetic tape, it was a mess. The tapes were formatted in strange ways, and thousands of incident records needed hand-correcting each year. We managed to push our data-cleaning operation back to January 1991, but that was all we could imagine accomplishing. The situation eventually improved. In 1999, the city adopted a database system storing everything in modern fashion. Data input screens now automatically correct the street names officers key in. By 2021, this database grew to include more than 14 million crime incidents. The post-1999 detailed arrest data examined here were downloaded *en masse* as individual records from the police data system, while the yearly arrest totals from earlier decades presented in Chapter 8 can be found in the department's annual reports.

Stop & Frisk Administrative Data

Central to several chapters are data created from the more than five million stop & frisk reports registered by the CPD during the timeframe of this project. Prior to 2016, data-driven news and reform organizations had to press the city hard with FOIA requests and even threaten lawsuits to gain access to these files. Large chunks of what they received eventually surfaced in the underground river of data now flowing through the city. Reporters and activists from organizations as diverse as The Trace, Lucy Parsons Labs, the Invisible Institute, and Chicago Public Radio are part of this growing data-sharing community. The acknowledgments page of this book extends thanks to many of those involved. After 2016, the CPD began posting investigative stop report data on its website, although with caveats no researcher would recommend. Chapter 6 describes the important roles played by the Illinois State Legislature and the Illinois branch of the American Civil Liberties Union in increasing the transparency of stop & frisks and traffic stops. In addition, the city's Inspector General's Office now provides continuously updated weekly stop & frisk counts (and other material) on their public safety dashboard.

Operations Data

Various chapters report on departmental records of gun seizures, arrests, ticketing, and other indicators of officer activity. These were released in response to formal FOIA requests, or as part of a signed data sharing agreement I have had with the CPD since the early 1990s. Some of the data came from them aggregated by month, but most were dumps of individual records directly from their data system. The Cook County Medical Examiner provides an independent assessment of the number of homicides in Chicago (the numbers differ by agency), as well as counts of deaths from drug overdoses, accidents and other indicators flagging communities in trouble. The independent civilian office managing 911 calls and dispatching (plus fire department calls, traffic management, and other public safety domains) is a home for Big Data. At this writing my database of some of the events they track exceeds 165 million records. For reasons made clear in Chapter 6, the Illinois Department of Transportation dispenses data relating to the many millions of traffic stops in Chicago. Data on complaints against the Chicago police were secured and made public through legal action by the Invisible Institute, a data-driven Chicago reform organization headed by Jamie Kalven.

Notes

Chapter 2

1. Every year the Chicago Police Department determines that a few homicides are "justifiable" because they involved self-defense, inadvertent killings, or justified killings by police officers. These are excluded here and elsewhere.
2. Estimates of the number of shootings presented here vary somewhat from reports released by the Chicago Police. Theirs rely on special, detailed coding at the district level; here, shootings are reconstructed from detailed crime categories available in the crime database described in the Data Appendix. The two series are very similar and track one another almost perfectly.
3. Smaller is better when choosing location size for examining crime concentration. Block groups were chosen because there is much more demographic and economic information available about them, when compared to smaller areas such as Census blocks or street segments. They are also the smallest area that could be reliably linked to data on police and other activities, which are sometimes released with truncated address fields to preserve privacy at individual addresses (see Eck, et al., 2017).

Chapter 3

1. They did not always have the same reaction. Jerry Sanders, a chief in San Diego, told me, "who would want to work for an organization that treats their employees like that."

Chapter 4

1. There is a very large body of research on procedural justice. For diverse introductions that relate directly to this project see: Tyler and Meares, 2019; Nagin and Telep, 2017; Worden and McLean, 2017; Skogan, Van Craen and Hennessy, 2015; Meares, 2014.
2. These calculations were made using STATA 14's Regression and Margins routines.

Chapter 5

1. For a rich ethnographic study of how officer's attitudes develop in contrasting city neighborhoods see Gordon, 2022.

Chapter 6

1. These figures were calculated from complaints data assembled from official sources by the reformist Invisible Institute. Note that complaints involving searches may refer to all forms of police action, including those attendant to traffic stops and arrests of all kinds, as well as any stemming from stop & frisks.
2. The *New York Times* data are available to researchers via the survey's sponsor, the Kaiser Family Foundation. The analyses reported here are based on their original data, but the conclusions are my own.
3. Public reports by Chicago police lump together guns that were seized, turned in during gun buy-back or turn-in events, and found by officers (usually after a citizen has called about it) into one category. The latter sources of recovered guns are subtracted here.

Chapter 7

1. Terkel, Amanda. "Ray Kelly On Stop and Frisk: 'No Question' Violent Crime Will Rise If Program Is Stopped," *HuffPost*, August 18, 2013. https://www.huffpost.com/entry/ray-kelly-stop-and-frisk_n_3776035.
2. Again, yearly counts vary a bit depending on where and when you look. These numbers are drawn from the crime incident database described in the Data Appendix.
3. Unusually for a police department, Chicago posts its orders and directives for officers on its searchable "Department Directives System" web page, which can be found via chicagopolice.org.
4. Kaplan, Jacob. Uniform Crime Reporting (UCR) Program Data: Raw Data. Ann Arbor, MI: Inter-university Consortium for Political and Social Research, February 2, 2019. http://doi.org/10.3886/E108361V1. These data were supplemented with custom searches for 2018 city data, plus some estimated values.

References

Abadie, Alberto, Alexis Diamond and Jens Hainmueller. 2010. Synthetic control methods for comparative case studies: Estimating the effect of California's tobacco control program. Journal of the American Statistical Association, 105: 493–505.

ABC7Chicago. 2015. Poll: Rahm Emanuel's approval rating sinks to 18 percent. Online. December 8.

Achen, Christopher H., and Larry M. Bartels. 2017. Democracy for Realists: Why Elections Do Not Produce Responsive Government. Princeton: Princeton University Press.

ACLU of Illinois. 2015b. Stop and Frisk in Chicago. Chicago. March.

Antrobus, Emma, Ben Bradford, Kristina Murphy and Elise Sargeant. 2015. Community norms, procedural justice, and the public's perceptions of police legitimacy. Journal of Contemporary Criminal Justice, 31: 151–170.

Apel, Robert, and Daniel S. Nagin. 2011. General deterrence: A review of recent evidence. Pp. 411–436 in James Q. Wilson and Joan Petersilia (Eds.) Crime and Public Policy. New York and London: Oxford University Press.

Arthur, Rob, and Jeff Asher. 2016. Gun violence spiked—and arrests declined—in Chicago right after the Laquan McDonald video release. New York Times: FiveThirtyEight. Retrieved April 12.

Ba, Bocar A., and Roman Rivera. 2019. The Effect of Police Oversight on Crime and Allegations of Misconduct: Evidence from Chicago. Philadelphia: Faculty Scholarship at Penn Law. SSRN: 3317952.

Bartlett, Robert, and Frank Partnoy. 2020. The ratio problem. SSRN #3605606.

Baumgartner, Frank R., Derek A. Epp and Kelsey Shoub. 2018. Suspect Citizens. New York and Cambridge: Cambridge University Press.

Bayley, David H., Michael A. Davis and Ronald L. Davis. 2015. Race and Policing: An Agenda for Action. Cambridge, MA: Program in Criminal Justice, Kennedy School of Government, Harvard University. New Perspectives in Policing.

Bernstein, David, and Noah Isackson. 2014. The truth about Chicago's crime rates. Chicago Magazine. April 7.

Better Government Association. 2015. Chicago tops in fatal police shootings among big U.S. cities. Chicago. July 26.

Block, Richard L. 1971. Fear of crime and fear of the police. Social Problems, 19: 91–101.

Bradford, Ben, and Paul Quinton. 2014. Self-legitimacy, police culture and support for democratic policing in an English constabulary. British Journal of Criminology, 54: 1023–1046.

Bradford, Ben, Jonathan Jackson, and Elizabeth A. Stanko. 2009. Contact and confidence: Revisiting the impact of public encounters with the police. Policing & Society, 19: 20–46.

Braga, Anthony A., and David Kennedy. 2020. A Framework for Addressing Violence and Serious Crime: Focused Deterrence, Legitimacy and Prevention. New York and Cambridge: Cambridge University Press.

Braga, Anthony A., and David L. Weisburd. 2015. Focused deterrence and the prevention of violent gun injuries: Practice, theoretical principles, and scientific evidence. Annual Review of Public Health, 36: 55–68.

Braga, Anthony A., and Philip J. Cook. 2018. The association of firearm caliber with likelihood of death from gunshot injury in criminal assaults. JAMA Network Open, 1: No. 3.

Braga, Anthony A., Brandon Turchan and Lisa Barao. 2019. The influence of investigative resources on homicide clearances. Journal of Quantitative Criminology, 35: 337–364.

Braga, Anthony A., David M. Bureau and Brandon S. Turchan. 2019. Hot spots policing and crime reduction: An update of an ongoing systematic review and meta-analysis. Journal of Experimental Criminology, 15: 289–311.

Braga, Anthony A., David L. Weisburd and Brandon Turchan. 2018. Focused deterrence strategies and crime control: An updated systematic review and meta-analysis of the empirical evidence. Criminology & Public Policy, 17: 205–250.

Braga, Anthony A., Edward F. Davis and Michael D. White. 2012. Boston, Massachusetts Smart Policing Initiative: Evaluating a Place-based Intervention to Reduce Violent Crime. Boston, Massachusetts: Smart Policing Initiative.

Braga, Anthony A., Greg Zimmerman, Lisa Barao, Chelsea Farrell, Rod K. Branson and Andrew V. Papachristos. 2019. Street gangs, gun violence, and focused deterrence: Comparing place-based and group-based evaluation methods to estimate direct and spillover deterrent effects. Journal of Research in Crime and Delinquency, 56: 524–562.

Brayne, Sarah. 2014. Surveillance and system avoidance: Criminal justice contact and institutional attachment. American Sociological Review, 79: 367–391.

Capellana, Joel A., Rachel Lautenschlager and Jason R. Silva. 2020. Deconstructing the Ferguson effect: A multilevel mediation analysis of public scrutiny, de-policing, and crime. Journal of Crime and Justice, 43: 125–144.

Caplan, Joel M., Phillip Marotta, Eric L. Piza, and Leslie W. Kennedy. 2014. Spatial risk factors of felonious battery to police officers. Policing: An International Journal of Police Strategies & Management, 37: 823–838.

Carr, Patrick J., Laura Napolitano and Jessica Keating. 2007. We never call the cops and here is why: A qualitative examination of legal cynicism in three Philadelphia neighborhoods. Criminology, 45: 445–480.

Cassell, Paul G., and Richard Fowles. 2018. What caused the 2016 Chicago homicide spike: An empirical examination of the ACLU effect and the role of stop and frisks in preventing gun violence. University of Illinois Law Review, 2018: 1581–1684.

Chicago Crime Lab. 2014. Tracing the Guns: The Impact of Illegal Guns on Violence in Chicago. University of Chicago.

Chicago Crime Lab. 2017. Gun Violence in Chicago 2016. University of Chicago.

Chicago Inspector General. 2021. Follow-up Evaluation of the Chicago Police Department's Random Reviews of Body-Worn Camera Recordings. June.

Chicago Police Department. 2012. 2011 Murder Analysis. Chicago.

Chicago Tribune. 2013a. Chicago murder toll drops. December 29.

Chicago Tribune. 2013b. Choosing Chicago's murder toll; Defy the odds; Push the body count lower in 2014 and beyond. Chicago Tribune (Editorial). December 29.

Christian Science Monitor. 2013. Chicago erupts in gun violence: 74 people shot, 12 killed over July 4 weekend. July 8.

Commission on Police Integrity. 1997. Report of the Commission on Police Integrity. Chicago. November.

Cook, Philip J., Anthony A. Braga, Brandon S. Turchan and Lisa M. Barao. 2019. Shooting clearance rates: Why do gun murders have a higher clearance rate than gunshot assaults? Criminology & Public Policy, 18: 525–551.

Cox, Ted. 2016. Too much police paperwork to blame for spike in murders, union boss says. DNAinfo. August 3.

Crews, Julian. 2015. Chicago, CPD face lawsuit over stop and frisk. WGN News (Online). 21 April.

Dai, Mengyan, James Frank and Ivan Sun. 2011. Procedural justice during police–citizen encounters: The effects of process-based policing on citizen compliance and demeanor. Journal of Criminal Justice, 39: 159–168.

Dardick, Hal. 2015. State's Attorney Alvarez defies calls to quit, urges U.S. probe of Chicago cops. Chicago Tribune. December 3.

Davey, Monica. 2013. In a soaring homicide rate, a divide in Chicago. New York Times. January 2.

Davis, Elizabeth, Anthony Whyde and Lynn Langton. 2018. Contacts Between Police and the Public, 2015. Washington, DC: Bureau of Justice Statistics, NCJ, 251145.

De Angelis, Joseph, and Aaron Kupchik. 2007. Citizen oversight, procedural justice, and officer perceptions of the complaint investigation process. Policing: An International Journal of Police Strategies & Management, 30: 651–671.

Decker, Scott. 2003. Advertising against crime: The potential impact of publicity in crime prevention. Criminology & Public Policy, 2: 525–530.

Desmond, Matthew, Andrew V. Papachristos and David S. Kirk. 2016. Police violence and citizen crime reporting in the black community. American Sociological Review, 81: 857–876.

de Maillard, Jacques, Daniela Hunold, Sebastian Roché and Dietrich Oberwittler. 2018. Different styles of policing: Discretionary power in street controls by the public police in France and Germany. Policing & Society, 28: 175–188.

Doering, Jan. 2017. Afraid of walking home from the "L" at night? The politics of crime and race in racially integrated neighborhoods. Social Problems, 64: 277–297.

Dugan, Laura, Daniel S. Nagin and Richard Rosenfeld. 1999. Explaining the decline in intimate partner homicide: The effects of changing domesticity, women's status, and domestic violence resources. Homicide Studies, 3: 187–214.

Dumke, Mick. 2011. New police chief sets out to show he's not the old police chief. Chicago Reader. June 6.

Dumke, Mick. 2012. Chicago's crime problem: A matter of "perception." Chicago Reader. June 16.

Durlauf, Steven N., and Daniel S. Nagin. 2011. Imprisonment and crime: Can both be reduced?. Criminology & Public Policy, 10: 13–54.

Eck, John E., and Dennis Rosenbaum. 1994. The new police order: Effectiveness, equity and efficiency in community policing. Pp. 3–26 in Dennis P. Rosenbaum (Ed.) Community Policing: Testing the Promises. Newbury Park, CA: Sage Publications.

Eck, John, Yong Jei Lee, Soo Hyun O and Natalie Martinez. 2017. Compared to what? Estimating the relative concentration of crime at places using systematic and other reviews. Crime Science (online only): doi.org/10.1186/s40163-017-0070-4

Engel, Robin S., and John E. Eck. 2015. Effectiveness vs. Equity in Policing: Is a Tradeoff Inevitable? Ideas in American Policing #18. Washington, DC: Police Foundation.

Epp, Charles. R., Steven Maynard-Moody and Donald P. Haider-Markel. 2014. Pulled Over: How Police Stops Define Race and Citizenship. Chicago: University of Chicago Press.

Epp, Derek A., and Macey Erhardt. 2020. The use and effectiveness of investigative police stops. Politics, Groups, and Identities, 2020: 1–14.

Fan, Andrew. 2015. Many superintendents have tried to reform the Chicago Police. Chicago City Bureau. December 18.

Fan, Andrew. 2016. Data plays central role in police reform efforts in Chicago and beyond. Chicago Reporter. April 28.

Federal Bureau of Investigation. 2016. Uniform Crime Report 2015. Washington, DC.

Fessenden, Ford, and Haeyoun Park. 2016. Chicago's murder problem. New York Times. 27 May.

Fletcher, Connie. 1990. What Cops Know: Cops Talk About What They Do, How They Do It, and What It Does to Them. New York: Villard Books.

Floyd, et al. v. City of New York, et al., 959 F. Supp. 2d 540 (2013).

Fontaine, Jocelyn, Nancy La Vigne, David Leitson, Nkechi Erondu, Cameron Okeke and Anamika Dwivedi. 2018. "We carry guns to stay safe": Perspectives on Guns and Gun Violence from Young Adults Living in Chicago's West and South Sides. Washington, DC: Urban Institute.

Ford, Quinn, and Alex Parker. 2013. "The murder mayor": CTU's Karen Lewis lashes out at Rahm Emanuel. DNAinfo. March 22.

Ford, Quinn, and Jeremy Gorner. 2015. Chicago's gun violence up from a year ago, topping 1,000 victims earlier. Chicago Tribune, June 8.

Gardner, John. 1969. Traffic and the Police: Variations in Law-Enforcement Policy. Cambridge: Harvard University Press.

Gerbner, George, and Larry Gross. 1976. Living with television: The violence profile. Journal of Communication, 26: 172–199.

Gibbs, Jennifer C., Jonathan Lee, Joseph Moloney and Steven Olson. 2018. Exploring the neighbourhood context of serious assaults on police. Policing & Society, 28: 898–914.

Gill, Charlotte, David Weisburd, Cody W. Telep, Zoe Vitter and Trevor Bennett. 2014. Community-oriented policing to reduce crime, disorder and fear and increase satisfaction and legitimacy among citizens: A systematic review. Journal of Experimental Criminology, 10: 399–428.

Goldsmith, Andrew. 1990. Taking police culture seriously: Police discretion and the limits of law. Policing & Society, 1: 91–114.

Gordon, Daanika. 2022. Policing the racial divide: urban growth politics and the remaking of segregation. New York: New York University Press.

Gorner, Jeremy. 2013. Police stops raise suspicions. Chicago Tribune. November 5.

Gorner, Jeremy. 2015. ACLU, Chicago police agree to changes on controversial street stops. Chicago Tribune. August 7.

Gorner, Jeremy. 2016. Police: Morale still low, emboldening criminals and contributing to violence. Chicago Tribune. November 25.

Gorner, Jeremy, and Peter Nickels. 2016. City homicide numbers spike. Chicago Tribune. March 1.

Graziano, Lisa. 2019. News media and perceptions of police: A state-of-the-art-review. Policing: An International Journal, 42: 209–225.

Gressier, Roman. 2019. Why tackling urban violence should be first on America's domestic agenda: Interview with Thomas Abt. The Crime Report (online). June 25.

Grunwald, Ben, and John Rappaport. 2019–2020. The wandering officer. Yale Law Journal, 129: 1676–1782.

Guarino, Mark. 2013. Rahm Emanuel is losing control of his city. Salon. June 16.

Hannon, Lance. 2020. An exploratory multilevel analysis of pedestrian frisks in Philadelphia. Race and Justice 10: 87–113.

Harp, Ryan D., and Kristopher B. Karnauskas. 2018. The influence of interannual climate variability on regional violent crime rates in the United States. GeoHealth, 2: 356–369.

Hartman, Hermene. 2018. Garry McCarthy: Sacrificed in Laquan cover-up. N'Digo Magazine. December.

Hausman, David, and Dorothy Kronick. 2021. When police sabotage reform by switching tactics. SSRN paper 3192908.

Heinzmann, David, and Emma Graves Fitzsimmons. 2007. Cops disband elite unit: Scandal-plagued division broken up under pressure of criminal probes. Chicago Tribune. October 10.

Heinzmann, David, Todd Lighty and Jeff Coen. 2007. Feds join in probe of city's elite police; Stakes get higher for accused officers. Chicago Tribune. August 16.

Herbert, Steve. 1998. Police subculture reconsidered. Criminology, 36: 343–369.

Hickman, Matthew J., Alex R. Piquero and Joel H. Garner. 2008. Toward a national estimate of police use of nonlethal force. Criminology & Public Policy, 7: 563–604.

Hinz, Greg. 2017. Chicago cops getting a bum rap, ex-chief McCarthy says. Crain's Chicago Business. September 19.

Hoerner, Emily. 2016. Cops and stops. Chicago: Injustice Watch. July 9.

Hope, Tim, and Alan Trickett. 2008. The distribution of crime victimisation in the population. International Review of Victimology, 15: 37–58

Hough, Mike, Jonathan Jackson and Ben Bradford. 2013. Legitimacy, trust, and compliance: An empirical test of procedural justice theory using the European Social Survey. Pp. 326–347 in Justice Tankebe and Alison Libeling (Eds.) Legitimacy and Criminal Justice: An International Exploration. New York and London: Oxford University Press.

Hureau, David M., and Anthony A. Braga. 2018. The trade in tools: The market for illicit guns in high-risk networks. Criminology, 56: 510–545.

Illinois Advisory Committee. 1993. Police Protection of the African American Community in Chicago. Chicago: Illinois Advisory Committee of the United States Commission on Civil Rights.

Independent Monitoring Team. 2020. Independent Monitoring Report 2. Case: 1:17-cv-06260 Document #: 844, Filed: 06/18/20 in the United States District Court for the Northern District of Illinois.

Independent Monitoring Team. 2021. Independent Monitoring Report 3. Case: 1:17-cv-06260 Document #: 939, Filed: 03/30/21 in the United States District Court for the Northern District of Illinois.

Isackson, Noah. 2012. Garry McCarthy under the gun. Chicago Magazine. July 5/August issue.

Jackson, Jonathan, Ben Bradford, Betsy Stanko and Katrin Hohl. 2012. Just Authority? Trust in the Police in England and Wales. London: Routledge.

Jackson, Jonathan, Ben Bradford, Mike Hough and Katherine H. Murray. 2012b. Compliance with the law and policing by consent: Notes on police and legal legitimacy. Pp. 29–49 in Adam Crawford and Anthea Hucklesby (Eds.) Legitimacy and Compliance in Criminal Justice. London: Routledge.

Jackson, Noah. 2013. Chicago's criminals are getting away with murder. Chicago Magazine. March 25/April issue.

Janssen, Kim. 2015. Michigan Avenue Black Friday protests cost stores 25–50 percent of sales. Chicago Tribune. November 30.

Janssen, Kim. 2016. Preckwinkle calls former top cop Garry McCarthy a 'racist bullyboy'. Chicago Tribune. November 2.

Jennings, Jay T., and Meghan E. Rubado. 2017. Preventing the use of deadly force: The relationship between police agency policies and rates of officer-involved gun deaths. Public Administration Review, 77: 217–226.

Jobard, Fabien. 2020. Policing the banlieues. Pp. 187-201 in Jacques de Mallard and Wesley G. Skogan (Eds.) Policing in France. New York and London: Routledge.

Jobard, Fabien, René Lévy, John Lamberth, Sophie Névanen and Elizabeth Wiles-Portier. 2012. Measuring appearance-based discrimination: An analysis of identity checks in Paris. Population, 67: 349–375

Johnson, Devon, and Joseph B. Kuhn. 2009. Striking out: Race and support for police use of force. Justice Quarterly, 26: 592–623.

Jones-Brown, Delores D., Jaspreet Gill and Jennifer Trone. Stop, Question & Frisk Policing Practices in New York City: A Primer. New York: Center on Race, Crime and Justice, John Jay College of Criminal Justice, 2010.

Jurek, Alicia L., Matthew C. Matusiak and William R. King. 2022. Ferguson as a distal crisis: Chief assessments of changes in the police institutional environment. Criminology & Public Policy, 21: 83–105.

Kalven, Jamie. 2018. Chicago finally released video of police officer shooting unarmed disabled Ricky Hayes. The Intercept. October 16.

Kelling, George L., and William J. Bratton. 2015. Why we need broken windows policing. City Journal. Winter Issue. https://www.city-journal.org/html/why-we-need-broken-windows-policing-13696.html.

Kemal, Samaa, Karen Sheeran and Joe Feinglass. 2018. Gun carrying among freshmen and sophomores in Chicago, New York City and Los Angeles public schools: The youth risk behavior survey 2007–2013. Injury Epidemiology, 5(Suppl 1): 47–53.

Kennedy, David M., Mark A. R. Kleiman and Anthony A. Braga. 2017. Beyond deterrence. Pp. 157-183 in Nick Tilley and Aiden Sidebottom (Eds.) Handbook of Crime Prevention and Community Safety. London: Taylor & Francis.

Klinger, David A. 1995. The micro structure of nonlethal force: Baseline data from an observational study. Criminal Justice Review, 20: 169–186.

Kochel, Tammy Rinehart, and Wesley G. Skogan. 2021. Accountability and transparency as levers to promote public trust and police legitimacy: Findings from a natural experiment. Policing: An International Journal, 44: 1046–1059.

Konkol, Mark. 2016. Chicago police street stops decrease dramatically amid sinking morale. DNAinfo. January 13.

Korecki, Natasha. 2015. Emanuel fires police superintendent amid protests over video. Politico. December 12.

Kotlowitz, Alex. 2016. Solving Chicago's murders could prevent more. The New Yorker. September 20.

Langdon, Lynn. 2010. Women in Law Enforcement, 1987–2008. Washington, DC: Bureau of Justice Statistics, NCJ 230521.

Lauritsen, Janet L., and Theodore S. Lentz. 2019. National and local trends in serious violence, firearm victimization, and homicide. Homicide Studies, 23: 243–261.

Lee, YongJei, John E. Eck, SooHyun O. and Natalie N. Martinez. 2017. How concentrated is crime at places? A systematic review from 1970 to 2015. Crime Science (online only): doi:10.1186/s40163-017-0069-x.

Lennon, Genevieve, and Kath Murray. 2018. Under-regulated and unaccountable? Explaining variation in stop and search rates in Scotland, England and Wales. Policing & Society, 28: 157–174.

Levi, Ron. 2009. Making counter-law: On having no apparent purpose in Chicago. British Journal of Criminology, 49: 131–149.

Levine, Jay. 2011. Inside peek: Top police administrators in the hot seat. CBSLocal.com. September 30.

Lum, Cynthia. 2021. Perspectives on policing. Annual Review of Criminology, 2021: 18.1–18.7.

Lum, Cynthia, and Daniel S. Nagin. 2017. Reinventing American policing: A seven-point blueprint for the 21st century. Crime and Justice: A Review of Research, 26: 339–393.

Lum, Cynthia, Christopher S. Koper, David B. Wilson, Megan Stoltz, Michael Goodier, Elizabeth Eggins, Angela Higgins and Lorraine Mazerolle. 2020. Body worn cameras' effects on police officers and citizen behavior: A systematic review. Campbell Systematic Reviews, 16: e1112. https://doi.org/10.1002/cl2.1112

Lurie, Stephen, Alexis Acevedo and Kayle Ott. 2018. Less than 1%: Groups and the extreme concentration of urban violence. New York: National Network for Safe Communities, John Jay College.

Lydersen, Kari. 2013. Mayor 1%: Rahm Emanuel and the rise of Chicago's 99%. Chicago: Haymarket Books.

MacDonald, John, and Anthony A. Braga. 2019. Did post-Floyd et al. reforms reduce racial disparities in NYPD stop, question, and frisk practices? An exploratory analysis using external and internal benchmarks. Justice Quarterly, 36: 954–983.

MacDonald, John, Jeffrey Fagan and Amanda Geller. 2016. The effects of local police surges on crime and arrests in New York City. PLoS One (online only): doi:10.1371/journal.pone.0157223.

Maguire, Edward R., Belén V. Lowrey and Devon Johnson. 2017. Evaluating the relative impact of positive and negative encounters with police: A randomized experiment. Journal of Experimental Criminology, 13: 367–391.

Manski, Charles F., and Daniel S. Nagin. 2017. Assessing benefits, costs, and disparate racial impacts of confrontational proactive policing. Proceedings of the National Academy of Sciences, 114: 9308–9313.

McCluskey, John D. 2003. Police Requests for Compliance: Coercive and Procedurally Just Tactics. New York: LFB Scholarly Publishing LLC.

McCluskey, John D., Stephen S. Mastrofski and Roger B. Parks. 1999. To acquiesce or rebel: Predicting citizen compliance with police requests. Police Quarterly, 2: 389–416.

McDowall, David, and Colin Loftin. 2009. Do US city crime rates follow a national trend? The influence of nationwide conditions on local crime patterns. Journal of Quantitative Criminal, 25: 307–324.

McGarrell, Edmund F., Steven Chermak and Alexander Weiss. 2002. Reducing gun violence: Evaluation of the Indianapolis Police Department's Directed Patrol Project. Washington, DC: US Department of Justice, Office of Justice Programs.

McQueary, Kristen. 2015. A task force to study the police? Please say you're kidding. Chicago Tribune. December 3.

Main, Frank. 2007. Guns in police custody fall into criminal hands. Chicago Sun Times, February 26.

Main, Frank. 2017. The watchdogs: Gun-shop burglaries helping fuel Chicago violence. Chicago Sun Times, May 5.

Main, Frank. 2018. More Chicago shooting victims being shot multiple times. Chicago Sun Times, January 2.

Mancik, Ashley M., Karen F. Parker and Kirk R. Williams. 2018. Neighborhood context and homicide clearance: Estimating the effects of collective efficacy. Homicide Studies, 22: 188–213.

Maple, Jack. 2000. The Crime Fighter: How You Can Make Your Community Crime Free. New York: Broadway.

Martin, Susan E. 1982. Breaking and Entering: Policewomen on Patrol. Berkeley: University of California Press.

Martinez, Natalie N., YongJei Lee, John E. Eck and Soo Hyun O. 2017. Ravenous wolves revisited: a systematic review of offending concentration. Crime Science (online only): doi.org/10.1186/s40163-017-0072-2.

Meares, Tracey. 2014. The law and social science of stop and frisk. Annual Review of Law & Social Science, 10: 335–52.

Mitchell, Chip. 2015. City fires investigator who found cops at fault in shootings. WBEZ News Online. July 20.

Mitchell, Chip. 2016. Chicago sets aside stop-and-frisk as deterrence strategy, police data show. WBEZ News Online. July 28.

Mitchell, Mary. 2016. Police data cast doubt on Chicago-style stop and frisk. Chicago Sun Times. May 5.

Nagin, Daniel S. 2013. Deterrence: A review of the evidence by a criminologist for economists. Annual Review of Economics, 5: 83–105.

Nagin, Daniel S., and Cody W. Telep. 2017. Procedural justice and legal compliance. Annual Review of Law and Social Science, 13: 5–28.

NBC5 Chicago. 2015. Alvarez defends herself, Mayor Emanuel in timing of charges in Laquan McDonald case. Online. November 24.

Neil, Roland, and Christopher Winship. 2019. Methodological challenges and opportunities in testing for racial discrimination in policing. Annual Review of Criminology, 2: 73–98.

Nivette, Amy E., and Manuel Eisner. 2013. Do legitimate polities have fewer homicides? A cross-national analysis. Homicide Studies, 17: 3–26.

Oliveira, Thiago R., Jonathan Jackson, Kristina Murphy and Ben Bradford. 2021. Are trustworthiness and legitimacy "hard to win, easy to lose"? A longitudinal test of the asymmetry thesis of police-citizen contact. Journal of Quantitative Criminology, 37: 1003–1045.

Pew Research Center. 2011. 2011 local news survey questions. January 12–25.

Police Accountability Task Force. 2016. Recommendations for reform: Restoring trust between the Chicago Police and the communities they serve. Chicago. April.

Police Foundation. 2018. Opinions of officers of the Chicago Police Department on the upcoming consent decree: A report to the State of Illinois Office of the Attorney General. Washington, DC. July.

Papachristos, Andrew V., and David S. Kirk. 2015. Changing the street dynamic: Evaluating Chicago's group violence reduction strategy. Criminology & Public Policy, 14: 525–558.

Papachristos, Andrew V., Christopher Wildeman and Elizabeth Roberto. 2015. Tragic, but not random: The social contagion of nonfatal gunshot injuries. Social Science and Medicine, 125: 139–150.

Papachristos, Andrew V., David M. Hureau and Anthony A. Braga. 2013. The corner and the crew: The influence of geography and social networks on gang violence. American Sociological Review, 78: 417–447.

Papachristos, Andrew V., Noli Brazil and Tony Cheng. 2018. Understanding the crime gap: Violence and inequality in an American city. City and Community, 17: 1051–1074.

Peacock, Robert. 2021. Dominance analysis of police legitimacy's regressors: disentangling the effects of procedural justice, effectiveness, and corruption. Police Practice and Research, 22: 589–605.

Pearson, Rick, and David Heinzmann. 2013. Emanuel's push to curb crime gets split verdict in Chicago poll. Chicago Tribune. May 9.

Peffley, Mark, Jon Hurwitz and Paul M. Sniderman. 1997. Racial stereotypes and whites' political views of blacks in the context of welfare and crime. American Journal of Political Science, 41: 30–60.

Pew Research Center. 2017. Most violent and property crimes in the U.S. go unsolved. March.

Pickett, Justin, and Justin Nix. 2019. Demeanor and police culture: Theorizing how civilian cooperation influences police officers. Policing: An International Journal of Police Strategies & Management, 42: 537–555.

Pizarro, Jesenia M., William Terrill and Charles A. LoFaso. 2018. The impact of investigation strategies and tactics on homicide clearance. Homicide Studies, 22: 1–22.

Police Accountability Task Force. 2016 Recommendations for Reform: Restoring Trust Between the Chicago Police and the Communities They Serve. Chicago.

Preib, Martin. 2010. The Wagon and Other Stories from the City. Chicago: University of Chicago Press.

Quig, A. D. 2016. Fairley holds disjointed short presser to announce new staff hires. DNAinfo. January 5.

Ramirez, Mark D. 2013. Punitive sentiment. Criminology, 51: 329–364.

Ramos, Elliott. 2019. Chicago seized and sold nearly 50,000 cars over tickets since 2011, sticking owners with debt. WBEZ News (online). January 7.

Roberts, Dorothy. 1999. Race, vagueness, and the social meaning of order maintenance policing. Journal of Criminal Law & Criminology, 89: 775–836.

Roman, Caterina G. 2021. An evaluator's reflections and lessons learned about gang intervention strategies: an agenda for research. Journal of Aggression, Conflict and Peace Research, 13: 148–167.

Rosenfeld, Richard. 2016. Documenting and Explaining the 2015 Homicide Rise: Research Directions. Washington, DC: National Institute of Justice. June.

Rosenfeld, Richard. 2018. Studying crime trends: Normal science and exogenous shocks. Criminology, 56: 5–26.

Rosenfeld, Richard, and Robert Fornango. 2014. The impact of police stops on precinct robbery and burglary rates in New York City, 2003–2010. Justice Quarterly, 31: 96–122.

Rosenfeld, Richard, and David Weisburd. 2016. Explaining recent crime trends. Journal of Quantitative Criminology, 32: 329–334.

Rosenfeld, Richard, Karen Terry and Preeti Chauhan. 2013. New York's crime drop puzzle. Justice Quarterly, 31: 1–4.

Rosenfeld, Richard, Shytierra Gaston, Howard Spivak and Seri Irazola. 2017. Assessing and Responding to the Recent Homicide Rise in the United States. Washington, DC: National Institute of Justice. November.

Ruthhart, Bill. 2017. ACLU: Emanuel's police agreement with Trump administration "a non-starter." Chicago Tribune. June 7.

Ruthhart, Bill, and Gregory Pratt. 2018. McCarthy crime plan: Remove politics, Emanuel's meddling from police department. Chicago Tribune. July 9.

Ruthhart, Bill, and Lolly Bowen. 2016. Distrust of Chicago cops helps drive Emanuel's low approval on crime. Chicago Tribune. February 3.

Safer, Ronald. 2014. Preventing and Disciplining Police Misconduct: An Independent Review and Recommendations Concerning Chicago's Police Disciplinary System. Chicago: Schiff Hardin LLP and A.T. Kearney Co. December.

Sampson, Robert J., and Jacqueline Cohen. 1988. Deterrent effects of the police on crime: A replication and theoretical extension. Law & Society Review, 22: 163–190.

Sargeant, Elise, Rebecca Wickes and Lorraine Mazerolle. 2013. Policing community problems: Exploring the role of formal social control in shaping collective efficacy. Australian & New Zealand Journal of Criminology, 46: 70–87.

Schafer, Joseph A., and Stephen D. Mastrofski. 2005. Police leniency in traffic enforcement encounters: Exploratory findings from observations and interviews. Journal of Criminal Justice, 33: 225–238.

Scott, Thomas L., Charles Wellford, Cynthia Lum and Heather Novak. 2018. Variability of crime clearance among police agencies. Police Quarterly, 22: 82–111.

Sekhon, Nirej. 2017. Blue on black: An empirical assessment of police shootings. American Criminal Law Review, 54: 189–232.

Sharkey, Patrick, Gerard Torrats-Spinosa and Delaram Takyar. 2017. Community and the crime decline: the causal effect of local nonprofits on violent crime. American Sociological Review 82: 1214–1240.

Shjarback, John A. 2018. Neighborhood influence on police use of force: state-of-the-art review. Policing: An International Journal, 41: 859–872.

Shjarback, John A., and Edward R. Maguire. 2021. Extending research on the "War on Cops": The effects of Ferguson on nonfatal assaults against US police officers. Crime & Delinquency, 67: 3–26.

Shi, Luzi, Yunmei Lu and Justin T. Pickett. 2020. The public salience of crime, 1960–2014: Age–period–cohort and time–series analyses. Criminology, 58: 568–593.

Shiner, Michael, and Rebekah Delsol. 2015. The politics of the powers. Pp. 31–56 in Rebekah Delsol and Michael Shiner (Eds.) Stop and Search: The Anatomy of a Police Power. London: Palgrave-Macmillan.

Silver, Jasmine R., and Justin T. Pickett. 2015. Toward a better understanding of politicized policing attitudes: Conflicted conservatism and support for police use of force. Criminology, 53: 650–676.

Simpson, Dick, Thomas J. Gradel, Michael Dirksen and Marco Rosaire Rossi. 2020. Chicago Still the Corruption Capital. Anti-Corruption Report #12. Chicago: University of Illinois at Chicago. February 17.

Skogan, Wesley G. 2006b. Police and Community in Chicago: A Tale of Three Cities. New York: Oxford University Press.

Skogan, Wesley G. 2009. Policing immigrant communities in the United States. Sociology of Crime, Law and Deviance, 13: 189–203.

Skogan, Wesley G. 2015. Surveying police officers. Pp. 109–118 in Michael D. Maltz and Stephen K. Rice (Eds.) Envisioning Criminology: Researchers on Research as a Process of Discovery. New York: Springer.

Skogan, Wesley G. 2018. The commission and the police. Criminology & Public Policy 17: 379–396.

Skogan, Wesley G., and Tracey L. Meares. 2004. Lawful policing. Annals of the American Academy of Political and Social Science, 593: 66–84.

Skogan Wesley G., Maarten Van Craen and Cari Hennessy. 2015. Training police for procedural justice. Journal of Experimental Criminology, 11: 319–334.

Skogan, Wesley G., Susan M. Hartnett, Natalie Bump and Jill Dubois. 2009. Executive Summary: Evaluation of CeaseFire–Chicago. Evanston, IL: Institute for Policy Research, Northwestern University. http://skogan.org/WorkInProgress.html.

Slocum, Lee Ann, and Stephanie Ann Wiley. 2018. Experience of the expected? Race and ethnicity differences in the effects of police contact on youth. Criminology, 56: 402–432.

Smith, Douglas A. 1986. The neighborhood context of police behavior. Crime and Justice, 8: 313–341.

Smith, Douglas A., and Craig D. Uchida. 1988. The social organization of self-help: A study of defensive weapon ownership. American Sociological Review, 53: 94–102.

Sobol, Rosemary. 2015. McCarthy defends officers' street stops, praises cooperation of ACLU. Chicago Tribune. August 7.

Spielman, Fran. 2013. Rahm says he has "absolute confidence" in Police Superintendent Garry McCarthy, but progress reducing gang violence "not good enough." Chicago Sun Times. November 19.

Spielman, Fran. 2015. Black Caucus renews demand for McCarthy's ouster. Chicago Sun Times. November 25.

Spielman, Fran. 2017. CPD revises street stop form yet again to boost police activity. Chicago Sun Times. January 6.

Stein, Rachel E., and Candace Griffith. 2017. Resident and police perceptions of the neighborhood: Implications for community policing. Criminal Justice Policy Review, 28: 139–154.

Stinchcombe, Arthur L. 1963. Institutions of privacy in the determination of police administrative practice. American Journal of Sociology, 69: 150–160.

Sullivan, Christopher M., and Zachary P. O'Keefe. 2017. Evidence that curtailing proactive policing can reduce major crime. Nature: Human Behavior, 1: 730–737.

Sweeney, Annie, and Jeremy Gorner. 2016. Ten shootings a day: The complex causes of Chicago's spiking violence. Chicago Tribune. July 3.

Tankebe, Justice. 2013. Viewing things differently: The dimensions of public perceptions of police legitimacy. Criminology, 51: 103–135.

Tarling, Roger, and Katie Morris. 2010. Reporting crime to the police. British Journal of Criminology, 50: 474–490.

Terkel, Amanda. 2013. Ray Kelly on stop and frisk: "No question" violent crime will rise if program is stopped. HuffPost, August 18. www.huffpost.com/entry/ray-kelly-stop-and-frisk_n_3776035.

Terrill, William, Jason Robert Ingram, Logan J. Somers, and Eugene A. Paoline III. 2018. Examining police use of force and citizen complaints. Policing: An International Journal, 41: 496–509.

Terry v. Ohio, 392 U.S. 1 (1968).

Tankebe, Justice. 2013. Viewing things differently: The dimensions of public perceptions of police legitimacy. Criminology, 51: 103–135.

Tiratelli, Matteo, Paul Quinton and Ben Bradford. 2018. Does stop and search deter crime? Evidence from ten years of London-wide data. British Journal of Criminology, 58: 1212–1231.

Toobin, Jeffrey. 2013. Bratton's endorsement of stop-and-frisk. The New Yorker. December 5.

Tyler, Tom R. 2004. Enhancing police legitimacy. The Annals of the American Academy of Political and Social Science, 593: 84–99.

Tyler, Tom R. 2006. Psychological perspectives on legitimacy and legitimation. Annual Review of Psychology, 57: 375–400.

Tyler, Tom R., and Tracey L. Meares. 2019. Procedural justice policing. Pp. 71–94 in David Weisburd and Anthony Braga (Eds.) Police Innovation: Contrasting Perspectives. Cambridge: Cambridge University Press.

Tyler, Tom R., and Yuen Huo. 2002. Trust in the Law: Encouraging Public Cooperation with the Police and Courts. New York: Russell Sage Foundation.

Tyler, Tom R., Jeffrey Fagan, and Amanda Geller. 2014. Street stops and police legitimacy: Teachable moments in young urban men's legal socialization. Journal of Empirical Legal Studies, 11: 751–785.

Tyler, Tom R., Patrick E. Callahan and Jeffrey Frost. 2007. Armed and dangerous (?): Motivating rule adherence among agents of social control. Law & Society Review, 41: 457–492.

United States Department of Justice. 2017. Investigation of the Chicago Police Department. Washington, DC: U.S. Department of Justice. January 13.

Van Craen, Maarten. 2016. Understanding police officers' trust and trustworthy behavior: A work relations framework. European Journal of Criminology, 13: 274–294.

Van Craen, Maarten, and Wesley G. Skogan. 2016. Achieving fairness in policing: The link between internal and external procedural justice. Police Quarterly, 20: 3–23.

Velasquez, Phil. 2016. Preckwinkle calls former top cop Garry McCarthy a "racist bully boy," Chicago Tribune. November 2.

Vitale, Alex S. 2017. The End of Policing. New York and London: Verso Books, 2017.

Walgrave, Stefaan, Amber E. Boydstun, Rens Vliegenthart and Anne Hardy. 2017. The nonlinear effect of information on political attention: Media storms and US congressional hearings. Political Communication, 34: 548–570.

Wandling, Michael, Jess Behrens, Renee Hsia and Marie Crandall. 2016. Geographic Disparities in access to urban trauma care: Defining the problem and identifying a solution for gunshot victims in Chicago. American Journal of Surgery, 212: 587–591.

Weisburd, David. 2015. The law of crime concentration and the criminology of place. Criminology, 53: 133–157.

Weisburd, David, and Clare White. 2019. Hot spots of crime are not just hot spots of crime: Examining health outcomes at street segments. Journal of Contemporary Criminal Justice, 35: 142–160.

Weisburd, David, and Malay K. Majimundar (Eds.). 2018. Proactive Policing: Effects on Crime and Communities. Committee on Proactive Policing: Effects on Crime, Communities, and Civil Liberties. Washington, DC: The National Academies Press.

Weisburd, David, Alese Wooditch, Sarit Weisburd and Sue Ming Yang. 2016, Do stop, question, and frisk practices deter crime? Evidence at microunits of space and time. Criminology & Public policy, 15: 31–56.

Weisburd, David, Elizabeth R. Groff and Sue-Ming Yang. 2012. The Criminology of Place: Street Segments and Our Understanding of the Crime Problem. New York: Oxford University Press.

Weitzer, Ronald, Steven A. Tuch and Wesley G. Skogan. 2008. Police-community relations in a majority black city. Journal of Research in Crime and Delinquency, 45: 398–428.

Wellford, Charles F., and James M. Cronin. 1999. An Analysis of Variables Affecting the Clearance of Homicides: A Multi-state Study. Washington, DC: Justice Research and Statistics Association.

Westley, William A. 1970. Violence and the Police. Cambridge, MA: MIT press.

Wheeler, Andrew P. 2020. Allocating police resources while limiting racial inequality. Justice Quarterly, 37: 842–868.

White, Michael D., and Henry F. Fradella. 2016. Stop and Frisk: The Use and Abuse of a Controversial Policing Tactic. New York: New York University Press.

Wilson, James Q., and Barbara Boland. 1978. The effect of the police on crime. Law & Society Review, 12: 367–390.

Wogan, J. B. 2016. Task force report finds Chicago cops racist and unaccountable. Now what happens? Governing Magazine. April 28.

Worden, Robert E., and Sarah J. McLean. 2017. Mirage of Police Reform: Procedural Justice and Police Legitimacy. Oakland, CA: University of California Press.

Wood, George, Tom R. Tyler and Andrew Papachristos. 2020. Procedural justice training reduces police misconduct and use of force. Proceedings of the National Academy of Sciences, 117: 9815–9821.

Wood, George, Tom R. Tyler, Andrew Papachristos, Jonathan Roth, and Pedro H. C. Sant'Anna. 2021. Correction for Wood et al., Procedural justice training reduces police use of force and complaints against officers Proceedings of the National Academy of Sciences, 118: e2110138118.

Worden, Robert E., and Sarah J. McLean. 2017. Mirage of Police Reform: Procedural Justice and Police Legitimacy. Berkeley, CA: University of California Press.

Wu, Xiaoyun, Christopher Koper and Cynthia Lum. 2021. Measuring the impacts of everyday police proactive activities: Tackling the endogeneity problem. Journal of Quantitative Criminology, 38: 1–21.

Zimring, Franklin E. 2011. The City that Became Safe: New York's Lessons for Urban Crime and its Control. New York: Oxford University Press.

Zimring, Franklin E., and Gordon Hawkins. 1999. Crime is Not the Problem: Lethal Violence in America. New York and London: Oxford University Press.

Zorn, Eric. 2018. The 16 shots were bad. The cover-up was worse. Chicago Tribune. September 6.

Index

Printed in the USA/Agawam, MA
November 1, 2022

800593.024